Praise for *City of Devils*

'In Mr French, who has spent years chasing Shanghai's ghosts, [the city] has its champion storyteller. *City of Devils* is based on real people and events. With a fabulist's flair, Mr French supplies whatever details were withheld by the archives he has ransacked . . . The story is brought alive by Mr French's Shanghai-noir telling, which echoes Dashiell Hammett and James Ellroy . . . He grips his reader to the end' *Economist*

'Written in a demotic, joyously profane and daringly idiosyncratic style . . . [close to] the urgent hepcat prose of James Ellroy's mid-career pomp. As with *The Black Dahlia* and *LA Confidential*, its style and subject matter are perfectly attuned, enhancing the book's doom-laden film noir atmosphere . . . deserves to replicate the popularity of *Midnight in Peking*' *Literary Review*

'When is a novel not a novel? When it's 'narrative non-fiction' . . . French's louche and moodily lit recreation of Shanghai is thrillingly done' *The Times*

'Plunge yourself deep into the mean milieu of Shanghai in the 1930s with this hard-boiled beauty of a chunk of noir . . . The atmosphere created runs the gamut from claustrophobic and dark to electric and menacing' *Sunday Sport*

'Such a rich tapestry of characters is every author's dream but weaving their stories together within the confines of a city that didn't exactly cherish the preservation of documents and proper names takes immense skill. It also requires a love for the ways of this labyrinthine settlement, nurtured by French's years spent navigating its back streets. French superbly conveys the surrealism of life in Shanghai' *Real Crime Magazine*

'An astonishing achievement, magically transporting the reader back to Old Shanghai, then sweeping us through its streets and its bars in a gripping, breakneck ultra-noir narrative reminiscent of vintage Ellroy' David Peace

'Few writers are more expert at mingling crime narrative and social history, journalistic precision and novelistic sweep than Paul French. His books paint tin stories so vivid and harrow thrall. If you love R *City of Devils*' Megan

Paul French lived in Shanghai for ten years and frequently comments on China for the English-speaking press around the world. French studied history, economics, and Mandarin at university and has an M.Phil in economics from the University of Glasgow. He lives in London.

Also by Paul French

Midnight in Peking

CITY OF DEVILS

DEVILS

A Shanghai Noir

PAUL FRENCH

riverrun

First published in the USA in 2018 by Picador
First published in Great Britain in 2018 by riverrun

riverrun
An imprint of

Quercus Editions Limited
Carmelite House
50 Victoria Embankment
London EC4Y 0DZ

An Hachette UK company

A CIP catalogue record for this book is available
from the British Library

Paperback 978 1 78747 034 7
Ebook 978 1 78747 032 3

10 9 8 7 6 5 4 3 2 1

Designed by Devan Norman

Printed and bound in Great Britain by Clays Ltd, Elcograf S.p.A.

For A.V.W.

The conduct of the people was so indescribably frightful, that I felt for some time afterwards almost as if I were living in a city of devils.

—Charles Dickens

Shanghai was a city of vice and violence, of opulence wildly juxtaposed to unbelievable poverty, of whirling roulette wheels and exploding shotguns and crying beggars . . . Shanghai had become a tawdry city of refugees and rackets.

—Vanya Oakes,
White Man's Folly (1943)

Shanghai. A heaven built upon a hell!

—Mu Shiying,
Shanghai Fox-trot (1934)

Truly the devil pulls on all our strings.

—Charles Baudelaire

CONTENTS

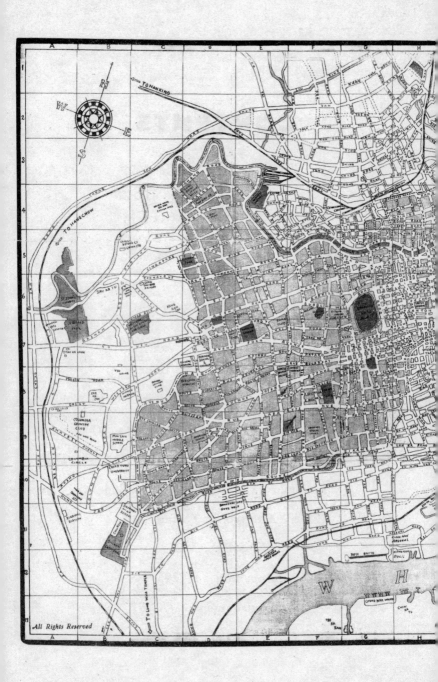

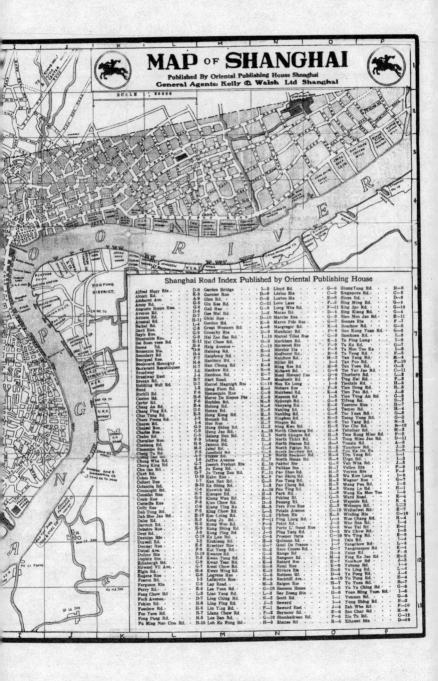

MAP OF SHANGHAI

Published By Oriental Publishing House Shanghai
General Agents: Kelly & Walsh Ltd Shanghai

SCALE : 36000

POOTUNG DISTRICT

Shanghai Road Index Published by Oriental Publishing House

Alfred Magy Rte.	D-8	Garden Bridge	I-5	Lloyd Rd.	G-6	Stung Ung Rd.	H-6
Alcock Rd.	K-8	Garnier Rue	D-9	Lorlou Rte	C-9	Singapore Rd.	C-5
Amherst Ave.	A-9	Glen Rd.	O-2	Lorton Rte	E-6	Sinza Rd.	D-6
Amoy Rd.	G-5	Gin Kee Rd.	G-5	Love Lane	F-6	Sing Ming Rd.	G-6
Auguste Boppe Rue	G-8	Gall Rue	I-2	Lung Wha Rd.	F-11	Sing Jao Rd.	G-10
Avenue Rd.	D-6	Gee Mai Rd.	I-2	Macao Rd.	D-1	Sing Kiang Rd.	G-4
Annam Rd.	D-7	Ghisi Rue	D-10	Marche Rue	C-9	Sieo Moo Jao Rd.	E-11
Arsenal Rue	H-11	Gordon Rd.	E-6	Marco Polo Rue	G-7	Soears Rte	F-7
Balkal Rd.	L-4	Great Western Rd.	A-8	Margregor Rd.	K-4	Soochow Rd.	G-5
Bard Rue	G-9	Grouchy Rte	G-8	Mandalay Rd.	F-6	Sun Kung Yuen Rd.	G-8
Bayti Rue	G-8	Hai Zao Sze Rd.	J-10	Marcel Tillot Rue	G-8	Szechuen Rd.	I-5
Bluntschle Ruw	L-4	Hai Chow Rd.	O-3	Markham Rd.	E-5	Ta Ping Lung	I-5
Bel Soon ruen Rd.	H-11	Haig Avenue	H-8	Marsonet Rte	C-9	Ta Ku Rd.	D-5
Boone	H-4	Haining Rd.	H-4	Mercier Rte	I-4	Ta Moo Ka	I-5
Bonsamn Rte.	G-9	Haiphong Rd.	D-6	Medhurst Rd.	E-6	Ta Tung Rd.	F-5
Boundary Rd.	H-4	Hanbury Rd.	F-7	Melchou Rd.	M-2	Tan Yang Rd.	A-8
Bourgeat Rue	F-7	Han Chung Rd.	H-8	Miller Rd.	I-4	Tao Foo Rd.	I-6
Boulevard Montigny	H-8	Hankow Rd.	H-7	Ming Koo Rd.	H-8	Ten Yuen Rd.	F-5
Boulevard Republique	H-7	Hardoon Rd.	J-4	Mohawk Rd.	E-7	Ten Yar Jao Rd.	C-11
Broadway	I-5	Hart Road.	B-7	Moni Morand Rue	G-6	Thorhorn Rd.	I-3
Broadway East	J-4	Marcel Magnigh Rte	D-7	Moulmein Rd.	F-7	Ting Hai Rd.	F-8
Brenan Rd.	B-7	Heng Foon Rd.	F-6	Mo Ka Loung	J-8	Tientsin Rd.	H-6
Bubbling Well Rd.	D-7	Hennequin Rue	F-8	Moliere Rue	E-8	Tien Dong Rd.	L-3
Bund	F-6	Herve De Sleyes Rte	E-9	Muirhead Rd.	K-4	Tien Fong Rd.	J-8
Burkill Rd.	F-6	Hochien Rd.	F-5	Museum Rd.	H-5	Tien Tsng An Rd.	G-8
Canton Rd.	G-5	Holung Rd.	H-5	Myburgh Rd.	M-3	Tifeng Rd.	B-7
Carter Rd.	D-5	Honan Rd.	H-6	Nanyang Rd.	E-6	Tournee Rue	H-7
Chang An Rd.	K-8	Hong Kong Rd.	H-6	Nanking Rd.	G-6	Teepoo Rd.	H-4
Chang Ping Rd.	K-3	Hoopeh Rd.	J-3	Nanhing Rd.	G-6	Tse Yuen Rd.	J-5
Chae Foona Rd.	I-4	Hue Rue	H-7	Ningkin Rd.	H-5	Tseng Yung Rd.	N-2
Chapoo Rd.	I-5	Hung Shing Rd.	G-3	Ningpo Rd.	H-7	Too Yang Rd.	N-3
Chapsal Rue	C-9	Hung Jao Rd.	A-10	Ning Kwe Rd.	H-5	Tso Che Rd.	H-6
Charles Rue	C-9	Holang Sun Rd.	G-3	North Chekiang Rd.	G-4	Tatsihar Rd.	M-2
Chafoo Rd.	G-9	Ichang Rd.	F-9	North Kiangse Rd.	H-4	Tau Kong Miao Rd.	D-11
Chevalier Rue	H-6	Jamson Rd.	I-4	North Szechow Rd.	H-4	Tsung Miao Jao Rd.	D-11
Cheklang Rd.	M-3	Jehol Rd.	G-4	North Thibit Rd.	G-3	Tunsin Rd.	L-3
Chewatoo Rd.	C-9	Josefield Rd.	I-5	North Shanse Rd.	I-4	Tunchow Rd.	I-5
Cheng Tu Rd.	D-6	Jinkee Rd.	A-8	North Saochow Rd.	G-4	Tun Ka On Ka	L-5
Chung Wha Rd.	L-8	Joffre Avenue	C-9	North Paochow Rd.	H-4	Urn Yang Rd.	L-3
Chung King Rd.	K-8	Joseph Frelupt Rte	E-8	Pakhol Rte	H-7	Urga Rd.	L-3
Chu sae Rd.	E-8	Ju Kong Rd.	F-11	Palikao Rue	H-7	Vah Wha Rd.	J-5
Chert Rd.	G-7	Ju Tseng Gun Rd.	F-11	Pao Shan Rd.	H-3	Vellex Rte	F-8
Cohen Rte	D-10	Kahn Rue	D-10	Pao Shing Rd.	H-2	Voyron Rte	H-8
Colbert Rue	I-2	Kan San Rd.	G-8	Pao Tung Rd.	H-2	Wa Kwe Lung	G-7
Columbia Rd.	B-10	Ka Shing Rd.	J-3	Pao Chong Rd.	J-3	Wagner Rue	G-7
Connaught Rd.	G-6	Keswick Rd.	A-8	Pao Ting Rd.	K-3	Wang Ka Rd.	L-5
Consulat Rue	H-6	Kiangse Rd.	H-6	Park Rd.	G-5	Wang Ka Meo Too	L-9
Conte Rue	G-9	Kiang Wan Rd.	H-3	Peking Rd.	H-6	Ward Road.	J-4
Cormille Rue	F-8	Kien Chow Rd.	D-8	Penang Rd.	D-6	Wayside Rd.	K-4
Cotty Rue	C-9	Kiang Ying Ka	G-9	Pere Froc Rue	G-8	Weimore Rd.	L-5
Doh Tong Rd.	F-2	King Chow Rd.	L-3	Petain Avenue	C-10	Wellentwel Rd.	E-7
Dah Moo Jao Rd.	E-10	Keo Ching Rd.	G-5	Plehon Rte	E-8	Winling Rte	C-10
Dalny Rd.	K-8	Kong Ja Rd.	F-11	Ping Liang Rd.	I-4	Woo Chang Rd.	J-5
Darroch Rd.	H-3	Kung Woo Rd.	E-9	Point Rd.	L-3	Woo Sun Rd.	I-4
Delastre Rue	E-9	Kung Shing Rd.	G-8	Porte L' Ouest Rue	G-8	Woo Tai Rd.	L-5
Dent Rd.	J-3	Kung Ping Rd.	J-3	Ping Yang Rd.	O-2	Wu Chow Rd.	L-5
Denium Rte	D-10	Ku Lun Rd.	I-2	Prosper Paris	C-10	Wu Ting Rd.	E-6
Doxwell Rd.	I-2	Klukiang Rd.	H-6	Quinsan Rd.	I-4	Yulo Rd.	L-3
Doener Rue	E-8	Kraetzer Rue	C-9	Quai De France	G-7	Yangchow Rd.	K-4
Dubail Ave.	F-9	Kul Yang Rd.	L-3	Race Course Rd.	O-2	Yangtszepoo Rd.	K-4
Dufour Rte	D-10	Kwanse Rd.	I-2	Range Rd.	H-4	Yates Rd.	D-6
Dupleix Rte	D-8	Kwen Tung Rd.	H-2	Rangoon Rd.	M-4	Ying Ka Jao Rd.	H-2
Edinburgh Rd.	C-8	Kwan Tsao Rd.	D-8	Rataral Rue	E-7	Yoochow Rd.	J-2
Edward VII Ave.	G-7	Kwei Chow Rd.	G-8	Remi Rue	E-9	Yuhung Rd.	I-5
Elgin Rd.	H-4	Kwen Ming Rd.	K-3	Riviere Rue	D-8	Yu Ling Rd.	L-3
Eugene Rue	G-8	Lagrene Rue	G-8	Robison Rd.	D-5	Yu Fong Rd.	K-4
Fearon Rd.	I-3	Lafayette Rue.	C-9	Rockhill Ave.	A-10	Yu Yuang Rd.	E-6
Ferguson Rte	C-9	Lay Road.	H-3	Saigon Rue	M-3	Yun Rd.	J-8
Ferry Rd.	E-6	Lee Yuen Rd.	G-5	Saosoon Houes	L-8	Yu Ya Ching Rd.	G-5
Feng Chow Rd	L-8	Liao Yang Rd.	L-3	Sey Zoong Rte	D-8	Yuen Ming Yuen Rd.	I-5
Foch Avenue.	D-7	Ling Ching Rd.	H-5	Scott Rd.	I-1	Yunnan Rd.	J-8
Fokien Rd.	H-6	Ling Ping Rd.	I-8	Seward	F-8	Yang Shing Rd.	F-10
Foochow Rd.	H-6	Lin Ying Rd.	H-5	Seward East	F-1	Zah Wha Rd.	F-10
Foo Yuen Rd.	H-7	Liang Chow Rd	E-8	Zau Char Rd	E-6	Zoo Char Rd	F-10
Fong Pang Rd.	H-8	Loe Ban Rd.	G-10	Shanhaikwan Rd.	H-6	Zis Tu Rd.	D-12
Fa Ming Nan Cho Rd.	H-10	Loh Ka Pong itd.	H-9	Shanse Rd.	H-6	Zikawei Rte	D-10

Prepared by Mr. Minshan Hu

PREFACE

I lived in Shanghai for many years. Daily I walked the city's streets, soaking up its unique atmosphere. Despite the myriad skyscrapers and overhead expressways, I spent my spare time looking for traces of what had been before, wandering a city of ghosts and trying to recapture the lives of those foreigners of so many nations who once knew the International Settlement of Shanghai as their home. In the last quarter of a century, Shanghai has become a city reborn. In the early 1950s, a virtual dust sheet was cast over the port, and little changed for more than forty years. It was only in the mid-1990s that Shanghai was allowed to thrive again. In the late twentieth and early twenty-first century I lived in a city that was building at breakneck speed, bulldozing the old and well worn seemingly without a care, keen to construct the new and shiny as fast as possible. But an older city still, just about, exists.

It's easy to succumb to nostalgia in Shanghai. The metropolis is constantly eroding the built environment of its past. It is rapidly losing the last remnants of both its art deco and modernist architectural heritage, as well as its traditional narrow, confined rookeries and alleyways, *shikumen* stone dwellings and *lilong* lane houses. Periodically Shanghai does try to recall its previous heyday between the world wars, but every renewed bout of nostalgia becomes more disconnected, more affected by hindsight. It takes increasing amounts of imagination to catch a glimpse of the old glamour and style of Shanghai (best done at twilight or dawn, I find) down an alley, in the lobby of an old building, along the banks of one of the city's creeks and streams. In my effort to understand what the city's inhabitants once thought and why they acted as they did, my quest has always focused on the lower depths of this once remarkably cosmopolitan city, Shanghai's foreign underbelly: those rarely written about, the men and women not covered in glory or fabulous riches, not feted or even remembered in the minutes and formal records of the city. I'm drawn to the flotsam and jetsam, the impoverished émigrés and stranded refugees, transient ne'er-do-wells and washed-up chancers, con men and female grifters. I seek out those foreigners who came to the China Coast and preferred to exist in the city's criminal milieu, to disappear into its laneways and backstreets. They're not distinguished or heroic. Invariably they're liars and cheats. They're rarely anything close to good, and all are terribly flawed, often living in Shanghai because they were one step ahead of the law and, invariably, other options were few and far between. But many of them had a certain style, panache; their own particular flair. They take a lot of seeking, but their traces—faint, sketchy—remain.

City of Devils is based on real people and real events, as best as can be divined from the witnesses, participants, and reports of the time. A complete record is impossible due to the nature of the people involved, their somewhat clandestine lives, purposely hidden pasts and false names, changed birthdates and the crimes they committed and/or abetted, all of which they would never willingly confess to. Where records do exist, they are rarely as complete and as detailed as the academic historian would accept—falsifications, clerical errors, and downright lies were exacerbated by war and devastation. Although assumptions have been made, I've done my utmost to adhere to historical accuracy. Of course all the main players are now gone, though I am sure they would have denied everything, just as they did at the time.

This story is drawn from a wide variety of sources, primary and secondary. As we are now three quarters of a century distant from the finale of the events in this book, primary sources are difficult. Fortunately, some people who lived through those times still remain with us, while others told their stories to their children and grandchildren—they are thanked in the acknowledgments. I trawled through a large range of secondary sources, including the archives of the Shanghai Municipal Police and the Shanghai Special Branch, the annual reports of the Shanghai Municipal Council, the archives of the British and American consulates, the records of the U.S. Court for China at Shanghai and the archives of the United States Marine Corps. I also drew upon the China Coast newspapers and periodicals of the time, especially the *China Weekly Review, China Press, North-China Daily News, Shanghai Times, Shopping News, Peking and Tientsin Times* and *Walla-Walla* (the magazine of the U.S. Fourth Marines in Shanghai). The excerpts from the *Shopping News* that appear in the text are genuine historical articles from the publication, with one or two minor additions in the interest of advancing the narrative.

I have tried to recreate the linguistic Tower of Babel that was the treaty port of Shanghai between the world wars. As well as English (in its British, Irish, American, and Australian variants), other commonly spoken languages were Yiddish, German, Russian, Portuguese, French, Italian, and Spanish, as well as Tagalog, Korean, and Japanese. Shanghai was also, of course, a melting pot of Chinese dialects—Mandarin-Pekingese dialect and Cantonese as well as, obviously, the local Shanghainese dialect. I have used the Reverend Donald MacGillivray's *A Mandarin-Romanized Dictionary of Chinese* (eighth edition, 1930) to standardise the Wade-Giles system of romanisation. That said, there is no definitive answer to most of these romanisations.

It's worth noting that most slang, curses, racial epithets, and colloquial words and terms used are specific to the time and place and may, if not viewed in the context of the period and place, trouble modern sensibilities. Throughout I have sought to use those words and phrases most commonly noted in memoirs and newspapers of the time. Many are now deemed offensive, and I have no desire to revive them except in the interest of historical accuracy. Between the wars Shanghai was certainly highly cosmopolitan, but it was, in many ways both formal and informal, segregated between the Chinese and the foreigners. At times the two communities interacted and overlapped—this went for the respective criminal minority as well as the law-abiding majority of the city's populace—but, for most of the characters in this book, Shanghai was a Chinese city where they invariably worked, played, and committed criminal acts largely with other foreigners.

At a time of ever-escalating inflation in Shanghai in the late 1930s and early 1940s, calculating any prices in the text into today's money is problematic. Shanghai used multiple currencies and did business in anything considered reliable, from gold bullion to Indian rupees. The Mexican silver dollar was the most trusted currency during the time of the Badlands and was imported in great volume. The Bank of China issued Chinese one-dollar, five-dollar, ten-dollar, fifty-dollar, and hundred-dollar notes, though inflation made these problematic, as did rampant forgery. Coiners also put out fake coppers—three hundred (real ones) equalled one silver dollar. As a rough guide, Shanghai Mexican silver dollar amounts can be multiplied by six for an approximate equivalent U.S. dollar sum in 2017.

—*Paul French, London, August 2017*

INTRODUCTION

Shanghai was a prize won after victory in an opium war, a war waged by Great Britain to open China to a drug that caused pain, waste, and death in the Middle Kingdom while enriching the western nations. The foreigners claimed Shanghai as part of their victory terms, cauterised it from the rest of China by a most unequal treaty signed in the face of British gunboats. And so a strange urban aberration grew up on the banks of the Whangpoo River, close to the mouth of the Yangtze River, gateway to the vast Chinese hinterlands. The foreigners who came to build the city described Shanghai as a shining light, an example to the heathen darkness of China of the benefits of free trade and modernity. To others, the freebooting city was little more than a magnet attracting adventurers and ne'er-do-wells; a festering goiter of badness; stolen territory. Yet good, bad, or not caring either way, grow Shanghai did, from walled fishing village in dread of marauding pirates to an international 'treaty port' and the world's fifth largest city by the 1930s— a deafening babel of tongues, a hodgepodge of administrations, home to hopeful souls from several dozen nations joined together by one simple guiding ethos: money and the getting of it. In a hundred Sunday sermons from the missionaries who hoped to bring the light to China, Shanghai was the insanity of Sodom incarnate.

Shanghai became a legend: the Wild East. By the 1920s, three and a half million people called the nine square miles of the International Settlement home.

The International Settlement governed itself—not a colony like Hong Kong or Singapore, but a treaty port, a place of trade and enrichment for the conquerors. The Settlement was administered by an elected Municipal Council composed mostly of foreigners—'Shanghailanders'—and, later, grudgingly a few 'Shanghainese' Chinese. The foreign-run Municipal Police enforced the law and, if needed, the Shanghai Volunteers would muster to reinforce the foreign troops stationed in the city to protect the Settlement. The Settlement represented fourteen foreign powers—Belgium, Brazil, Denmark, France, Italy, Japan, the Netherlands, Norway, Portugal, Spain, Sweden, Switzerland, Great Britain, and the United States—who had extracted treaty port rights from a weak and teetering Qing Dynasty China. Each had its own consulate and courts within the Settlement, for within the Settlement a foreigner was not subject to Chinese justice but only to that of his or her own nation. This extraterritoriality meant that an American could only be called before the American court, a Briton before the British court and so on and so on. A mixed court was created to resolve legal issues between foreigners and Chinese, with a foreign assessor sitting alongside a Chinese magistrate.

The French refused to join the Settlement and maintained their own adjacent concession with their own municipal council, police force, troops, and justice system. The vastness of China abutted the foreign concessions to the north and to the west. Those areas, the roads just beyond the Settlement's borders, became contested no-man's-lands. As China spiraled downward towards war with Japan, the once leafy and suburban Western Roads area of the city transformed into a 'badlands' of gambling, dope, and vice.

Shanghai's existence was the most direct manifestation of the weakness of the ailing Qing Dynasty—Chinese soil taken by foreign powers. In 1911 the 267-year-old dynasty collapsed, and a Chinese republic was born. That republic descended swiftly to infighting and fratricidal dispute. Warlords rose and ruled giant swathes of China the size of Europe with their own private bandit armies throughout the 1920s. China appeared constantly on the point of collapse, about to fragment into a hundred warring states. Against this chaos Shanghai stood solid, prospered, and grew.

Shanghai between the world wars was a home to those with nowhere else to go and no one else to take them in. Its International Settlement, French Concession, and Badlands district admitted the paperless, the refugee, the fleeing; those who sought adventure far from the Great Depression and poverty; the desperate who sought sanctuary from fascism and communism; those who sought to build criminal empires; and those who wished to forget. The city asked nothing of them, not visas nor money nor status. Shanghai became a city of reinvention. It reinvented old China as something modern, glittering and golden, where a Chinese peasant didn't have to *chi ku*, 'eat bitterness', as generations of their forebears had, but could grow rich and flourish. It transformed an unwanted orphan, born in a cold-water tenement in the American Midwest, on the run from a maximum-security prison, into a millionaire through slot machines, roulette wheels, and violence. It transformed a hungry and ambitious Jewish boy from the Vienna ghetto, dreaming of an escape from poverty, into a master impresario who created dazzling dance hall spectaculars with chorus lines that rivalled anything New York, London, or Paris could muster, alongside a casino empire such as the Far East had never seen before.

But no city, not even Shanghai, was big enough for all those who sought to profit from it. And so inevitably men, nations, and ideologies clashed in an ever-expanding orgy of violence and retribution, while an invading Japanese army raped and ravaged outside the gates of the International Settlement.

Shanghai was surrounded—by sea to the east and south and by

the ferocious pillaging armies of Japan to the north and west. In August 1937, the Japanese bombed the Chinese-controlled portions of the city. They avoided attacking the foreign concession, not yet wanting war with the European powers and America, and so the International Settlement and the French Concession became the 'Solitary Island' (*Gudao*, as it was dubbed by the Chinese). Lines long demarcated and agreed upon were crossed, negotiated spheres of influence were laid to waste, and thousands of innocent people were killed. While the phosphorous flames of the fox demons of war swirled through the burnt-out streets and devastated quarters of the Chinese portions of the city, the Japanese entered the house and took everything. Those who could escape did so, but many were left behind in the City of Devils.

This book is a true account of the lives of two men who inhabited Shanghai in its last, dying days before Pearl Harbor, when it fell definitively to the Japanese occupation. Joe Farren, born in the Vienna ghetto as penniless Josef Pollak, had come to Shanghai as an exhibition dancer and risen to become 'Dapper Joe', the city's own Flo Ziegfeld, running the best chorus lines in the swankest nightclubs, and finishing up with his name in neon above the Badland's biggest casino. His partner in that last, most lavish Shanghai venture was another man who changed names and identities—Jack Riley, ex–U.S. Navy, wanted prison escapee, who began his China Coast criminal career as a bouncer in the toughest rookeries of northern Shanghai and rose to be the city's slots king, controlling every slot machine in the city.

Over the years the two men edged warily around each other as they became rich and powerful, as between them they created much of the city's reputation as an international capital of sin and vice. Joe constantly sought more and accepted the city's temptations if they facilitated his rise; Jack greedily grasped any and every opportunity that presented itself. 'Dapper Joe' and 'Lucky Jack' collided, collaborated, clashed, and then made truce and partnered, a thing nobody could have predicted.

In November 1940 they bestrode the Badlands of Shanghai like kings, the streets their kingdom, their gigantic nightclub and casino their palace, while all around the Solitary Island were desperation, poverty, starvation, and genocide. They thought they ruled Shanghai; but the city had other ideas.

This is the story of their rise to power, as part of Shanghai's foreign underworld; it is also the story of their downfall and the trail of destruction they left in their wake. Shanghai was their playground for a flickering few years, a city where for a fleeting moment even the wildest dreams seemed possible.

PROLOGUE

The Devil's Last Dance

February 15, 1941—Farren's Nightclub,
Great Western Road, the Shanghai Badlands

Shanghai is not the city it once was . . .' She heard it over and over again, repeated so often it had become received wisdom. At the still-swank cocktail parties just off the stunning waterfront Bund; at dinner parties in the still-elegant apartments and villa houses of the French Concession . . . Since August 14, 1937, Bloody Saturday, Shanghai was not what it once had been.

She disagreed.

Not that the war, the bombings, the Japanese hadn't changed things, but that change wasn't all bad. Shanghai clouds had silver linings. Her father, a bullion dealer, was making more money than ever: inflationary and uncertain times meant demand for gold had soared. The Japanese encirclement of the foreign concessions was an inconvenience; fewer ships came and went; airplane service was erratic to nonexistent. Life in the protected Solitary Island could be tiresome as it meant many of life's goodies didn't make it to Shanghai anymore, but nothing was insurmountable.

For Alice Daisy Simmons, just turned twenty-eight, a Shang-hailander by birth, unmarried and a partner in her father's firm,

Solitary Island life was exciting. From her Frenchtown penthouse, the wardrobe stuffed with tailor-made gowns and Siberian furs, Alice looked out on a city that twinkled at night like a jewel box. They all knew war raged in the hinterlands, that the wartime capital at Chungking was bombed nightly, that little seemed to stand in the way of the Japanese Imperial Army and their desire to subjugate all China. But here, in Shanghai's foreign concessions, the neon still shone brightly, taxicabs still hustled for fares, and the night-clubs swung just like before.

While other Shanghailander girls had been shipped out—down to Hong Kong, away to far-off Australia—she had stayed. Her father believed in Shanghai, believed the Japanese would want it to remain a special place that generated profits for them. There-fore they would leave it alone, ring-fence it, and let Shanghai do what it had always done: make money. She believed that too.

And so she had remained in the Solitary Island, and found it a surrounded citadel where those who could afford it continued to dedicate themselves to pleasure as the rest of the world burned around them. This was Shanghai in 1941, and she was part of it.

A chill Shanghai February, close to midnight. Alice arrives at Farren's on the Great Western Road, her favourite nightspot, sup-posedly the largest in the Far East. The place enthrals her. After the Japanese invaded the western districts of the city and allowed the cabarets, casinos, dope dens, and brothels of the Badlands to spring up cheek-by-jowl alongside the streets and boulevards of the Settlement and Frenchtown, she had begun making excuses to avoid the stuffy drawing room soirées; the boring tittle-tattle of lunchtime tiffins and Frenchtown cafés. What she discovered, under the neon lights, beyond the velvet rope, was Farren's and its three floors of roulette, chemin de fer, and craps.

She is known here, treated with respect, among people who feel the same thrill. The young Austrian refugees who man the doors swing them wide open and usher her in with exaggerated bows and cheeky winks. The head doorman, Walter, a great bear of a Viennese but always charming, helps Alice out of her fur as a coat-check girl has a hanger ready. He motions her towards the bar, where Joe Farren, the patron of the club and master impresario of Shanghai's wartime nightlife, pours her a glass of champagne from an ice bucket that stands on the corner, always full, ready for Dapper Joe to toast his most favoured clientele. He kisses her cheeks and raises his own glass. They clink flutes. He whispers in her ear over the sound of the band whipping up a storm on the dance floor. She doesn't quite hear what he says but nods and smiles. With Gentleman Joe it's always compliments.

Alice moves through the diners and dancers, those left in Shanghai lucky enough to be able to afford steak and champagne, to shrug off their cares and dance. It's a dwindling group, but those best able to party and gamble come to Farren's. She heads up the staircase to the gambling floors and makes for the roulette tables where her cohort of fellow gamblers gathers nightly. Alice favours roulette, a game of pure chance that rewards only those willing to believe in the long odds and with the money to stay in the game all night. It is always surprising that so many in Shanghai, a city that few bet on surviving much longer, should worship at the roulette table. But the tables are packed. There are no spare stools, though she knows they will always find a place for her.

Usually she would begin her evening talking with the pit boss, Gentleman Joe Farren's partner, Jack Riley. Where Joe is suave, all middle-European elegance, Jack is American bluntness with a rough charm. But she knows Jack wouldn't be around tonight; she'd heard Jack had trouble with the courts and was lying low. Some thought he'd skipped town; others that he was hunkered down over in Hongkew, up by Little Tokyo, and wouldn't be reappearing anytime soon as the law, or what was left of it in Shanghai, had sworn to jail him.

She stops to drink a good-luck toast with a few friends who also spend their evenings at the Farren's roulette tables. Then she decides to see if the gods of good *joss* are with her that evening and heads towards the table. Albert Rosenbaum, Jack's number two and stand-in pit boss, sees Alice and winks. He taps the shoulder of a Chinese dandy and whispers in his ear. The dandy has been betting low amounts and coming up evens, so neither he nor Farren's is ahead. The dandy refuses the croupier's offer to bet and decides to call it a night, pocketing a few chips in a pile that Rosenbaum has added to as an incentive to vacate his place. Rosenbaum motions to Alice to take the vacant spot. He places a pile of chips on the table for her, and she sees him make a note in his little notebook of the amount. A good pit boss always makes sure the regulars with money to burn have chips in front of them.

Alice sips the last of her champagne. She nods to Joe as he comes up the stairs from the bar and heads up one more flight to his top-floor private office with Rosenbaum.

Suddenly, she hears shots and screaming from downstairs. She knows what's happening. This is the Badlands; desperate gunmen had raided other nightclubs and casinos. She watches the players at the next table scramble underneath. Then more screaming, shouting, glass shattering. More gunshots, this time on the gambling floors. A light fitting shatters; wood splinters fly as a shot hits the wall opposite the roulette table. She hears footsteps heavy on the stairway and turns round. Alice is surprised to see Jack Riley, shotgun in hand, with his German bodyguard, Schmidt, waving a Mauser, scattering people looking to get down the stairs. Jack shouldn't be here; the police are hunting him; he is Shanghai's most wanted man. He smiles at her, his usual broken-tooth grin she knows so well. He looks embarrassed, and then he looks away. Jack and Schmidt point their guns up at the ceiling and fire. Croupiers are diving for cover. Jack glances back at her momentarily. Then she feels a sharp burning sensation in her back and falls to the floor.

March 28, 1941—Young Allen Court,
Shanghai International Settlement

Alone and friendless, Jack Riley is holed up in the Young Allen apartments on the Chapoo Road, Hongkew. He is not so Lucky Jack now. Only the vast stretches of Shanghai's Eastern District—Hongkew, Yangtzsepoo, the Northern External Roads—offer the possibility of sanctuary. This is predominantly Chinese Shanghai, effectively outside Shanghai Municipal Police day-to-day control. It's policed by the Japanese, its northern edge raked by Imperial Japanese Army snipers and trashed by civilian Japanese looters who call themselves ronin. Hongkew is now inhabited only by transients, Chinese refugees from the countryside, Japanese army deserters, and marauding *pi-seh* hoodlums for hire. Jack is on the lam and paying over the odds, in cash daily, for the flop. Everyone knows he's on the run, the newspapers revelling in the fact that, finally, the odds are stacked against the Slots King of Shanghai. His crew, dubbed Riley's Friends, have evaporated. All of his former allies are in the wind.

Shanghai is a dead end, a lethal cul-de-sac. There's no way out. No white man would last five minutes in the occupied countryside outside the city, where Japanese Navy bluejackets roam. The sea is twenty Jap-infested miles downriver, and the Whangpoo River is on lockdown, with Little Tokyo's marine gendarmerie on patrol. Frenchtown is too small, with too many enemies—the Sûreté, the Vichyites, the Frenchtown Corsicans he's crossed before. The Badlands is crawling with trigger-happy, dubiously fresh-badged faux-police goons of the Chinese collaborators and nasty Japanese Kempeitai, Tokyo's homegrown version of the Gestapo, military police fingernail pullers, who'd love to give him a beating and then claim the bounty. They used to smile like friends, take his fat envelopes stuffed with cash, break bread and parley. Every last one of them knows Jack's mug intimately—they took money off him for long enough. Jack won't get any help from the Shanghai Badlands Syndicate either. Thanks to him, it's over. He's interfered with business, broken rule number one: don't draw undue attention.

It's not that he doesn't have regrets; it's just that he doesn't have many. He feels bad for not having treated Babe and Nazedha, the only two real women in his life, better. He wishes things had worked out better with Joe. He can't get the image of that girl, Alice, out of his head, at the roulette table, falling down to the floor, her eyes on him all the time.

So here is Jack, among the rubble and the smouldering timbers, the result of Imperial Japanese Navy bombs aimed at the main railway line out of the city. The room is bare, cold, the fireplace useless, even if he had coal—and nobody without serious connections in Shanghai has had coal for months. He's left with a Japanese hibachi stove and precious little charcoal to fuel it. The place reeks from his chamber pot, the toilet broken. An iron bedstead, an ancient mattress made rancid and lumpy by a thousand arses, a thin red eiderdown that's never seen a laundry. A little balcony, but he dare not show his face. Late at night he hears the ping of the solitary shots from Type 97 sniper rifles picking off poor indigents out scavenging firewood. Their bodies are left in the street. The first night he woke up scratching, the wallpaper covered with bugs, a seething mass. He sleeps fully clothed, but the lice get in anyway, marking his arms and legs like the worst kind of track marks. Jack never took to the toot juice or the needle; he was always a caffeine and Benzedrine junkie. He'd kill for a cup of joe now, and he's down to a handful of bennies his old squeeze Babe cadged for him under the counter at the Sine Pharmacy on the Hongkew Broadway. He knows he has to stretch them out to keep alert and stop the tremors from kicking in.

He is too well known to leave the building—who doesn't know Slots King Jack's trademark chipped-tooth grin? Every schmuck who ever bought a two-cent beer or a dollar hooker down at the

Jukong Alley brothel shacks, or cruised Avenue Eddy for better-class working girls, or took in the floor show at DD's, ritzed at the Paramount, spun a wheel at Farren's, bet on the mutts at the Canidrome, attended the Friday night fights in Frenchtown, watched the baseball, caught the super fast Basque boys at the jai alai, shot the shit at the Fourth Marines Club, slummed it in the Scott Road Trenches or huddled out back of Blood Alley for the bareknuckle Square-Gos knows him, every single one of them now a betrayer.

There are rifle butt–sized holes gouged in the masonry where the Japanese used the building to snipe Nationalist soldiers in '37. He can't bathe or shower and uses an increasingly blunt razor to shave his face. He is deteriorating and he knows it—his collar grimy, cuffs filthy. His teeth ache, his gums bleed, and the cold makes his fingers hurt. Jack Riley is, for the first time in a long, long time, desperate.

Crouched by the window he hears the end, the growling engine of the Red Maria. Men spill out the back, taking up position in full body armour—they're expecting him to shoot it out. The Municipal Police riot squad has come with wide-bore guns, the safety catches flicked off, corporals shouldering ugly Chinese knockoff Mauser M.1896 semi-automatics with broom-handle grips—old-school and nasty. There are huge white boys with the red hair of Ireland, the meanness of Ulster, and the menacing grins of England; oilskin-clad Sikhs standing ramrod straight, handpicked for the elite squad and armed with .303 carbines. Snipers take up positions, alongside a man with a teargas bomb.

The Young Allen apartment complex is strangely silent. The riot squad won't hesitate. Their standard orders? Shoot to kill, then count to ten. How the hell had it come to this? Jack slides under the bed frame in the hope it'll offer some protection. He stares up at the rusty springs of the iron bedstead; he can almost feel the men's fingers caressing the triggers outside. Maybe he'll be Lucky Jack just once more . . . before it all gets shot to shit.

PART ONE

The Rise to Greatness

Shanghai is a big city. It is a modern city. It is also a unique city. Its up-to-the-minute citizens live in skyscraper apartments and pent-houses, listen and dance to the latest in swing music.

—*China Digest*, 1940

Shanghai: saturated in riches and crimes, in vanities and vices, in miseries and poisons . . .

—Marc Chadourne,
Tour de la terre: Extrême-Orient (1935)

Let us sing of that old tavern, where dark Louis used to dwell
Where the Olgas and the Sonyas cast their spell
Of Whitey Smith, Bo Diddley and the little Carlton girl
Of Joe Farren and his own sweet Russky Nell

—'*Maloo Memories*', a pastiche
of an old Shanghai Volunteer Corps song

1

Born Fahnie Albert Becker, the custodians called him John. His origins were a subject of rumour and conjecture, an ever-changing story as the years and then the decades passed. But the man who would be Jack Riley to all in Shanghai was probably born in a Colorado logging camp near Manitou Springs in 1897, the son of a certain Nellie Shanks and Albert Azel Becker. His old man, a violent alcoholic, was gone before his son's first birthday. His mother, broke and deserted, dumped him in a Tulsa orphanage, where the custodians beat the boys and left them hungry at night. Becker decided to bail when he was seven. He bummed around and somehow reached Denver, where he got a job polishing brass and emptying spittoons in a nightclub, sleeping out back; the joint was part casino, part dive bar, part brothel.

At seventeen he found a home and a family in the United States Navy. He shipped out of San Francisco for Manila on the U.S.S. *Quiros* as an apprentice seaman for two years on Yangtze Patrol, the 'Yang Pat' of the United States Asiatic Fleet. The *Quiros* was part of a squadron that patrolled upriver from Shanghai to Chungking and all ports in between, protecting U.S. citizens and interests, guarding the tankers of John D. Rockefeller's Standard

Oil Company, the up-country terminals of Texaco, and the packed warehouses and go-downs of British-American Tobacco.

Discharged in 1919, Becker couldn't think of anything better to do than re-enlist for another tour, this time Manila to Shanghai. Nights off he spent playing craps in the Hongkew and Chapei sailor bars and drinking along Blood Alley with money won in prizefights out back of the bars. Righteous bucko mate, rated fighter, all-round good guy. Then he was back aboard and upriver to Wuhu, Nanking, and Chungking, his downtime spent boxing on deck, going ashore to play baseball, or shooting craps in the mess. The Yang Pat rotated and the *Quiros* headed home. John Becker was honourably discharged in 1921.

John Becker stepped ashore in San Francisco and wandered the port towns of California, staying in one-night cash-only flops, eating corned beef in sawdust-floored restaurants or chop suey in all-night Chinese diners, oyster shells crunchy underfoot. Then came Prohibition, and he switched to speakeasies and shebeens, sucking down rotgut hooch, sandpaper gin, and near beer. Eventually he ran out of money and headed back to Oklahoma, to Tulsa County; the only city he could vaguely call home, though his memories of that orphanage and the violent custodians were far from warm.

He got a gig at a taxi company. He knew engines, and the company could save a mechanic's wage by having him service his own vehicle. In 1923 Becker was still driving drunks home on the late shift, but he knew for sure Tulsa was a bust. Darktown was in cinders after the Greenwood race riots, and crime was out of control.

One night he picks up two guys at the Cave House speakeasy out on Charles Page Boulevard. It's a good fare, and Becker has been drinking and feels like he can handle these boys. When they get to the destination, a house in the suburbs, the men tell John Becker to wait while they pick something up, and then they'll head back to town. The meter's still running, he's supping a quart of rye, so what the heck. The men walk up to the house across the lawn, the outline of their hats visible as they open the door and smoke wafts out into the dark night air. There's shouting, commotion, and a shot; the men come out fast, dragging a third who doesn't look like he wants to leave.

If you believe John Becker, he didn't know anything till he heard the shouting and the shot. The men threw the third in the back and jumped in, punching the daylights out of the poor sap. Becker drives them to another house, and they drag the beaten guy in with them, but not before one of the men hands him a hundred-dollar bill and tells him to vamoose. The next day the cops show up and bust Becker for kidnapping. His fare had boosted an illegal dice game, killed one of the punters, and kidnapped another. There's a kidnapping epidemic in the Midwest, and it's re-election year, so the judge is not inclined to go easy. John Becker goes down for thirty-five years in the Oklahoma State Penitentiary, McAlester.

His civvies are confiscated, his head shaved to prevent lice; he's fingerprinted and photographed. On the cellblock: big guards with black batons; seven-by-three-foot cells; a disinfectant-filled bucket for your shit; a deafening siren in case of escape or riot; bad, bad food; men praying; hardened cons deranged with untreated syphilis, sobbing for their mamas; the mad and the bad of McAlester.

Becker plays dice for smokes. He becomes a trusty and gets a job in the shop. An old lag shows him how to make a pair of loaded dice that will always come out the way you want, if you learn to throw them just so and distract the heels. Those hours of pitching with the Yang Pat crew prove useful; he becomes the starting pitcher on the prison baseball team. They head for an out-of-pen game in McAlester City, and when the team heads one way with the guards, Becker heads the other. Walking away, the sweat streaming down his back, he waits for a guard's bullet to smash into his spine. Not running, not turning back, heart beating fit to jump right out of his chest. But the bullet never comes. He hops a freight running the St. Louis–San Francisco line. He's just skipped out on the lion's share of a three and a half decade stretch.

On the run, he's in a San Francisco boardinghouse down on the Embarcadero—as far west as you can get without swimming. He's spent nights in hobo camps where nobody asks your name. Now he needs to hunker down, stay out of sight, hope Oklahoma forgets about him. He knows he got lucky; he got a second chance. He quits the booze and the smokes—no profit in either. He rolls a drunk tramp on the waterfront and nabs his papers, and he's Edward Thomas Riley now. Fahnie Albert Becker is history. He likes Jack better than Edward, thinks he'll keep the T, and Riley suits just fine too—anonymous, everyday, all-American. There must be thousands of Jack Rileys out there. But some things are more difficult to change than your name.

Jack sits at a small table, rolls up his sleeves, and pours caustic soda in a glass. He takes off his leather belt and puts it between his teeth, then lays two hand towels out next to the glass. He takes three deep breaths, looks out the window at the scrappy backyard of the boardinghouse, and dips the fingers of his left hand in the chemical mix. The acid burns, and he snorts through his nose, forcing himself to dip each finger, then switches to his right hand, breathes really deeply, and repeats the process—thumbs and all. He takes his last finger out and relaxes his jaw, lets the belt fall out on his lap. He manages to wrap the towels around his hands and staggers over to the bed. He lies there for days, in satisfied agony. The whorls on his fingertips are gone, and they slowly heal and harden into callused skin. It ain't pretty, but he's a new man with a new start. He signs on as a mechanic with a tramp freighter heading across the Pacific to the Philippines.

Jack had liked Manila on his two Navy tours. First he stays at the Seamen's Mission, but then gets wise to where things are really happening. He hangs out at Ed Mitchell's Rhonda Grill, swings by a hole-in-the-wall called Tom's Dixie Kitchen that cooks tender steaks and sells imported Scotch for nine pesos a shot. He laps up the scene at the Metro Garden and Grill Ballroom, watching the Navy boys of the United States Asiatic Fleet drinking iced Pabst. On Christmas Day, the joints round Manila Bay and the Metro are a sea of white hats. It seems those boys can't spend their wages fast enough—booze, girls, dope.

Jack trades up to a room at the Manila Hotel. He gets himself into some craps games and wins himself a stake with those magic Oklahoma State Pen dice. He attends the afternoon tea dances at the genteel Bayview Hotel to tickle the ears of the Navy wives and buys himself some Saigon linen suits to smarten up his act. Early afternoon he takes in the movies at the theatres near the Malacanyan Palace until he realises the seat cushions are teeming with lice; he has to wash his hair with kerosene to kill the bastards. He likes walking the wealthy streets where the rich mestizos and the expat Americans live: the quiet, wide, tree-lined thoroughfares by the Bay or Dewey Boulevard with high-end American compounds, a LaSalle convertible in every driveway.

Down at the Metro, Jack hooks up with a local called Paco who shows him the sights. Paco has a British gal called Evelyn who's got a Russian surname, Oleaga, on account of having been married to a Russian some time back. Paco and Evelyn spot Jack for a bucko-mate-on-the-lam right off the bat. They hang out nightly at Ed Mitchell's before hitting the Metro: determinedly teetotaling Jack on the seltzer, Evelyn on the house Dubonnet cocktails. Paco invariably gets shit-faced with his Manilamen brothers, leaving Jack and Evelyn to talk. Jack breathes in her chypre perfume and digs her fancy cut-glass accent. He tells her he wants out. Manila is a steamy version of Tulsa, but Shanghai is the real deal. She confesses she hates this swamp and wants to go to Shanghai too. Jack tells her to look him up.

A couple of weeks later Paco pulls a bank heist with his brothers on Evelyn's tip-off and walks away with forty thousand pesos. Evelyn had her claws into the manager and sweet-talked everything out of him that Paco needed to know to rob the place right when the teller's drawers were full to bursting. Evelyn asks for her share, and Paco laughs, spits in her face, and slaps her across the room before throwing her out on the street and calling her evil. Evelyn, black-eyed, finds Jack drinking coffee in the Rhonda Grill and tells him the sorry story. Jack takes umbrage on her behalf and walks her back to her Chinatown apartment, where he finds Paco liquored up and smooching a Japanese whore. Jack beats the living crap out of Paco and hands Evelyn her cut, only to watch while she kicks Paco repeatedly in the cojones. Paco was right, Jack thinks, you are evil, Evil Evelyn. She stays the night in his hotel room, leaving the scent of chypre on Jack's sheets. The next morning he takes her to the harbour and watches her board a steamer for Shanghai, Paco already forgotten. Evil Evelyn pecks him on the cheek and says she owes him one.

In Manila Jack sees his first real industrial-size slot-machine operation and the gawk-eyed leatherneck marines lining up to lose their coin on payday. He'd seen slots in Tulsa, but only one at a time in a speakeasy or a blind pig. Nobody had much coin to spare back there. But in Manila, they cover whole floors. He watches the coins go in, the wheels spin, and a fuck of a lot fewer coins come out. Later, a thick-necked guy comes over and empties the back of the machine into a bucket, right up to the brim. Sweet business. Jack gets friendly with the lanky overseer, some ex-army Canadian called Penfold, or Pinfold. He explains the slots business to Jack. Easiest money on God's green earth, no wages wasted on croupiers, machines don't thieve the take, the dumbest hick could figure it out: just pop a peso in the slot, pull the lever, and wave it goodbye. Then do it again . . . and again . . . and again. It's rigged to the house and pays out ten per cent max on a good day.

It's time to move on. Jack buddies up with the Navy boys and jumps a U.S. Army transport heading for Shanghai. The U.S.S. *Chaumont* does the run regular and the crew are always willing to do a favour for a Yang Pat vet. Maybe they could carry the odd cargo from Manila for an old U.S. Navy man trying to make a go of it on the China Coast? Maybe they could at that.

The cold weather lingers late in Shanghai the spring of 1930. Jack Riley's fingers feel the cold bad. He's got a one-room flop with a shared can up in Hongkew that's a pay-by-the-day establishment. It's run by an old Swedish seaman's widow who's soft on sailors and doesn't hassle him for the rent. He keeps warm in his single divan with a leaky old kerosene heater and stashes his clothes in a mothball-smelling closet pushed against the mouldy blue walls. By night Jack's got a gig bouncing the door of the Venus Café, a late-late-night cabaret up on the North Szechuen Road, close by the dive bars of Jukong Alley. Babylonian Jewish Sam Levy runs the joint with his sister-in-law, Girgee, and they take a liking to Jack. Sam schmoozes the patrons while Girgee keeps the business side of things ticking over—ten cents a dance with the White Russian hostesses. Sam's happy to have Jack take care of the door, pay him some, and have his company for the Venus's traditional four a.m. ham and eggs, when the riffraff is sent on its way.

The Venus is a quiet joint till about midnight, when it becomes a bad-news mix of off-duty marines, British squaddies, Shanghai's foreign lowlife, and slumming swells. Jack is packing knuckle-dusters and a leather cosh, and there's a cutthroat Bengal razor in his breast pocket if things go truly south. Feet and fists will deal with ninety-nine per cent of the trouble at the Venus, and Jack's rep as a tasty amateur Navy boxer helps some. He's partnered with another ex-Navy tough guy called Mickey O'Brien, who's solid backup. The two hit it off from day one.

He's taken up with a regular at the Venus, Babe Sadlir, who's been in Shanghai 'since Christ only knows when'. Brown-eyed Babe is originally from Nevada via some dark times in San Francisco after stabbing a girl who took her man. She ditched the man, dodged the police, and lit out for Shanghai. Babe is one of the legion of 'White Flowers' of the China Coast, semi-high-class tramps who drift the Settlement, grifting the newly arrived British 'griffins', those young businessmen with money to spend who work at the great corporations, or *hongs*, as they're known, or the soldiers with pay to waste and the sojourners looking for company while they're in port.

By day you'll find Babe topping up her tan by the pool at the Columbia Country Club, scandalising the taipan wives with her Mei Li Bah cigarettes and short shorts that don't leave much to the imagination. By night you'll find her drinking champagne and snaffling free caviar in her tight-fitting linen dresses—all on some British or French officer's tab at the Cercle Sportif Français. She stays out all night a lot and lets Jack crash at her place in the Young Allen apartments on Chapoo Road. They even get it together occasionally. Jack likes Babe: the jagged scar on her neck from some ancient catfight, how she can't speak without cursing, her blonde ringlets. She teaches him the funny-sounding China Coast pidgin English and a smattering of Shanghainese patter. But she's got an awful bad dope habit and disappears for days, getting glassy-eyed on the divans in Leong's opium den out back of the Moon Palace dance hall, a ballroom with a mostly Chinese clientele, on the Hong-kew Broadway. Leong's sweet on her blonde hair, calls her a 'fox spirit girl' and lets her have dope gratis till she can find another sucker to sub her.

Jack finds Sam's four a.m. crew are mostly Jewish. There's Al Israel, who runs the Del Monte Café out in the Western External Roads on Avenue Haig; the Wiengarten brothers, Sammy and Al, who front the Red Rose Cabaret and a bunch of hooch shacks north of the Soochow Creek; Albert Rosenbaum, who'd come to Shanghai from Mexico City via New York; a Swiss heist merchant called Elly Widler, who has you counting your fingers after you've shaken hands with him; and the exhibition dancers Joe and Nellie Farren. Babe knows Nellie from the Majestic; Joe's in tight with the Israelites, being of that persuasion himself.

One night after the ham and eggs Joe tells Jack there's a long-standing craps game close by, out back of the Isis Cinema, organised by the White Russian band that accompanies the silent flicks. There's an old army blanket rather than felt for a shooting surface. Get low down against the wall and roll them dice. The suckers fresh out of California or just off the boat from England let Jack Riley use his very own special rolling bones, his sole souvenir of the Oklahoma State Pen. Six the hard way, easy eight, hard ten. Jack rolls a four, 'Little Joe from Kokomo'; a snake-eyes, comes up with three on each dice and calls it 'Jimmie Hicks from the sticks'. He keeps up the patter to keep the dice flying, the money moving, and nobody looking too closely. The sailor boys and the griffins are in awe of Jack, and they lap up his schtick.

They're long games; they go on till way past dawn. Jack ups the stakes, lures the mugs in, stares down anyone who would like to suggest Jack Riley's dice ain't straight. He prowls the Trenches bar strip after the Venus closes, hearing the Chinese touts crying 'Poluski girls, Poluski girls', taking the punters in the craps games out back of the shacks that run the length of the Scott Road and always building his stake a little higher. The next step is to gain some real estate of his own, put down some Shanghai roots.

In the shadow of the North Station train lines, the filth and driftwood of Shanghai pile into bug-infested lodgings along Jukong

Alley, a ghetto no decent resident of foreign Shanghai—that's a Shanghailander to you—would stand for. It's a million miles from the top joints like the Majestic Ballroom with smoothly mixed whisky sodas—*stengahs*, as everyone calls them—and a cloakroom stacked with Siberian furs. Or about a mile and a half in reality. The rows of tenements with shacks out back and passages between like veins on a doper's arm are a disgrace to the good name of Shanghai, says the uptight Municipal Council; a festering dunghill of sin and vice, say the two-faced Shanghai Municipal Police; a rookery no honest white man should enter and expect to leave alive, says the pompous *North-China Daily News*. Yet it stays because it pays—the SMP takes the squeeze and lets it run.

The Alley's pretty much sewn up. The boys from the back room of the Venus own it all, with the Wiengarten brothers, originally from Romania, ruling the roost. Hard for a newcomer to get any of the action there, but just over the Soochow Creek and then across the Avenue Eddy, across the Settlement lines and into Frenchtown, there's Rue Chao Pao San—that's Blood Alley to you, sailor boy—and Jack knows that sordid strip of old from his Yang Pat days.

Opportunity knocks. Jack chows nightly with Sam, Girgee, and Joe at the Venus. While Nellie and Babe swap gossip, Joe tells Jack there's a lush on Blood Alley for the taking: a dipsomaniac ex-Navy cook discharged in Shanghai who's bought himself a bar. He's got a taste for the dice and the bourbon but a firm belief that Lady Luck is with him. Joe makes the introductions and swears Jack's kosher; Jack drops tales of his Yang Pat past, acts like a hopeful naïve civilian and he's in the game. Jack plays the lush nightly for two weeks, losing, winning some back, always coming out slightly worse off than the heel. Then he ups the stakes until he gets the guy into debt, bad debt, and now the only way the sucker can get out of the hole is to play some more and hope for the best. But soon he gets so deep all he's got left is his bar—and then he doesn't even have that. Jack subs him the price of the Dollar Line steamer ticket back to San Fran and waves him off with a genuine au revoir.

And just like that, Jack Riley becomes the owner of one of Blood Alley's lowest and most knock-down-and-drag-out shebeens—the Manhattan Bar, proprietor Jack T. Riley, Esq. He invites Joe, Nellie, Sam, and the after-hours Venus crew for a drink. Mickey changes the locks while Babe sets them all up at the cigarette-burned mahogany bar. Sam tells Jack that it's a shithole sailor bar on Blood Alley . . . and Joe finishes his sentence: 'You'll make a fortune—mazeltov!' They all toast to that.

2

Josef Pollak, a Viennese Jewish boy, lives in the cramped quarter of the city's Leopoldstadt Yiddish ghetto. It's home to the *Ostjuden* pogrom refugees, those forced to be pickers of rags, peddlars of tat, roasters of chestnuts or brothel pianists, all coming home to watery broth and poverty. Twelve to a tenement room; fifty, sixty, or more packed into flea-ridden pensions, families huddled tight above small workshops . . . but at least it's Vienna and not the Jew-hating lands of Bessarabia or Galicia.

Josef moved from boyhood to manhood as the post–Great War depression destroyed the city's economy. Suicide cults hit the headlines—young people, all hope gone, all money lost, ordered coffee, added potassium cyanide, drank it and died writhing on the floor minutes later. The Pollaks are a large family—brothers, sisters; never enough money, never enough work. Vienna and the Pollaks shiver through the long winters amid shortages of coal and fire-wood; influenza takes the young and the elderly; the *zitterer*, literally 'those that shake', the shell-shocked of a lost war and a destroyed empire, live in doorways begging for spare *krone*.

Josef wants more. His eyesight is too poor for the sweatshops; he's too slight to be of interest to the Leopoldstadt gangs. He sneaks in the side door of the Wien Raimund Theatre, gazes at the chorus lines on stage, hears this new thing called 'ragtime' and dreams of a life in the spotlight. He learns to dance, slicks down his hair with pomade, keeps his fingernails clean. Josef grifts the city's teeming dance halls as a taxi dancer for hire to solo ladies and maybe, if he needs the money and the mood is all right, a tchotchke, a gigolo. The *frauenzimmer* like his charm, his style; he entertains them, they tip big. He becomes an exhibition dancer, with different partners each night, showing the dance-hall crowds how it should be done, with effortless grace, feet that slide.

He gets noticed. In 1924 he's recruited to join a troupe of continental entertainers called the Midnight Frolics, heading for a tour of the Far Eastern ports. It's a mixed bag—tap dancers, Russian ballerinas, a mouth organist, a singing violinist, a magician, and an Italian tenor. Among the recruited Frolics are two White Russian sisters, Nellie and Eva, trained in the ballet and performing mild comic numbers. He's paired with Nellie, the older sister; she's a beauty with jet-black hair, rouged cheeks, and eyes ringed with kohl. Black tails for Josef, silk chiffon for Nellie, and a mutually beneficial partnership. Josef Pollak changes his name to Joe Farren and escapes Leopoldstadt for a new life away from the poverty of the ghetto. They bill themselves as Joe and Nellie Farren. That they should fall in love was really no surprise.

The Frolics, billed as the best of *Mitteleuropa*, turned out to be a hit across the Orient; but they were a temperamental troupe— the ballerinas fought, the tenor drank, the magician doped. They dance in Kobe and Yokohama, Batavia and Singapore; they move on to Manila, across to Tientsin, Peking, and then Shanghai—the top spot on the Far East circuit.

It's 1926: two years later, a lot of steamers between humid Far Eastern ports and cross-country trains, bug-ridden hotels, and claustrophobic dressing rooms later. In the Plaza Hotel on Shanghai's Hankow Road, behind the imposing Bund and in the heart of the International Settlement, the troupe sees a crowd that spends silver dollars like pennies. They see 'Slick' Jack Carter and his Serenaders, an all-Negro band, pack the dance floor. They hear scat singer Bo Diddley improvise nonsense songs and wow fashionable Shanghai. They hear Black Broadway hoofer turned trumpet player and singer Valaida Snow, backed by the demon piano player Teddy Weatherford. Here in the sumptuous Plaza Hotel, Shanghai's wealthiest foreign taipans in evening dress, sipping stengahs and smoking fat cigars, their wives in satins and jewels, make whoopee among the modern youth of Shanghai's Chinese elite. Valaida finishes her set on a still-warm September Shanghai evening with 'Someone to Watch Over Me', while the ultramodern Chinese *mopu* boys, their handkerchiefs folded in the jacket pockets of their tight-fitting *pongee* suits, smooch with their slightly diffident *moge* girls in slimline flapper dresses. That night, breathing in the camphor scents and street smells of Shanghai, Joe knows where his future lies. But he and Nellie are committed to the Frolics for two more years.

By December 1929, times are challenging for Shanghai; the fallout from the Wall Street crash has reached the Settlement. Still, for the most part, the rich stay rich and the Majestic Hotel Ballroom on the Bubbling Well Road is now the place to be, and it's packed. Joe and Nellie bag a gig as the hotel's exhibition dancers, thanks to the house bandleader Whitey Smith. Whitey has been based in Shanghai since '22, after skipping out on Prohibition-wracked San

Fran. He'd caught the Farren act down in Singapore as part of the Frolics, and told Joe there'd be a job for him and Nellie at the Majestic, if they ever wanted it. Joe definitely does want it. Shanghai had been his Mecca—the best clubs, the best opportunities, and the best pay packets. They finally ditch the Frolics and take one more cramped steamer voyage to Shanghai and the Majestic.

Joe, with Nellie in his arms smelling sweetly of Guerlain Mitsouko, glides across the floor of the Majestic's clover-leaf–shaped ballroom in white top and tails, shoes polished like mirrors. Their dancing was meant to be sensuous; they were an example of how to do it right. He pulled her close; she fell into his arms. It was a trick, an illusion, a set of rehearsed and performed motions to persuade the watching crowd of amateurs that they too could glide and swoon across the dance floor as effortlessly and with such passion, looking as good as Joe and Nellie Farren. They couldn't know that Joe and Nellie still surprised themselves by how easily they came together. His thin, tallish frame felt perfect to Nellie. He noticed none of her hard angles and boniness—they fitted each other, joined perfectly for at least those moments on the dance floor, under the spotlight, thrilling the crowd.

Shanghai's got dance madness, and they're the best exhibition dancers in town. Joe and Nellie make it seem so easy, so refined. Eight hundred swells sit down to dinner, and Joe and Nellie are part of the show, along with singers and comedians, accompanied by a ten-piece orchestra led by Whitey. The Majestic comps their food and cleaning bills, Whitey's boy shines Joe's shoes, and Nellie has her own seamstress. After the exhibition you can dance with Joe if you're a lady of a certain age or a wife with a roving eye for a slick continental with the accent to match. The men, dance tickets clutched in their fists, queue to dance with Nellie, to hold her slim figure in their arms, to dance with a woman who knows what she's doing. They look into her round, dark eyes, highlighted by crow-black kohl, breathe in her scent, and think they might have a chance.

But those eyes are only for Joe and for the tips they'll make. Occasionally she and Joe catch each other's eye and share a lightning-quick smile.

They've got a single-room cold-water place on Woo Foo Lane, not far from the Majestic. Typical Shanghai: a lane house with creaky wooden stairs, boiling in summer, freezing in the winter. The old oak bed is draped with mosquito nets that never really keep the bastards out, the legs in old tins of kerosene laced with arsenic to stop the bugs crawling up into the mattress. Nellie hates the flies, whose bulbous corpses await them on the flypaper Joe has hung up. She can't get used to the strange sour taste of the milk from the Shanghai Dairy or the smelly petroleum lamp that casts long shadows across the eaves. The raggedy curtains barely cover a window that is not quite three feet from the apartment opposite. They keep the drapes permanently closed, but the piercing Shanghai sunlight slices in. There's a stained oak dressing table, the drawers lined with old copies of the *Deutsche Shanghai Zeitung* chewed at the edges by voracious ants. The mirror has foxing creeping from the edges, which distorts Nellie's face as she tries to make up. There are two rickety cane chairs and a table, a small porcelain washbasin with a tap, chipped, of course; they get hot water from a shop at the end of the lane. It's a couple of cents for a Chinese coolie to fill the enamel sit-and-soak bath; they cook on shared charcoal-fuelled hibachi stoves on the landing one floor down. It's a noisy place, stuffy with charcoal fumes, populated by a mix of Chinese not long from the countryside, several White Russian families who seem to live on a shoestring, an argumentative Portuguese woman formerly of dubious employ, and an old Englishman who never leaves his room.

They usually get to sleep about the time the Shanghainese early-risers start caterwauling across the lanes at full volume. Each morning they hear the cacophony of raucous throat clearings, coughing with the first smoke of the day, the clank of tooth glasses on porcelain, the swilling and spitting, the sizzling hot plates, the shouting in Russian and guttural Shanghainese, the nose-blowing and the feet stamping to the shared privy out the back. Boiling kettles whistle, pans clank, and tin mugs slosh with the morning tea. But it's just a start, Joe promises. They'll save, they'll move on. Shanghai is a place where you can do that.

The crisp chill of a Shanghai winter morning, the first of the new decade. A celebration. A first anniversary in Shanghai. Joe breaks his regular hours and is up early and out shopping. Brioches from Bianchi's on the Bubbling Well Road, Nellie's favourite taro cakes from a Shanghainese street vendor, Turkish delight from the Velvet Sweet Shop (where, Jack tells him, the Chinese confectioner is known to sell a white powdery substance under the counter to his more red-eyed regulars), salted almonds, champagne on ice from behind the bar of the Manhattan (courtesy of recently installed proprietor Jack Riley), kir from Egal & Cie, Frenchtown's best vintner—a collection of all Nellie's newfound favourites, the sort she'd only dreamt of as a young girl.

Nellie Farren is Shanghai's heartbreaker—sweet, dark, Russky Nell. There isn't a member of the Volunteer Corps, an off-duty SMP man, or a fresh-off-the-boat griffin who doesn't fall hard for Nellie. Joe puts up with it; it's good for business. She takes the orchids and the Nestle's chocolates. She flirts, laughs, plays the coquette, improves her English, rounds out her vowels, flutters her big, dark eyes. Male hearts break a little when she comes out in silk and slides across the floor in Joe's arms. By now they all know she's his, even if Joe isn't always hers.

A year in Shanghai, through the dripping heat of the city's long, humid summer, the short-lived balmy autumn as the leaves fall from the London plane trees of Frenchtown. Then a bone-chilling winter with snow at Christmas before the rainy spring and then, every year with no exception, the furnace of another long Shanghai summer. They've realised the Majestic's a sweet gig. Good wages, topped up with tips from the swank crowd—Shanghai's elite, the so-called '400', the wealthiest and most influential foreigners in the International Settlement, the richest razzle-dazzlers of the town. There are Frenchtown's *nouveau riche* looking for new nighttime thrills and curious wealthy Chinese after jazz and Western-style dancing. The crowd sits on big rattan chairs around plain deal tables laid out on a thick Peking carpet, among palm fronds set in bamboo boxes. They sip drinks in the Winter Gardens conservatory on tables layered in white linen. Joe and Nellie even dance one night for Douglas Fairbanks and Mary Pickford, who are visiting town selling their silents. Joe dances with 'America's Sweetheart', her rubies and sapphires against his chest, while Nellie takes a turn with Fairbanks for the press, and Joe and Mary watch that old dog goose Nellie's backside.

Even at the Majestic, summer is a trial. The place is a sweatbox despite the rattan fans worked all night by unseen white-gowned coolies. There are a dozen large blocks of ice in the middle of the dance floor to cool off the dancers, and Chinese with mops clear the water off the floor between dances. Joe and Nellie slide round the blocks like they're on skates. But it still gets so men sweat buckets and the ladies' makeup streams. By midnight it's sodden collars and panda eyes, the men stepping out to switch damp collars for fresh—on humid Shanghai summer nights the men bring maybe a half dozen additional collars with them in anticipation of having to change them. Backstage Joe does as much 'tidying' as Nellie—powdering his nose to stop the shine under the lights, darkening the eyebrows, a little spot of colour on the cheeks. After midnight the band steps it up and cuts loose. The management installs a model train that runs round the dance floor, and Whitey calls out the name of Chinese train stations through a megaphone, with his band all hollering 'choo-choo' every time. The big-shot Chinese lap it up; they spritz on any kind of gimmick. They soak up the band's closing number, 'When it's Night Time in Dear Old Shanghai and I'm Dancing, Sweetheart, with You'.

Joe and Nellie choreograph a dozen White Russian girls Babe knows from the Moon Palace for a chorus line. They call them the 'International Review', and the girls high-kick across the Majestic's floor before knocking out the crowd with a can-can to a Gay Paree backdrop. Then the clincher. Forget yesterday's vogue for prim 'grass skirt dances'; Joe has Nellie come out dressed—or virtually undressed—as an Aztec princess, to shimmy across the floor showing almost all God gave her. She's Shanghai's Josephine Baker and, had she been on the Champs-Élysées, she'd have given La Baker a run for her money.

Jack and Babe drop by most nights; Jack is making it his business to know everyone who counts, since Blood Alley is only the start. He introduces Joe to two Chinese guys who love the whole Majestic setup. The two look like some kind of Oriental Laurel and Hardy. They call themselves Tung and Vong, wear Western-style suits, with their thumbs in their trouser pockets, gold watch chains on show, sesame cake crumbs on their shirtfronts. They're aiming to start a new club in Frenchtown, and they want the best dance-and-dine in Shanghai. Maybe Joe'd like to come over and supervise, bring Nellie, line up some music and chorus lines. Jack says that's where the real money is; Joe says sure, maybe, call me when you're up and running. That's Shanghai—city of big dreams and bigger dreamers. He figures he'll never hear from those two clowns again.

Now, one year in, Nellie and Joe sit at the small table on their two rickety chairs and watch the sun rise through the window, drinking the champagne and kir out of their tooth glasses. Joe passes a small, dark-red Morocco leather box across the table to

Nellie: it's a travel alarm clock, not cheap, a Movado Pullman with a gold face. A month's tips from eggy-breathed old taipan wives waltzing in his arms right there.

Jack has tipped Joe that he's heard that the Majestic is bust and will close soon. He tells Nellie he thinks they should form a troupe of their own, take it on tour round the outports and cities of the Far East. 'Farren's Follies'—their own thing. Nellie likes the sound of that. They've got enough to front it—all those tips and taxi dances; putting up with the bugs, smuts, and hawk-spitters in their building. And lately Joe and Nellie have been making extra gelt on late-night parties for select groups. Ragtime parties, Dixieland swings, with Dusky Nell and Gentleman Joe hosting—he in silk pyjamas and a cravat; she in a scarlet silk kimono bagged in Yokohama on the Frolics tours. Everybody's doing it, aping the pyjama parties of London's West End and Manhattan with Shanghai twists: cheap, cheap local opium wreathing the room with blue smoke and its distinctive treacly odour. Endless highballs and stengahs mixed by Nellie, opium courtesy of Babe's friend Leong, the Victrola cranked up for Nellie to lead the select few in the Turkey Trot and the Grizzly Bear, the Oriental fox-trot 78s. Nellie takes a toot or two—everyone knows it's slenderising, and of course Joe wants his Dusky Nell to keep her figure. Wild nights, lazy days. Time to plan for the future.

3

A big weekend, the Double Fifth—fifth day of the fifth month. Shanghai's 1932 celebration of Chu Yuan, the Dragon Boat Festival, is in full swing. And Jack's got something to celebrate: he has turned the Manhattan into the top bar on Blood Alley.

It's more a strip than an alley, really; 110 yards max. Two dozen bars, maybe more, mostly holes in the wall; plenty haven't even got electricity and you don't want to think about the latrines out back. Punters wander from one to another, crawl from one counter to the next. Stick to the hooch, however bad it's watered down, because the local water's got cholera and amoebic dysentry. Each bar stinks of sweaty linen, hair oil, pomade, brilliantine, cigarette smoke, rotten breath, cheap working-girl perfume. Mix that with the petrol stink from the paraffin vapour stoves and kerosene lamps, and there's a hell of a funk. These dive bars aren't afraid to give themselves some grand names, though—the Palais Cabaret, the 'Frisco, Mumms, the Crystal, George's Bar, Pop's Place, Monk's Brass Rail, the New Ritz . . . and, of course, the Manhattan. The working girls are a League of Nations—Cantonese from the south, unfussy fat Koreans, French-speaking Annamite girls with wide hips, and really skinny, gorgeous 'Natashas', the collective Shanghailander noun for White Russian women of dubious occupation.

The latter are double the price of any other girl, except the Americans tucked away in the higher-end bordellos on Kiangse Road and away from the groping paws of the soldiers and Navy boys. They all work the bars alongside dead-eyed Eurasian Macanese and hardworking Filipinas and Formosans. The dim lights of Blood Alley disguise the track marks and pox scars.

Jack is straight in for the army crowd—Fourth Marines, Seaforth Highlanders, Welsh Fusiliers, Savoia Grenadiers, and French *matelots,* along with the men of the Liverpool tramps of the Blue Funnel Line. They love him and his hooch. Jack lays out plates of ham sandwiches and bowls of watery slumgullion stew, gratis, for the boys to keep them drinking. Men with empty bellies don't booze hard, they just fall over early and get picked up by the shore patrol. A marine private is pulling in thirty bucks a month, a gunnery sergeant maybe eighty bucks, and Jack is selling beer at two cents, a bottle of top-shelf London gin for sixty-seven cents, and a bottle of legit Johnnie Walker for under a dollar. Meanwhile back home they've got the Great Depression and Prohibition. The Alley's a slum, but these schmucks think they got lucky winding up on it.

Jack's got a small combo playing on the tiny stage—Manilamen with a wailing sax and blasting trumpet. The Manhattan and Pop's Place are the two best joints to hit on Blood Alley, but if you're smart and sober, you keep your hands on your wallet at all times. Jack's barman and bouncer is Mickey O'Brien, his old pal from the door over at the Venus Café. Mickey is Jack's equal in the muscleman stakes and keen on the work too. Babe, also from the Venus, is his main girl. When she's not off on the end of the pipe, she sits in the window and pulls in plenty of randy marines and Highlanders. Jack buys her white linen dresses from Madame Greenhouse's on the Bubbling Well Road to keep her looking good. He tells her to quit the smoke, it gives her a runny nose and glassy eyes, but she just smiles and avoids his glare.

There's a hierarchy to Shanghai bar streets. Bottom of the heap is Jukong Alley up north of the Soochow Creek—'Varicose Alley', Jack jokes—with bathtub gin that'll blind you. That year Aimee Semple McPherson and her band of holy rollers hit 'the wickedest city in the world' and started patrolling Jukong Alley looking to save souls and baptise the working girls. Jack makes a donation to keep the Bible-thumpers out of Frenchtown. To everyone's surprise, McPherson does actually baptise and save the souls of eight working girls and one poor punter before she sails back to America.

But too many drunk squaddies are getting rolled for their pay, so Jukong gets declared out of bounds by order of the British Army Red Caps and the American Miltary Police. Also to the north of the Settlement is Scott Road, which has been called 'the Trenches' since the 1890s and isn't much better. It too is out of bounds for any man in a uniform. Consequently Blood Alley, marginally a step up from Jukong and the Trenches, gets the soldier and sailor traffic.

Jack branches out. He invests his Blood Alley profits and opens Riley's Bamboo Hut up on the North Szechuen Road, not too far from the Venus—kind of a luau theme mixed with rattan furniture round the bamboo-lined walls, waitresses wearing Honolulu leis and not much else. North Szechuen in Hongkew is marginally classier than Blood Alley, though far from top drawer. Jack taps Nellie to get in some dancers who didn't quite make the cut for the Follies; Joe finds him a band looking for a gig who can work up a few ukelele tunes to fit the theme. Hongkew is mostly out of bounds to squaddies and leathernecks, but not to officers. And so Jack covers the bases—the Manhattan coins it in from the leathernecks and the ranks; the Bamboo Hut gets the NCOs and the brass.

The money is rolling, and Jack is building a stash as 1932 rolls into 1933. But he's still trying to wipe out his past. He takes a steamer to Yokohama. Some all-American dollars get Jack T. Riley a Chilean passport from the consul general before he's inevitably recalled after, equally inevitably, another military coup in Santiago. Jack stays and relaxes in the Grand Hotel, wastes a few nights in the famous Nectarine bordello, gets bored and jumps a steamer back to Shanghai. At dockside he tells customs he's Jack T. Riley, bar proprietor in Shanghai and proud to be a Chilean citizen. He is waved through with a low bow and a smartish salute.

Tonight he's out back of the Manhattan decanting cheap apple cider into champagne bottles. He'd have gone for apple juice at half the price, but it needs a little fizz when it comes out of the bottle to look real. Still, apple cider knocked out at champagne prices is a good margin for the Manhattan. Later on he'll baptise the whisky with a little holy Shanghai water to boost his margins a touch more.

He can't stop thinking of those lines of slots pouring coin into buckets back in Manila, with that lanky Canadian collecting the dough. There aren't any slots in Shanghai, just illicit high-end roulette for the swells, which keeps on getting busted by the Shanghai Municipal Police, and the Hwa-Wei Chinese lottery for everyone else. Business has been booming in Manila, with the rackets down there running booze across the Pacific into Prohibition-dry San Francisco and bringing back three-reel 'Liberty Bell' slot machines in parts in the empty whisky barrels. Jack wires Joe, who's on tour down in Manila with Nellie and their Follies. Maybe Joe can look into it? Joe wires back, sure thing, finds a supplier; Jack orders his first shipment, wires the guy the money, and they arrange delivery. Shanghai is about to welcome the reign of the Slots King.

4

The rumours had been true: the Majestic folded, was pulled down, demolished, the four-leaf-clover-shaped ballroom reduced to rubble. Where once Shanghai taipans danced, Hagenbeck's Circus pitched its tent and hawked tickets for coppers to Chinese and Shanghailanders alike to gawp at the listless Indian elephants. It had been a good time for Joe and Nellie to go on tour.

Joe hires the Russian girls from Al Israel's joint, the Del Monte. California-born Al has been in Shanghai since before the Great War, running the joint with his wife, Bertha, and his two-hundred-pound Great War vet brother-in-law 'Demon' Hyde. Folks said Al was crazy to open out in the western suburbs, but he laid out a car park, hired a turbaned Sikh watchman, and strung coloured lights up to the entrance. Shanghai duly fell in love with the automobile. Now Al has a long line of Buicks, Packards, and Caddies driving out to his Versailles-themed place, where things don't get going till two a.m. Al is a mensch and doesn't mind Joe poaching his girls—they're tight up at the Red Rose early mornings kvetching with the Wiengarten brothers or at the Venus for the ham and eggs, and Al knows there are always new hoofers up in the White Russian slums of Harbin and Dairen ready to tread the boards of the Del Monte.

The Farren's Follies tour starts in the outports—Tientsin, Weihaiwei—then goes on to Manila, Yokohama, Tokyo, and Kobe, down to British Hong Kong, Dutch Batavia, French Saigon and Hanoi, and even across as far as Bombay to entertain the Raj. It's an incestuous, claustrophobic world: the girls four to a room, the boys sharing as best they can manage. They bunk up on train couchettes, cram into steamer cabins, their rooms lined with strung-up laundry. The girls smoke incessantly, steal each other's lip-sticks, flirt with the bachelor griffins in Tientsin and Hong Kong and the bored planters in Kuala Lumpur and Batavia; a few disappear, lured away on the promise of a better life. The Malay States rubber planters see an end to their lonely nights; they give ship stewards and hotel porters something to dream of. The Follies annoy the staid old wives of the port towns they visit; the missionaries try to get them banned for indecency. The boys stay out late with older women, making money on the side.

Nellie is charged with keeping the girls in line. They need doctors; they need shoulders to cry on. They're a type—mostly Russian émigrés prone to extremes of temper; Nellie clones, chosen by Joe personally, with large, dark eyes. They mascara their eyelashes heavily, rouge their cheeks to accentuate their good bone structure, stay out of the sun to keep their skin marble-white, eat intermittently to keep their figures. Hair is cut short, styled close to their heads, with a satin sheen; they use salt and baking soda to whiten their nicotine-stained teeth.

The girls are often trouble. They can come on like good Russian Orthodox girls, but many whore for easy money in Singapore. Doc Borovika, who hangs out with the ham and eggs gang up at the Venus, is the man girls went to when they get back to town. In Shanghai the doc is essential, always on Joe's payroll and those of several dozen bordellos and cabarets. The doc claims to be a former Austrian Great War flying ace forced to decamp east amid the breakup of the old Austro-Hungarian Empire. Maybe he had been some kind of Red Baron; maybe he hadn't. But he's a legit doc, and his services are specialised. The girls have track marks from the doc's shots of arsenic compound to counteract the syphilis, and more track marks for the shots of bismuth to counteract the toxic reaction to the arsenic shots. Miss a few shots and you relapse fast. The doc looks after the scrapes the girls get when they get unlucky, the pox treatments, and those little pharmacy powders that keep the girls that use straight. He keeps Jack in supplies of Benzedrine for the long nights and sorts Babe for heroin pills, what the Shanghai dealers call Cadillacs, when she comes up short to pay for the good stuff.

Onboard ship and between rehearsals everyone is relaxed. They gather on the ship's deck for group photographs—fifteen, sixteen girls in canvas shorts and linen shirts knotted to reveal their flat stomachs; a half dozen boys with suntans and tight black swimming trunks; Joe, still good-looking but his hair receding fast, in white flannel trousers, a white shirt and always a tie, whatever the humidity; Nellie in a linen suit and floppy hat to keep the sun off her face. Joe has his arm round Nellie's waist. He holds her close and means it. The world is his oyster; the Follies are a hit in the treaty ports, the remoter outports wherever foreigners trade, and colonial towns. Where's the harm in doing a favour for a mensch like Jack back in Shanghai? Little does Joe realise that in taking on that side business and sorting those slots for Jack, he has changed the course of their futures forever and set them on a path of doomed codependency.

5

Jack Riley's got a shipment coming. The bill of lading says rattan furniture, or maybe ebony picture frames, or the workings for clocks . . . Inside it's slots machinery, one-armed bandits, ready to be assembled. Jack's old Manila contacts had come through, shipping direct courtesy of U.S. Navy transports in exchange for cash wired via Joe, and with the supply sergeants bought off at both ends.

Jack and Mickey park up on East Broadway by the gates of the Shanghai–Hongkew Wharf in a borrowed flatbed truck. It's early October 1933, and already there's a chill in the air. They sign the paperwork, slipping the customs squares a few bills. Mickey has rousted some ex-marines who never made it home and opted to keep on enjoying the Shanghai good life to act as trusted stevedores for a few bucks apiece. They load the crates onto the flatbed.

Shanghai is getting slotified, courtesy of Jack T. Riley—every Settlement bar, Frenchtown boîte, and Hongkew honky-tonk joint wants one. Fifteen Chinese bucks for the rental per week and the lion's share of the take for Jack, with enough kicked back to the venue to make it a worthwhile investment. The Chinese love the new 'dime-eating tigers' too, and every Chinese palais de danse wants them.

Back at the Manhattan, the men crowbar open the crates, and Jack puts all that Navy mechanical training to work assembling the things. Riley is the self-declared exclusive supplier of slot machines in Shanghai—from the Northern External Roads up by the Settlement's border with Chinese Paoshan across to the Western Roads and out to semi-rural Hungjao; Yangtszepoo ('Y'Poo' to cops and Shanghailanders) to the far east of the Settlement's borders down to Frenchtown; from the back-alley juke joints to the uptown parlours and gentlemen's clubs. If anyone thinks they're going to take a slot from some other arriviste get-rich-quick driftwood bum who thinks it might be a good idea to start importing, there'll be trouble. Jack owns and controls every slot machine in a city famously hooked on gambling.

The Navy transports keep on coming, and by Christmas 1933 the Settlement is swimming in slot machines. The SMP didn't even notice them coming in—they'd never seen them in Shanghai before, didn't know what they were. Slots are the new big thing and, though the missionaries and the Shanghai Women's Purity League don't like them, Shanghai's got no laws against them. Jack's got a new nickname courtesy of the *North-China Daily News*: the 'Slots King of Shanghai'. Jesus, he even puts his name on the tokens! Immortalised in brass, stamped 'ETR', which every leatherneck, squaddie, driftwood, and civilian knows stands for Edward Thomas 'Jack' Riley—five cents, ten cents, twenty cents, a dollar 'good-fors' redeemable all over town. Jack has effectively created a new alterative currency in Shanghai.

Business is good, and soon Jack needs more muscle than just Mickey to collect the coin. Those same ex-marines gone AWOL come in handy. They're big lugs who don't think too much and have a lot to lose—in other words, folks who can't call the cops. Most have past careers as standover men, robbing small-time Chinese and Russian drug dealers and boosting illegal back-alley casinos. Jack figures they're just the sort who'd rob him, so he puts them on the payroll instead and charms them with his old Yang Pat patter and Tulsa vowels. What they lack in polish they make up for in intimidation, warning off anyone thinking of grabbing Jack Riley's take for themselves. Jack pays them, liquors them up at the Bamboo Hut, lets them take their pick of the Manhattan's girls, and makes sure they get suited, booted, and shaved, even forms them up on weekends as a baseball team. Jack's Town Team of ex-marines and nightlife types wins the city league and also funds an orphanage for abandoned baby girls out in Hungjao on slots money. The men are all loyal to Jack. Soon they're known all over town as the 'Friends of Riley'; think twice before you cross them, start brawling in one of Jack's joints, or question the honesty of his slot machines too loudly, or the Friends may acquaint your head with the filthy flagstones of Blood Alley.

6

The Follies return home to Shanghai in the steamy summer of 1934, to a new revue at the Paramount, a humungous new ballroom up on Yu Yuen Road by the old Bubbling Well Cemetery where the Settlement meets the Western External Roads. It has a neon tower that proclaims the Paramount a dreamworld, with Tokyo café décor, art deco lamps, and a mixed Chinese–Shanghailander crowd. It's the latest thing—the Chinese call it *Bailuomen*, the gate to a hundred pleasures. The moneyed Shanghainese love the place; the Shanghailander 400 enjoy the sprung dance floor. It's the new place to be seen. The Paramount's status is sealed when Shanghai's richest bullion dealer, Simmons, hires out the entire place for his daughter Alice's twenty-first birthday party, and the social pages of the China Coast newspapers can talk of nothing, and nowhere, else. Immediately afterwards, the junction of Yu Yuen and the Bubbling Well Roads is a seething mass of chauffeured limousines jostling to pull up curbside and disgorge the young, rich, and beautiful of the metropolis into the stunning foyer of the Paramount.

Joe lines up the house chorus girls and calls them his Peaches—the Paramount Peaches, no less—and sets up Shanghai's longest tap line with Nellie front and centre. The theatre is gorgeous, but the dressing room is distinctly less so, with low ceilings and one tiny window-cum–air vent that lets in little more than the screech of the municipal trams and nonstop car horns. A couple of low-watt bulbs provide barely enough light. Chinese dressers cluster by the door, and an old Russian seamstress sits in the corner.

But this is the life—out of the dim dressing room and towards the brightly lit stage comes the chorus. Joe is at the top of the stairs, checking the line for dirty fingernails, too much greasepaint, visible track marks. Then later he's at the stage door, crowded with fans and young griffins eager to escort the showgirls to one of the Yu Yuen Road cabaret bars round the corner. It's hopeless; the girls have better places to go, older, better-heeled patrons to spend time with. The swells offer dinner at Ciro's with white-uniformed waiters and young boys serving tea, or late-night cocktails at Victor Sassoon's brand-spanking-new Tower Club at the top of the Cathay Hotel. For the Peaches, the trick is to get dinner, go dancing, snag a little treat or two they can pawn later or some cash, all without giving it up. Late-night motorcar rides round the circular Rubicon Road, a shady back table at the Black Cat cabaret in Frenchtown, tableside at the private roulette wheels illicitly spinning in the suites of the Burlington Hotel courtesy of old-time Brit gangster Bill Hawkins, Sasha Vertinsky's late-night Russian cabaret with the bad boys at the Gardenia on Great Western Road, champagne and Viennese torch songs courtesy of Lily Flohr at the Elite Bar on Medhurst Road—then always the fumble, the grope, the wandering hands.

Nellie herself is still the main object of everyone's desire; Joe's got the spot man keeping a light on her, and her alone, all the time. Every head turns when she enters the Paramount—red crêpe de chine dress, long black fur with the collar up, a black cloche hat, dark eyes, red cheeks, ruby-red lipstick, and a waft of Mitsouko. If every man who claimed to have bedded Nellie really had, she'd have been the busiest woman in the Settlement. But Nellie is above and beyond the reach of them all.

After the early show at the Paramount, Jack and Babe roll up in Jack's new sportscar to take in the city's largest ballroom for themselves. Nellie makes sure the coffee is strong for Jack and there's some dope for Babe. Once Babe has kvetched with Nellie some and Jack has chewed the fat with Joe, the Slots King's got business to attend to.

Jack Riley's Friday night bag run starts before the mass of punters rolls into the Manhattan looking to get drunk and laid, while the bored Natashas are still passing the time dancing with each other to the gramophone. It's out into a sweltering, humid Blood Alley, soon to be a roiling, roistering strip of sweat-stained uniforms, cajoling working girls, and curious slummers. A Chinese driver is at the wheel of the Packard with Mickey O'Brien riding shotgun, a new Friend called Schmidt with a Mauser under his armpit in back along with Riley, and a large padlocked trunk for the coin haul.

Business first: the boys head to the Bamboo Hut to check the shroff office and see that the ledger keepers are minding the chits and there are no seriously bad debts mounting up. Shanghai's chit system means the officer types and the swells can just sign for their booze and scoff and settle up later with the shroffs, but there are always a few who think they can run up a tab and then skip town without settling. Then Jack is off to the 37427 Club to see the Portuguese about shipping arrangements for more slots. Demand is high, and Manila can't spare any more, so Joe is tapping Macao for more machines, and Macao is Portuguese territory. Then the nightly slots run: three circuits of machines across the city, each visited once every three days, except for the Fourth Marines Club on the Bubbling Well Road, which is emptied nightly, sometimes twice.

Jack and Mickey head into the joints, collect the coin, sort the machines with tokens, rejig the mechanisms to pay less or more, depending on the take, and schmooze the barkeeps. They sling the canvas coin bags into the back of the Packard where the German Schmidt, with a crooked nose that has to have been broken at least twice, sits with his burly arm round the trunk and his Mauser in full view.

Tonight's run? The Settlement, starting with Van's Dutch Village Inn, Love Lane, back of the Bubbling Well Road. A Dutchman named Van, unsurprisingly, and his Japanese wife run the place. It's small and intimate; Van and his kimonoed *voor vrouw* boss lady keep watch from a small square enclosure in the middle of the joint. A three-piece orchestra and plenty of sing-alongs entertain the regular crowd, which invariably includes a bunch of off-duty SMP, while the house special—Schiedam *moutwijn,* malt wine—lays out more than one customer before the end of the night. Up Love Lane to the St. Anna Ballroom, aka Santa Anna's—a big dance floor with a full band, Earl Whaley and his Red Hot Syncopaters delivering big-band music and broadcasting live over the radio from their studio upstairs. Santa Anna's is Marine-heavy, a long-time fave of the Fourth Marine Corps given its close proximity to Maggie Kennedy's long-standing bordello. Next up is the Handy Randy bar and then the Jinx on Bubbling Well Road: German, beefsteaks and beers, small dance floor with Russian and Jewish hostesses, favoured by the Royal Navy's Jack Tars. Parsimonious and poorly paid Jack Tars never pump as much coin into the one-armed bandit as the always-lucky leathernecks. Finally, the Marines Club for the big haul. The slots are emptied, the owners squared on their cut. The next night it's Frenchtown, then Hongkew to complete the circuit before repeating it all over again, bringing in bigger and bigger hauls of coin.

By three-thirty a.m., they're in the Manhattan's back room again, with only solid regulars out front boozing, Friends armed on the doors front and back. It's time for the night's hard count; all that small change needs to make some serious dollars. Jack is on one of his regular caffeine binges, crumbling in bennies to stave off exhaustion. Mickey makes up a big pot of coffee the consistency of Pootung marsh mud for the boss on the percolator hot plate, strong and mean just as he likes it. Riley drinks gallons of the stuff daily, wired to the gills, yet makes Mickey smoke his cigarette outside. The windows and doors are shut tight despite the stifling August night.

Count, count, count. Coin piles across the table, with one pile equalling one dollar—bagged and ready to be banked. Jack, Mickey, and Schmidt are counting fast, marking off ten-dollar amounts on slips of paper for a final total. Pile after pile after pile—dollar after dollar after dollar. Jack is the living embodiment of the ethos 'watch the pennies and the pounds take care of themselves'.

All done, all tallied, all sorted and squared away. Cash is stashed out in the back room of the Manhattan in Riley's gigantic American-made and specially imported safe, ready for banking with some discreet Ningpoese moneymen next morning. The men from Ningpo who'd moved to Shanghai and created banking empires are just the type of bankers Jack likes: tight-lipped. Dawn up, first daylight, birdsong over the big-band swing from the jukebox—Paul Whiteman's 'Smoke Gets in Your Eyes', the Settlement's big hit that year. It really does—out front in the bar the ashtrays are piled high, the whisky bottles with dregs left for the boys. Jack's blinking fast and sketchy, but the job is done, and he's a richer man courtesy of the slots addicts of Shanghai. Schmidt and a couple of other Friends are left to guard the safe till the bank opens. It's time for another pot of coffee, maybe some ham and eggs at the Venus with Sam, Joe, Nellie, and Babe. If there was a better business than this, Jack Riley believed it to be the best-kept secret in all of God's great kingdom.

7

In September, Jackpot Jack decides to expand and go legit. He takes eighty per cent of what goes in the slots, and his stash has grown exponentially. He's filled several safes in the Manhattan and his pad, not to mention what's with the Ningpoese moneymen. He's bought Shanghai Power Company shares, Shanghai Telephone Company Shares, gas company shares, shares in the tram companies in both the Settlement and Frenchtown. But still it keeps on coming in and needs investing.

Don't be thinking Jackpot Jack has no ambition. He's looking to move up and move on from the drunks of Blood Alley. Even old Sam Levy at the Venus Café is going upmarket with his Manila Rhythm Boys and a troupe of thick-legged, high-kicking Korean dancers Joe has taught to cancan, while Al Israel's Del Monte swings till three or four in the morning with another Joe Farren–choreographed floor show, and Demon on the door keeping the drunks and the squaddies out. Jack has taken in the shows at the Moon Palace up on the Szechuen Road. He's seen the Peaches at the Paramount, and he's cogniscent of what 'Ziegfeld' Joe Farren does. Joe's got a three-score hoofer chorus line and a hundred dance hostesses over there. Jack wants some of that, some of the crowd that orders champagne and knows the real stuff from the apple cider fizz. Joe might be a yid from some shithole in Europe but he's treated like a king: the swells love him and his dame. Jack plans to buy himself some of that class. It's all about the big Shanghai money, the taipan money. Those gents spend large and long, all night, and don't start swinging fists when they're tanked.

How to make the leap? Joe tells Jack about a chain of joints up for sale that are just the thing. So Jack buys into DD's, a trio of swell clubs a brisk walk from Blood Alley, but a million miles in clientele, with a flagship on the Avenue Joffre, Frenchtown's major boulevard. 'DD's: the place to go for swank and swing.' It's dinner and dance with some good entertainment after Joe hooks Jack up with suave Romanian crooner Tino and his orchestra, who also needed a move up from the Red Rose. Now Jack is in competition with the Paramount and the swankier joints of the Settlement and Frenchtown. It's all done, except for one thing: if Jack is going uptown, putting on a tux, chitty-chatting with the 400, he can't do it with a bleary-eyed hophead in tow.

Jack has told the doc to stop slipping Babe Cadillac heroin pills. Nellie hears from her chorus-line girls that Leong has cut Babe off from her long, long lines of credit at the Moon Palace den. Now Babe is ranting and raving and tearing the place up. Joe finds Jack stocking the bar at his new joint, and they head over to Leong's place. The Chinaman's moaning that Babe is scaring off punters, and they find her rolling on a divan with stomach cramps and sweating like it's high summer. Jack is mad at her, tells her they're finished if she can't quit the dope. Babe screams and begs for just one more pipe. Jack walks out, and Babe tears up and collapses. Joe calls Doc Borovika, who knows a German hypnotist guy who cures dopers. Joe pays off Leong and checks Babe in with the German. He tells her to forget Jack, concentrate on the cure, get herself together.

A week later, outside DD's on the Avenue Joffre, the Little Russia strip, a gaggle of Natashas—all blonde, approximately half of them natural, are flirting. Yank Marines salute them, Brit squaddies wolf-whistle them, Italian Savoia Grenadiers push their greased hair back under their tousled kepis and wink big at them.

Jack greets them from the door. 'Come in sometime, boys, plenty more where they came from. We've got a surfeit of Natashas nightly. But ditch the uniforms, it scares the swells.' They chorus back, 'Indeed you do, Mr. Riley, indeed you do; indeed we will, Mr. Riley, indeed we will.'

But they won't. DD's isn't really for the Army boys; the drinks are five times the price of what they are in Blood Alley—think champagne at a whopping forty bucks a bottle; cocktails with large measures; the kind of place the swells like to patronize before the late-night frolics, taipans with their secretaries on Friday nights, the moneyed dames like Alice Daisy Simmons and the griffins looking to impress them.

Jack knows better than to front DD's himself. He's got a Russian émigré girl to really bring in the quality, a class act with all the charms and graces of the old world. Nazedha is a sweet gal who keeps the books straight in the shroff and captains the taxi dance girls, who dance for ten cents a ticket. At the front there's a liveried Sikh and an old-school St. Petersburg maître d' bowing to the big cheeses. The girls come and go, Russian mostly, and Nazedha keeps them in line. They earn fifteen per cent of what their partners spend at the bar, and the Natasha who cashes the most dance tickets come end of the week gets a ten-dollar bonus. Jack likes Nazedha's looks and how she keeps the girls in line. Might even the Slots King be in love?

Meanwhile, Jack and Mickey take care of the slots and stay mostly ensconced in the Bamboo Hut or the Manhattan with the Friends. DD's earns its own legit coin, no need to interfere. And Jack's got new Friends now, including one who wants plenty of gossip and insider schtick, former Baltimore tabloid hack turned Shanghai entrepreneur Robert 'Don' Chisholm. Jack has put in some cash to help Chisholm set up a newspaper telling all about the cabarets and the nightclubs, the tiffins and the fire sales, with money-off coupons and plenty of advertising. It'll be called the *Shopping News*, with dodgy Don writing the scurrilous editorial. He'll lambast the titans of the gas company, the tram company, and the phone company till they take full-page advertisements at high, high rates. He'll trash-talk the Municipal Council and then he'll titillate his readers with innuendo, dishing the dirt of their private lives, peccadilloes, mistresses, and drunken night-time misfortunes unless they care to place an advert or make a donation. It's an old-school sting. Make the chit payable to Mr. R. Chisholm. What Don needs is tittle-tattle of the highest order, and Jack's a supplier.

SHOPPING NEWS
—'BREVITIES'—
MONDAY, OCTOBER 15, 1934

We don't have to tell you, dear reader, that the cost of living is soaring in the Settlement. Our investigations have discovered some local firms exhibiting an attitude of generous sympathy towards their employees. For instance, we find the Asia Theatres (who haven't increased admissions) increasing the wages of their Chinese employees by 19%, their foreign employees by 15%. On the other hand we find the Shanghai Power Company dishing out a 250% increase to some of their employees entitled to home leave. WHICH MAY EXPLAIN ONE OF THE CAUSES OF THE 120% SURCHARGE NEXT MONTH, a 25% increase to locally employed Chinese and foreigners alike. To our way of reckoning a 40% pay increase will just about let the average wage earner break even.

The *North-China Daily News* Women's Page says crochet turbans are all the rage this winter from London to Paris to New York to . . . Shanghai, of course.

Shopping News offers you 30% off all new arrival crochet turbans for ladies, in all colors at CLEO CROCHET, 944 Bubbling Well Road. Just take this issue in with you. And don't forget they have all your pillow, bedspread and tablecloth needs covered. Tel: 36755 for an appointment.

If, and when, the Municipal Council's Old Guard gets busted open like a termite tasted leg of rotten timber, it will be a direct outcome of their own blind avarice and their increasing diligence in safeguarding and increasing their own riches. The Council, besides being a gathering of the people . . . says who? . . . is the finest Big Business Club in town. Well represented are landlords, public utilities, shipping, insurance, banking and the membership of the venerable old Shanghai Club. The first principle of justice is that 'No man shall be a judge in his own house' . . . or are we wrong?

Got a tale to tell? Editorial: Rm 540, 233 Nanking Rd. Tel: Shanghai—10695

8

Joe is called to the phone while busy rehearsing the Paramount's new Christmas show for 1934. He can hardly believe his Viennese ears: Laurel and Hardy, the two Chinamen Jack had introduced him to at the Majestic way back when, are for real. All Mr. Tung and Mr. Vong have ever wanted to do, it seems, is run the hippest joint in Shanghai. Knowing early that the Majestic was going to close down, they'd sold their shares to mugs less knowledgeable and moved on. They have the cash; they have the connections. Tung and Vong are blood brothers with Du Yuesheng, the man who really pulls the strings in Frenchtown.

Big-Eared Du is a Pootung wharf rat risen through the ranks of the city's Green Gang to become Shanghai's undisputed Chinese gangster king—the *zongshi*, the grand master of crime. He is a freakish looking man—ugly, short, coarse—but feared. It is believed that every prostitute, robber, drug dealer, lottery ticket seller, and sing-song house owner pays Du in one way or another. He has forged the Green Gang into Shanghai's dominant underworld force. He is the city's premier extortionist. He is said to control the Frenchtown detective bureau, the city's largest shipping firm, and at least two banks. But more important, Du is connected politically to the government and personally to Chiang

Kai-shek, the leader of Nationalist China. Chiang rules China, but in 1927 when the communist-controlled unions tried to overthrow his rule in Chinese Shanghai, Du's Green Gang thugs massacred the leftists, beheading them in the streets. Chiang Kai-shek owes Du Yuesheng. How else to explain that Du is both a member of the city's Board of Opium Suppression supposedly committed to eradicating the vice of dope trafficking and addiction in the city, and also Shanghai's largest drug dealer? How else to explain that he is a man who owns his own temple—dedicated to his ancestors—but operates China's largest heroin factory within it with seeming inpunity? He is a massive Frenchtown property owner, landlord to thousands, and anyone wanting to operate in the French Concession ultimately needs Du's permission.

Du is himself an opium addict, spending his days holed up in his European-style modernist mansion on Frenchtown's Route Doumer. Tung and Vong sit down with him, are granted an audience. He favours them with permission to run the Canidrome Ballroom, up on Rue Lafayette, next to the dog track and where there's quality boxing on Wednesdays and Fridays, and super-fast jai alai with the slick Basque, Catalan, and Argentine boys every night and twice daily on the weekends—sixteen *quinielas* daily, twenty-five points *partidos* on Saturdays.

Soft-spoken Mexican gambling impresario Carlos Garcia is behind the Canidrome. Garcia is a Shanghai crime veteran—he'd had a casino until '29, when he was busted by the SMP. After a one-year stretch in the city's Ward Road Gaol, he'd parlayed his profits, and friendship with Big-Eared Du, into building the Canidrome. The complex took up the whole Frenchtown block of Lafayette, Rue Cardinal Mercier, Avenue du Roi Albert, and Route Hervé-de-Sieyès. It's a genuine Shanghai gold mine. It's all fronted by a straight-as-a dye French banker called Louis Bouvier whom you'd trust with your life savings, unless you knew that Du considers him a blood brother too. Garcia keeps a low profile but oversees the whole thing—the dogs, the jai alai fronton, the fights and the nightclub—through his own straw men on the board.

With financing from Du, Tung and Vong were now on board, and Garcia tells them to get the best showman in town. The man in question, Joe Farren, asks for a Buick with a chauffeur thrown in, like Whitey Smith had at the Majestic, and he gets what he wants. Garcia tells them to keep it classy: black tie for men, dresses for women, a sophisticated show, no shimmy girls or cooch dancers; no brawling or whoring, no dealing or watering down the booze.

It has all the makings of Frenchtown's best joint, but there's competition for Shanghailander attention. Sir Victor Sassoon is oozing class over at Ciro's, while Jack has DD's. Meanwhile, the Elite gets the late-night European moneyed crowd, the old Chapei joints like the Venus still kick, and Sol Greenberg's Casanova club down on Avenue Eddy pulls in the after-hours Chinese money. In between are all manner of dives, blind pigs, juke joints, cabarets, and holes in the wall. Joe's mandate is simple: he needs to come up with something that will rip the shit out of the other joints, and that includes the Paramount. This has to be swanker, cooler, sexier, and altogether more spectacular than anything he's done before—the Frolics, the Follies, the Majestic, the Peaches, the Del Monte. Joe thinks back to that day back in '26, in town with the Frolics, watching Teddy Weatherford and Valaida Snow at the Plaza Hotel, and he decides he wants a black band. Negro syncopation, the Turkey Trot, the Charleston, the Black Bottom, the Twelfth Street Rag, the Rumba . . . that's the thing Shanghai needs, and Joe will provide it to put the Canidrome at the top of the pile.

Joe's prayers are answered when black Buck Clayton, his girl Derby and his band, the Harlem Gentlemen, decide to blow California and take ship to Shanghai. Buck and his crew are the real deal: Negro musicians who roll Cab Calloway, Louis Armstrong, and all that good jazz vibe into one set, and have Derby with her Ethel Waters routine to boot. It'll be like the good old days at the Plaza all over again, but with better suits and someone to clean the ashtrays more regularly. Joe signs them up; Tung and Vong advance the money but moan about the cost—Buck wants American salaries in American dollars; they grudgingly agree. Chinese Laurel and Hardy, one fat as a Buddha, the other skinny as a rake, and both rich as Croesus, are known to be mean with money. Carlos Garcia, up in the Canidrome's tower, smoking a Cuban cigar, looks out over his dog track and smiles.

Buck and his troupe dock on the *President Hoover*, clear customs at the Dollar Line shed, and head over to Frenchtown. Buck is grinning ear to ear, newly wed to gorgeous Derby, the pair all loved up and smooching dockside. The Harlem Gentlemen have had a high time onboard, shooting the shit with big-mouthed Hollywood actor Joe E. Brown, who clowned his way to Hawaii with them. A stopover in Kobe saw some antics ashore before the leg to Shanghai. Tung and Vong pull some strings in quickfire Shanghainese and get the band through customs fast. Black American Shanghai legend Teddy Weatherford, who's been playing piano in town since the early twenties, turns up for a Tung and Vong banquet and teaches Buck and the boys how to hold those pesky chopsticks, spin the Lazy Susan, and show they enjoy the chow.

Joe takes them on a tour of the town—Buck and Derby in his chauffeured car, the boys following in taxis—past the burgeoning neon of the city that lights up from sunset till dawn. They eat up the Shanghai nightlife, ogle the White Russian chicks, spit melon seeds like the locals, and check out the musical competition—Filipino, Chinese, and Russian. Joe shows the boys the Canidrome, and they are impressed: a big art deco barn of a place with lawns for tea dances in the summer, the roar of the crowds from the dog track behind. Carlos Garcia shows up, backslaps all round, and pours tequila from his own distillery back in Mexico for all while offering a box of Cubans to the boys. The Harlem Gentlemen are wide-eyed. They take in the jai alai and watch those lean Basque boys move slick as lightning; at the Wednesday night fights they see Billy Addis, the 'Marine Ace', deck his Japanese marine opponent and wrap himself in the Stars and Stripes for the assembled crowd. Joe takes them to his tailor, Pingee, and gets them all handmade pieces on the Tung and Vong account—white tuxes, black-and-grey dress suits, scarlet tails with satin hems. Pingee is barely five feet tall and stands on a tea chest to reach Buck's broad shoulders to fit him. There are a dozen white shirts for each band member, and Derby orders up a rack of silk gowns from the Parsee woman in Hongkew who stitches for Nellie sometimes. Joe wanted a real swank jazz troupe looking fine—Derby, Buck, and the Gentlemen were the real McCoy.

Joe lines up a mixed show for Tung and Vong. Mistress of Ceremonies is Ursula Preston, a British exhibition dancer with a cut-glass accent. She handily does a Fred and Ginger act with her boyfriend to 'Bolero' when Joe and Nellie don't want to take a turn themselves. The band plays straight payday classical from nine, then out come a dozen long-legged girls in a chorus line called the Hollywood Blondes, all supposed to be purebred California girls, though a few have telltale Russian accents. After nine-thirty it's pure Harlem. Joe sits down with Buck and works out a killer set that blows the roof off Frenchtown from the first night.

The Canidrome's position as the premier nightspot of Frenchtown is assured when Soong May-ling with her retinue take the best tables while Tung and Vong bow low to China's First Lady. The *generalíssimo* is in total control of China, and May-ling is his wife, translator, and closest confidante. He is the leader of China's government and military; she is China's most photographed and admired woman. The press photographers follow her wherever she goes. From the capital in Nanking Chiang maintains a wary relationship with the foreign powers controlling the concessions as well as Du Yuesheng's Green Gang—a triple alliance founded on their mutual opposition to the emerging communists. Madame Chiang maintains and bolsters the relationship with the foreigners, with her American education, flawless English, flaunting of Western ways, and being a daughter of the Soong family, perhaps Shanghai's most influential Chinese family. Madame Chiang loves everything she sees at the Canidrome—the stage, the dance floor, Buck and the boys, Derby, the Hollywood Blondes, Joe and Nellie gliding under the spotlight, the sophisticated crowd. Her patronage guarantees that Shanghai Chinese high society flocks in. She hits on the band for tap lessons, charms them all with her Wellesley accent, and is the only woman allowed in wearing slacks—even Carlos Garcia wouldn't think of imposing a dress code on Madame.

Joe hooks Buck up with some local musicians so he can build in some Chinese sounds, like Whitey did over at the Majestic years before. It's Oriental swing—and the cashed-up Chinese come out to hear it. Joe persuades Teddy Weatherford, still working four clubs a night, to add one more nightly gig and come in and sit down with Buck and the boys for the first few numbers. They'll do a big version of 'Rhapsody in Blue' and then Teddy can vamoose to his next gig. The guy never sits still, even when he is at the ivories.

Nowhere swings like the Canidrome swings—Tung and Vong just sit back and watch the money roll in. Joe schmoozes nightly with Nellie, charming all and sundry. Buck and the Harlem Gentlemen love Shanghai, and Buck and Derby become celebrities overnight—her honey voice contrasting with her lowdown dirty manner. The crowd whoops when she raises her skirt to show her thighs and shimmy for a tap number. Joe makes her centre spot, and the lighting guys are told to stick on her like glue. Derby looks amazing in those dresses, pure silks and satins, her hair straightened with Mary's Congolene, the Conk pasted on each night, noxious up close, but looking good under those gels. Betty Wang, who does the women's page for the *China Press*, says Derby looks 'heavenly' and Buck is perhaps the handsomest man in all Shanghai. Men ogle Derby's curves, and the ladies love Buck and the Gentlemen in their L.A.-style zoot suits (courtesy of Pingee, who pored over American magazines and got the cut just right), straightened hair and pencil-thin moustaches like Negro Clark Gables. The crowd won't let them leave the stage. A couple of weeks in and the Canidrome Ballroom is the place to be.

Through Christmas and the New Year, as '34 slides into '35, hot swing jazz keeps the place packed. Buck and the boys want a raise, in American dollars, and Joe argues they deserve it. Tung and Vong whinge but eventually cough up. To celebrate, Joe lets Buck and the boys cut loose after the show. Derby goes home to wash out the Conk before it burns her scalp. The fun starts with a few toots of good-grade Cadillac backstage, a few speedy hands of tonk, before hitting Frenchtown for high times and low life. The boys party hard. They get into fights with the marines at the Santa Anna. When fights break out, the house band's instruction is always to keep on playing, loud. Then they're off to the Golden Eagle just off Szechuen Road, a wild hop for the sailors on shore leave. Farther north into Chapei and they're at the Wiengarten brothers' Red Rose Cabaret for *smallbottlsvine* at twenty dollars Mex a quart. They scarf late-night chow at the Nanking on Foochow Road and then cruise the nearby brothels of the 'Golden Circle' for Chinese girls. They sling dice out back of the Isis with the Italian marines. They feast on sukiyaki and Asahi in Little Tokyo's beer halls; they chase Chinese and white dames at the Casanova Club—Korean girls and Natashas hurling *'Americanski durak!'* after them as they dance and then split without buying anything. They're not welcome at the Cathay Hotel—no coloureds— so in the early hours they generally go to Sam Levy at the Venus, with his traditional ham and eggs, or have breakfast at Teddy's crib—home-style fried chicken, hot biscuits, and gravy washed down with freshly mixed highballs.

Joe fixes them up with Doc Borovika, whose retirement fund and opium money are significantly boosted by the boys—and everyone else. Don Chisholm offers the doc free advertising in the *Shopping News* in return for gossip, but the doc keeps schtum. The Harlem Gentlemen line up Monday mornings with clap, pox, syph, crabs: a jigging queue of horny young men with burning piss and sores on their *schvantzes* outside the doc's spare room. The doc tells the startled neighbours that the boys are used to hot weather, and Shanghai gives them colds that just won't shift.

For Joe and Nellie, the Canidrome money is everything they'd dreamt of. Nellie finds a decent Frenchtown apartment, and their Woo Foo Lane days of bug tape, chipped enamel sit-and-soak baths, and communal stoves are long over. They move in and move up. Not that all is great in the garden—Joe can't leave the Follies, the Peaches, or the Hollywood Blondes alone, and that rankles Nellie. He's getting sloppy about it too—the whiffs of chypre and lily of the valley that linger, lipstick on the collar, blonde hairs caught on the lapels of his winter tweeds, the telltale signs of Joe's nonstop philandering. They fight but keep it together for the Canidrome punters who want them to glide and slide on the dance floor, Joe slapping backs and shaking hands, Nellie drinking with the big spenders. They're on the up, and it should have been enough. But Shanghai always offers other temptations: sex, money, success and, of course, the city's oldest temptress, its single greatest source of profit and wealth and its founding obsession—opium. And the world is about to get an unprecedented hit.

Shanghai is a bastard son of a city, an offspring nobody wants until it has something worth taking. It's Chinese land surrendered after defeat in battle and a subsequent unequal treaty by a weak China to a powerful England determined to sell opium and wanting the key port that controls the Yangtze trade. The city is an embarrassment to the Nationalist government in Nanking, a symbol of defeat, of historic weakness. Yet it has risen to become the China Coast's richest metropolis, a repository of treasure, a beacon attracting all of China's hopeful, ambitious, determined. Shanghai is now a prize worth taking, a son who's grown to outstrip the father that languishes in poverty, disease, floods that turn to droughts. The neon-bright city feeds off its host of four hundred million peasants barely surviving in China's fetid hinterlands and laughs at their degradation. Shanghai is an abscess on the country, a contamination. It will be cauterised, cleansed, disinfected—but not yet. For now, the *generalíssimo* and his Nanking government will let Shanghai persist in the hope that, perhaps, the Western consuls and businessmen, their soldiers and battleships, will keep the greater menace from the east—Tokyo—at bay.

Four times a year the city's sky turns black at midday, the sun blotted out, the streets choking as the quarterly bonfires of Chiang Kai-shek's Opium Suppression Force rage. Seized opium, heroin, cocaine, and vials of morphine stoke the flames. Convicted dope dealers are forced to shovel the haul into brick kilns on wasteland in Pootung, the muddy marshes across the Whangpoo, and ignite it in immense bonfires after customs agents determine the wind is in the right direction. The sweet, sticky, black cloud will descend on the Settlement opposite, reminding its citizens of their transgressions. The men who shovel will later be executed and buried in unmarked graves in those same Pootung marshlands. They are buried alongside the nameless impoverished addicts they fed, the lost opium ghosts they have created.

When the Whangpoo swells, rises, and bursts its banks, the corpses of the dealers and the addicts will reappear—bloated and blackened. But for now, all the black cloud does is remind the pedestrians on the Avenue Joffre, on the Bubbling Well Road, on the Avenue Haig, that the eternal truth of Shanghai is dope, is opium. It's a metropolis raised on dope, its foundations permanent reminders of that trade. The cloud that envelops the city is a fraction, a minuscule percentile, an insignificant amount of that which has flowed in and out of the city's arteries, creating wealth for some and hell for many. As long as a city stands on the banks of the Whangpoo River, dope will flow through its veins.

They haunt the banks of the city's creeks—the Soochow, the Saw-gin, the Siccawei. They crowd into bamboo-matted lean-to shacks in the western slum villages of Fah Wah and Zau de Ke. Some exist aboard rickety and leaky beggar boats, tarp-covered sampans permanently moored in the remoter sections of the fetid creeks. They are slaves to the Foreign Mud, the poisioned chalice of the West: opium. Those that work to suppress the vice estimate that the city contains 100,000 addicted souls. They throng the countless dens of Shanghai on Foochow, Kiangse, Yu Yuen Roads. There are too many flower-smoke rooms on too many streets to name. By day they beg, walking the city, scrounging coppers. By night they smoke, wreathed in the blue smoke of the juice of the poppy. Their complexions are grey, their skin as though bleached, with the consistency of papyrus. They stumble as though weak. Their noses run freely; their eyes water. Their teeth loosen and fall out, leaving bleeding gums; their pupils contract to points; they grow old quickly, with grey hair, stooped backs, cracked fingernails. Their souls are shattered, their minds deranged. Most die prematurely.

But others live and remain slaves. They survive on the dregs of juice left by others—that considered too poor-quality to keep: the so-called longtou zha. *It's sold to poor men in alleyways by servants from wealthier houses where addicts reside. In their shacks they boil it with water over coal stoves and smoke the residue. The truly desperate buy the pulp left over after this process for just three or four copper coins begged on the street. They then boil that residue down further, securing the last and final dregs. People consider these addicts neither dead nor alive, neither real nor illusory. They have ceased to exist except as opium ghosts, with no ambitions, no future cares, no past rememberances. And so they are known, and avoided, cast out to the far reaches of the city, the dope slum villages, to the beggar boats and the bankside bamboo shacks. The undead slaves of opium—ghosts.*

This, people believed . . .

9

The money had gone out of booze real quick when Prohibition was repealed in America in 1933. Technically the ban on drinking had applied to Americans in Shanghai too—the downside of extra-territoriality. But nobody, including the U.S. Court for China and the U.S. Marshal's office in the city, had been dumb enough to try to enforce the Volstead Act in the Settlement, and Americans in Shanghai had just gone right on drinking and whooping it up throughout. With the city's minuscule import duties, customs officials notoriously susceptible to bribery and looking the other way at the dockside, and no excise or license fees to pay on booze, American rum-runners brought in case after case of whisky from Ireland and Scotland, brandy and cognac from France, and shipped it all straight back out again as contraband to the States—the long but very profitable way round. Carlos Garcia had made a small fortune shipping his own distilled Mexican tequila into Shanghai and back out again to America's West Coast in crates marked 'Chinese Pig Bristles'. Higher-end California speaks and blind pigs relied heavily on shipments of decent liquor from Shanghai. Yes, Prohibiton had surely been good to the Settlement while it lasted. Still, everyone knows dope can make liquor look like small beer.

Dope is the future, but the killjoys in Washington, D.C., are intent on cracking down on heroin, cocaine, and morphine. Stealth and multiple trafficking routes are urgently required. New York mob boss Little Louis 'Lepke' Buchalter dispatches his top procurement mensch, Jacob 'Yasha' Katzenberg, east. Yasha hits the 'Hai in time for Chinese New Year 1935—the year of the pig—looking to buy opium and Cadillac pills for shipment to Lepke's processing plant up on Brooklyn's Seymour Avenue. Big-Eared Du and his Green Gang have a monopoly on the dope. To facilitate an introduction to him, Yasha needs a Shanghai connection.

So Yasha looks for his own kind, people he can trust. You can't just stroll up to Du's Frenchtown mansion-cum-fortress and get a meeting; you need local go-betweens. Yasha finds what he is looking for in Albert Rosenbaum, sipping schnapps at the Red Rose Cabaret. Rosenbaum had known Yasha somehow or other, some connection back in the old country, Romania, though people said Rosenbaum was Bulgarian—nobody was sure either what he was or what the difference was. Rosenbaum is tight with Sammy and Al Wiengarten, old-time Shanghai bad hats and owners of the Red Rose.

Like the Venus close by, the Red Rose is where the city's Jewish demimonde and underworld gather, kvetching about business, tightwad punters, meshuggeneh showgirls and schlemiel associates. Joe Farren still hangs out at the Red Rose after hours occasionally, even though he's now the 'dapper Ziegfeld' of the *North-China Daily News* society column, slurping goulash at the end of the bar with nightclub legends Sol Greenberg of the Casanova and Monte Berg, who runs the longtime popular Little Club. Joe likes Sammy Wiengarten; he's an old-timer, a mensch, an all-round nice guy if you don't cross him. Sammy should have retired long ago, but he'd just shrug, look up at the ceiling, and ask where he was supposed to retire to: fucking Jew-hating Romania? Sammy and Joe introduce Yasha to Rosenbaum, who's a moneyman and dealmaker with a finger in plenty of pies across town. All business, all deals; Jews without any romanticism or nostalgia for any old country, any shit-hole shtetl or slum tenement. They're all looking to make money, get rich, move up.

When the Paramount and the Canidrome close for the night, the Red Rose carries on till dawn with the late, late crowd, cars lined up all down the street, local Chinese kids paid to guard each one from car thieves. The Red Rose is nothing special; it's drafty and threadbare, with a White Russian manageress always dressed in black, still in mourning for her long-dead husband killed fighting the Bolsheviks. Close-to-past-it hookers grift the crowd while slumming swells jig to gypsy jazz from a White Russian balalaika band plinking away, done up like Kalderash clan *gitanes*. No Joe Farren–choreographed hoofers here; instead it's all Russians singing late-night torch songs mourning lost homelands over lukewarm borscht. Stateless Russians cry into their vodka alongside second-rate Ukranian gypsy boulevardiers, Shanghailanders swilling Japanese rotgut whisky. But it paid—*vunbottlvine* two dollars Mex to a known face, five dollars to a drunk sailor, ten bucks to a sojourning tourist, and never more than a buck twenty to a down-at-heel fellow Russian. Sammy is cheap with the acts—the night's big joke comes when a particularly croak-throated crooner starts their favourite Russian dirge, 'Dark Eyes'. The patrons empty their pockets of change, and the clatter of coppers generally drowns out the rotten sound, while the singer scoops up the coins and disappears offstage.

Early morning it's Farren, Rosenbaum, and the Wiengarten brothers backstage, all Yiddish bonhomie, old-time Shanghai stories from the twenties, checking out the new Russian and Jewish girls down from Harbin. The old gag: those girls dressed on credit and disrobed for cash. Joe checks several of his Follies and Peaches doing a little off-the-books business. They smile back; they know Joe's got the roving eye and the keys to half a dozen apartments he can take them to. Sammy Wiengarten and Al Rosenbaum lay it out: Du can supply the dope, but Yasha wants contacts to run his routes, and he only trusts his own. There's no crossing Yasha: his backers are Lepke Buchalter and Meyer Lansky of New York's Lower East Side mob, and both have reputations that cross the Pacific.

Buying off the Shanghai ports is no problem—Chinese customs officers are soon queuing up at the Buick showrooms with hundred-dollar bills shipped straight from Brooklyn. But Yasha drops major coin buying up U.S. customs to establish a direct route, and he urgently needs plenty of mules. Then Yasha and Lepke hear the U.S. Treasury is pushing the SMP to watch sailings from Shanghai to the States. Sammy thinks back to his pimping days and remembers how ladies travelled hassle-free. Go counterintuitive: zig when the Treasury boys expect you to zag. Girls board at Shanghai and go to Marseilles, then either go straight to New York or overland to somewhere like La Rochelle or Hamburg, and then on to the East Coast. No American citizens, foreign passports only. Send some alone and some with 'husbands' as cover. A few could go west via Manila or Yokohama and cross to mob-friendly L.A., maybe sail up to British Columbia and Vancouver, to be met dockside by someone with a train ticket to the East Coast. All it needs is girls, girls, girls. And all the boys know a mensch who can be trusted, a guy who knows girls, plenty of foreign girls—ones who could be encouraged to move on and have a stake waiting for them in America.

Nobody ever talks about who brokered the deal, but Joe Farren, choreographer, exhibition dancer, hirer of more young women for the purposes of dance-hall entertainment in Shanghai than anyone else, puts out feelers to take out a lease on a big nightclub somewhere on the western edge of the Settlement and Frenchtown, out where Al Israel's got the Del Monte coining it, out where the law gets a little sketchier. He's planning to staff it up, put a floor show together, poach the best chefs in town and let it be known there might a casino on the top floors. He says he can do it with no debt. Albert Rosenbaum sets him up with a front company to secure the licences and keep the Municipal Council happy. Serious gelt is spent; good luck to you if you want to see the accounts. Guess where the money came from? You'll never prove it; nobody will ever talk. But Joe Farren worked at the Canidrome: Carlos Garcia–owned, fronted by the smooth French banker Bouvier with Big-Eared Du as a silent partner; connect Du to the girls on the boats via Yasha, with the Red Rose as the meeting place for New York–trusted Albert Rosenbaum handling the money, and Sammy Wiengarten serving the drinks.

Joe Farren puts out casting calls all over town for any girl with a slim ankle and a wide smile who ever wanted to dance in a revue. A few get hired; plenty of others get offered other options that involve a boat ticket and a new opportunity. Albert Rosenbaum hands them passports, letters of transit, some cash for a new start, a package of dope for their false-bottomed suitcase, and the name of a man who'll meet them at the Chelsea Piers in New York.

The shipments start in December 1935. All is copacetic; everyone who is anyone is involved. The only catch is there's so much dope there just aren't enough girls willing to ship out. New York is exerting pressure, demanding more shipments. Rosenbaum is stumped, but Joe tells him he's got an idea. Remember Jack Riley and those slot machines? The Navy transports? Rosenbaum gets it: rotating marines and nurses head back stateside constantly with packs that'll hold a stash and no serious customs checks on the military. But Rosenbaum's no dummy, and he's not so keen on Riley; he tells Joe to make sure the independently minded Slots King knows exactly whom he's working for in New York, and understands their reputation.

Joe fixes it with Jack, who assures him there are any number of leathernecks, sailor boys, and army nurses more than happy to make a little extra on the trip back. He'll work his Fourth Marines contacts. Jack whistles when he hears who he's working for and shows respect, but thinks, *fucking New Yorkers; Tulsa's tougher.* It's on, but Joe reminds him that there are no side deals; you cannot fuck with these mensches. Joe finds the showgirls who want passage home; Jack works the Fourth Marines Club for rotating leather-necks. Yasha's men wait dockside in Manhattan and along the West Coast, from Seattle to L.A.

10

Nobody in Washington or the SMP thinks to look beyond the passenger liners departing Stateside. Long-established protocol means nobody interferes with the U.S. Navy transports heading to Manila and back home. Nobody checks as the heroes march down the gangplanks in California and Seattle, a sweet stash in their backpacks, straight to a back-alley bar where a man in a large suit with a bulge under his arm relieves them of their packages in return for some cash. Joe and Jack are in on the dope business.

The dope runs start up, and it's all running smooth as Shantung silk. By Chinese New Year 1936 Jack's got Nazedha in his bed and keeping things straight, ensuring DD's business is a decent-sized mint, despite losing some business to the Canidrome, and the slots all over town are still paying well. But he knows a roulette wheel could make in twenty minutes what a craps game takes ten hours to make and a line of slots a whole evening to earn. Tables are the ultimate—high stakes, appealing to the swells who can't throw a die more than they can do a day's hard work. Rig the wheels to high heaven, courtesy of wannabe gigolo Manilamen croupiers who learnt their trade back in the twenties from operators like Garcia, and reap the rewards. He's heard the late-night rumours up at the Venus, the Red Rose; the scuttlebutt that Joe intends to use his dope money to front a major joint out to the west of town and wants roulette wheels and a full casino. That could be Jack's chance too; he can run the casino and leave Joe to set up the floor show and get the whole shebang right to bring in the high spending crowd. Joe might just be his ticket to ringside. The Manhattan, the Hut, DD's, the slots, delivering willing leathernecks and nurses to the Red Rose dope ring—it's all paying, but fronting a casino for Joe's joint, cash cow as he's sure it will eventually be, will initially cost still more than all these ventures earn, much more, and he doesn't want to miss this shot.

Temptation. So many empty knapsacks heading Stateside; so many more leathernecks, nurses, and assorted military personnel who could be carrying dope. And it's dope that only he would profit from. He promised Joe no side deals. But if Joe doesn't know, then he won't care.

Jack notices a DD's regular who eyes up Nazedha lasciviously from the bar. He's about to sock him one when scandal rag proprietor Don Chisholm intervenes, gives Joe a wink, and introduces the two. The guy's an American by the name of Crawley, Paul Crawley. Word has it Crawley came out east after the Great War, spent time in Vladivostok and Tokyo, picked up the lingos. He worked out a way to make pirate copies of American movies with some guy called Goldenberg in the mid-twenties. They'd sold the flicks to a Tokyo entrepreneur for screening in cinema tents in the Japanese boondocks where Hollywood hadn't yet reached and made forty thousand bucks. Goldenberg managed to cash the check right before he was found dead in his Ginza hotel room, penniless and missing his signature diamond pinky ring. A few months later Crawley pitches up in Harbin, married to a smoking-hot Russian, *nyet*-ing and *da*-ing, running a gambling den and selling guns and dope on the side to the ever-feuding, ammo- and dope-hungry Northern warlords. Everyone knew how to recognise Crawley in Harbin— he was the guy wearing a diamond ring on his little finger.

By the late twenties Crawley is in with a Russian gang working out of Harbin's Hotel Moderne. They move down to Shanghai and invest in a couple of bars, selling guns and dope. As the warlord gun racket cools, they up their dope sales in league with a Cantonese confectioner with ambition who runs the Velvet Sweet Shop on the North Szechuen Road. Ah Lee mixes bonbons and Turkish delight by day and turns opium into heroin by night. He's really good at both trades. Meanwhile, Crawley starts looking for a route to the U.S. for the product.

Once dodgy Don Chisholm introduces sleazy Paul Crawley to ever-ambitious Jack Riley, they work out a deal sweeter than any of Ah Lee's confections. Riley kicks in some slots profits to up production over on the North Szechuen Road and takes his surplus marines and army nurses to create a new heroin route straight to the West Coast and to local interests of his acquaintance in San Francisco. It bypasses the New York syndicate and yields plenty of cash for Riley, Ah Lee, and Crawley. But it's a seriously risky game—the feds coming at you one way; maybe a pissed-off Yasha and the Hongkew Jew boys the other—but for now those roulette wheels are getting ever closer. Pull it off for a time without anybody getting wise to it, and Jack's got the stake he'll need to persuade Joe to let him manage the casino end of the business. He sits down with Joe at the Venus and makes a proposal. Joe listens.

Nellie Farren performing the Aztec Shimmy, 1929
(Courtesy of Peter Hibbard)

Joe Farren—'The Dapper Ziegfeld of Shanghai'
(North-China Daily News)

Jack Riley—'The Slots King of Shanghai'
(North-China Daily News)

Shanghai Crime Squad chief John Crighton with unidentified man, 1939
(Courtesy of Robert Bickers & Visualising China)

Sam Titlebaum, 1941
(China Weekly Review)

Chief Deputy U. S. Marshal Sam Titlebaum, who took a formal oath of office
in Shanghai on February 7.

Alice Daisy Simmons, 1941
(*China Weekly Review*)

Murdered

Miss Alice Daisy Simmons, who was an innocent victim of Shanghai's first inter-gambling gang shoot up at Farren's last Saturday night. Miss Simmons died almost at once from a bullet wound in the back.

Walter Lunzer

Walter 'Wally' Lunzer, 1941
(*China Weekly Review*)

Boobee & Vertinsky at the Gardenia
(North-China Daily News)

The Gardenia on Shanghai's Great Western Road
(Courtesy of Katya Kynazeva)

ABOVE AND BELOW:
Paramount Peach chorus line, 1937, with Nellie Farren centre-stage
(Photographs courtesy of Vera Loewer)

At the House of Surprises

JOE FARREN *says:*

"I have never had the pleasure in many years in Shanghai of satisfying my friends so much as with the great floorshow which we are presenting nightly. See it and hear it — early or late."

Sandra and Fredric Hartnell
(Sensation of London nightclubs)

Aristocrats of Harmony
(Greatest male quartet ever in the Far East)

Svetlanoff Duo
(Dancers de luxe)

Watch and wait (a little) for the next big surprise

COVER CHARGE $2   RESERVATIONS TELEPHONE 23113

Always the leader of Gaiety

To-night—Enjoy
Farren's Newest Sensation
Volsky's Midnight Follies of 1941

ABOVE, RIGHT, AND BELOW:
Farren's ads, 1940/1941
(The China Press)

☆
DANI SISTERS   TANIA SVETLANOVA   LANTZOF ☆

Shanghai Finest Dance Band
MIKE'S MUSIC MASTERS OF SWING

Under personal supervision of
For reservations   JOE FARREN   Convert
Dial 23113-23112   · $2

All Dressed Up . . . And ONE Place To Go!

FARREN'S
The House of Surprises

takes pleasure in announcing, in conjunction with the forthcoming presentation at the Roxy Theatre of the super-colossal film "Gone With The Wind" that

'A GAY GALA' NIGHT
featuring

AN OLD-FASHIONED WALTZ CONTEST

will be held to-morrow, Friday, June 14. Plan to enjoy some of that grand old Southern charm and hospitality by making your reservations now.

Special Floor Show Programme
Cover Charge $2

Personal Direction: JOE FARREN
Reservations Telephone 23113

Summer 1936 is starting to heat up. All's running sweet for Joe and Jack—stashes building up, clubs coining it, mugs still lining up three deep to play the slots, the dope getting through and the New York money flowing back. Seems Yasha, and by extension Lepke and Lansky in New York, are happy. Joe sees his nightclub-casino dreams becoming reality, and thinking maybe Jack is the man to run the casino; Jack is feeling easy knowing Joe and the Hongkew boys haven't wised up to his side operation, which is giving him the extra gelt he'll need to go into business with Joe.

At the Canidrome, the dogs run three times a week to a sellout crowd of fifty thousand punters betting small, large, and everything in between. Jack and Joe got mutts and trained them up. Neither is the horsey sort; the race club is for stuck-up Brits and the kind of Chinese who send their brats to university in Oxford or Massachusetts. Though they like to bet on the gee-gees, they have never worked out a surefire system for winning on the ponies. Joe can't work the odds in his favour reliably enough, and Jack can't figure how to nobble a horse. For a crooked town, the race club ponies are startlingly legit—so the nightlife boys stick to the dogs. Plus, the ponies run in the daytime, and they prefer the Canidrome evening races for their breakfast entertainment before the night's work begins.

Now Joe and Jack are in the stands behind the large concrete entrance, waiting for the big race with their crews in tow. Joe is with Nellie, wrapped up in her trademark black sable from the Siberian Fur Store on the Avenue Joffre, even though it's early June and the afternoon is warm with an occasional sudden rain shower. Joe's crew of assorted pouty Peaches, frisky Follies, and hot Hollywood Blondes is there, plus Albert Rosenbaum, Doc Borovika, and the Wiengarten brothers, Sammy and Al. Jack's just up back behind them with Nazedha looking sweet in a fox stole and a crew of Friends led by Mickey and Schmidt. Babe's there too, back in Jack's good books after taking the German hyp-notist's dope cure. She's trying to straighten herself out while being gracious in losing the heart of the Slots King to Nazedha. They're gal pals now and the 'look into my eyes; look into my eyes' cure seems to be holding.

The first races are perfunctory, no-good mutts, skinny little pups that might one day make the grade or be tossed in the Canidrome groundsman's stew—too green, not worth betting on. The dark still comes in fast this time of year in Shanghai, and the racetrack is an oval of electric light beneath the black sky, blink-ing neon signs at either end.

EWO BEER: HERE'S LUCK
FLIT: THE WORLD'S LEADING INSECTICIDE

Everyone is hassling the Chinese boys in neat white monkey jackets working for the pari-mutuel, who rush up and down the aisles with betting slips, shrilly calling the odds, grabbing the cash lightning quick, fluttering hands back to the touts.

It's race four, and Joe's excited—he's got his cream greyhound Pretty Peach running. His Chinese kennel man in a liveried jacket and white riding breeches leads the silk-jacketed dog out; there are big laughs as the mutt pauses, crouches, and shits in the dirt. Jack cracks wise about losing the extra weight; the old superstition says if they shit before the off, they'll be two lengths up. Joe's got fifty bucks riding on Pretty Peach, and he's not alone: Buck, Derby, and the Harlem Gentlemen are back up in the stands with their betting slips held high.

The bugle sounds, and the kennel men shove the dogs into the traps one by one, Pretty Peach going in last. The cloudless sky reveals a few stars over the city. The odds are right for Joe's hound, and with the dogs in the traps the bookies wipe the prices off their blackboards. There's a rumble as the electric hare ricochets out and starts flying round the circuit. The dogs fall silent themselves a moment, and then the traps bang up as the hare rattles past. The six thin hounds burst out of the cages and chase that hare for all they're worth.

Pretty Peach breaks clear and sweeps into the first bend holding the rails with a two-length lead, Jack shouting, 'Told you so.' Pretty Peach sticks to the rail, chases the hare and keeps the lead into the finishing straight. The other mutts trail like they're going backwards, and Pretty Peach scorches the winner's line half a dozen heads in front of the second dog. Joe and Nellie are hugging, Buck and his Harlem Gentlemen backslapping, and all those who bet on Pretty Peach are bowing towards Joe, who's provided their payday. The rest of the folks in the bleachers tear up their ticket stubs and fling them in the air, worthless confetti falling through the arc-light beam.

Then the last race of the night. Jack's got his mutt ready to go. Mickey O'Brien has been racing that dapple-grey dog round Hongkew Park daily, feeding her the best first-quality steak from Hongkew Market—the same steak the taipans get at DD's for twenty bucks Mex. Blood Alley Babe's got the big money on her, with the Friends and Fourth Marines all betting large on Jack's hound. They're not the only ones—Jack tells Joe to bet big on Blood Alley Babe—wink, wink.

The bookies have pinned new cards to their stands, and the layers are chalking up the prices. The boys of the pari-mutuel pass through the crowd once more. The 'Ships', young Chinese boys, are making ready to run the results from the track to the punters who don't like to leave their stools, betting from off-track bars and cafés nearby. Joe nods to Jack and waves his ticket—fifty bucks on Blood Alley Babe. The bugle sounds again, and Mickey O'Brien is leading out Jack's dog to the traps with his jockey cap on askew. The hare's out on the rail, and the expectation is high.

The dogs fly out the traps, but Blood Alley Babe broke bad and is losing by four lengths to another dog. Then the lead dogs bump, and throw the third and fourth mutts wide, with the fifth getting tangled in its own sinewy legs and crashing out into the fence. Carlos Garcia's dog, Black Dolly, is now out in front, and the swells in the Canidrome's exclusive high tower are cheering, but Blood Alley Babe is catching up on the back straight, keeping tight to the rail and gaining yards. They're level into the third bend and Jack is screaming from the stands, Nazedha jumping up and down. Babe shouts curses to make a sailor blush, her neck scar flushed red, and a hundred marines are on their feet and willing that bitch to edge ahead.

The dogs run stride for stride for twenty yards. Black Dolly is looking tired now, tongue lolling, visibly slowing, and Blood Alley Babe is on the outside pushing past, teeth bared, gums covered in foaming spittle. Riley's pooch cruises across the finish line. Jack is delighted, salutes Joe, who raises an eyebrow in return. Then a grumble from somewhere up back of the stands and a loud voice, pure Glaswegian, calling out, 'Dogs dinnae go slow like that, they doped that canine, sure as hell.'

Jack moves over the bleachers towards a bunch of Highlanders in kilts. Now there are marines and Friends and Jack throwing the first punch, and it's on. The fight sprawls over the benches as women scramble out of the way. Joe and Nellie watch and the Harlem Gentlemen cheer while the Highlanders, outnumbered, back off from the coshes and lead pipes of the Friends. There's a crush at the gate to get out and someone's killed the arc lights, and Joe is hustling Nellie off the stands, and there's thumping and shouting and clothes getting torn, and a Peach falling out of her shoes and getting trampled, and the off-duty Frenchtown Tonkinese *flics* who do the Canidrome's security are getting between the brawlers, and a bookie's stand is upset and then another, and a man topples off his steps and is thrown to the ground, and then someone yells 'Razors, Razors!' and there's a Highlander with a badly gashed face holding his cheek together as someone who looks a lot like Jack Riley turns and walks away, patting his jacket lapels, smoothing back his brilliantined hair, and the *flics* are blowing whistles, and the loudspeakers are oblivious to the fracas, telling everyone to remember there's a meet tomorrow at two-thirty, come rain or shine.

Jack is out a side entrance with Nazedha, Mickey, and some Friends, as Schmidt shows his Mauser in a shoulder holster and clears a path real fast. They pile into a Packard and head for DD's. Buck and his boys have formed a circle round Derby and are edging out, staring down anyone who might want to see a genuine California switchblade up close. A platoon of Peaches, Follies, and Hollywood Blondes are swinging handbags, pulling well manicured but seriously sharp fingernails down the cheeks of anyone who gets in their way. Joe's got Nellie up the stairs and through a side entrance into the Canidrome Club kitchens while down in the bleachers the driftwood and trash of Frenchtown along with the *pi-seh, lieu-maung* beggars and loafers are rolling in the dust of the track, grabbing coins flung from the bookies' smashed stands. And the loudspeakers repeat—tomorrow, two-thirty, cash sweep, come rain or shine.

Carlos Garcia, up in the members' bar in the tower, sipping

stengahs with Louis Bouvier, doesn't give a shit; it's a full house. The bookies all kick him back ten per cent of their take just to operate trackside. The Central Bank of China has built one of its biggest branches right next door to the stadium, there's so much money flowing through the complex, every day, come rain or shine.

12

U.S. Treasury Agent Martin 'Nick' Nicholson was no novice. He fancied himself the Elliot Ness of the Orient, and was evangelical about stamping out American involvement in the dope business. He'd worked hard to smash the dope rings at home. Now he'd come to Shanghai to do the same and declared that the summer of 1936 would be the hottest on record for the dope traffickers.

Nicholson isn't much to look at: five foot two in his brogues, with a blue small-brimmed hat. His grey pinstriped suit with its Brooks Brothers cut makes his short legs look even shorter, his body even stockier. He's as wide as he is tall in those suits. Jack Riley dubs him 'Little Nicky', which pisses him off but sticks. Little Nicky can't miss those slot machines all over town and wonders just who Jack T. Riley is. He checks the card index of U.S. citizens resident in Shanghai at the U.S. consulate and finds nobody of that name registered. He figures, correctly, that Jack bunkers down in Frenchtown, but the notoriously easily bought Frenchtown police, the *Garde Municipal,* aren't proving cooperative in confirming that hunch. Yet every slot in the Settlement and Frenchtown pays out tokens stamped 'ETR'. The man swaggers up and down Blood Alley backslapping marines, bankrolling their in-house newspaper with his advertising. He passes out the punch at the Bamboo Hut to senior U.S. military officers, and funds Don Chisholm's *Shopping News* scandal rag while charming the taipans of the American business community at DD's. Little Nicky is not unaware that the income from hosting Riley's slots is the biggest single earner for the Marines Club. Little Nicky thinks Jack T. Riley needs a little closer scrutiny. He contacts the FBI back home to find out what they have, but the feds come back with no records on file. Little Nicky is stymied on that front.

But he makes life tricky for everyone else. He gets the Federal Bureau of Narcotics in D.C. to formally petition the SMP to get tough on the dealers. Nicky gets proactive and joins them in a raid on Leong's Moon Palace dope den, they pull in a few bleary-eyed marines and some China Coaster dames, those foreign women of various nationalities who live by their wits along the China coast and whom the generous call 'courtesans' and the less generous have other names for. Nicky pulls Babe off a cot and gets a righteous stiletto scrape down the shins for his trouble; it seems the German hypno's cure didn't take. The SMP cart them off to the cells, but they all get let go the next day. The marines are back to barracks while Babe screams the place down until Jack Riley sends his henchman Schmidt over with bail money and an envelope for the SMP's Christmas party fund.

Still Little Nicky keeps on digging in the Shanghai dirt. He gets a tip-off that a Eurasian nurse is carrying dope back to the States. Nicky finds her with a stash of dope in her trunk, a fresh-stamped Macao visa in a newly issued Portuguese passport, and a ticket to California on a Dollar Line boat. The passport comes from a Portuguese gang; the visa appears genuine enough. Nick knows the Portuguese consulate in Shanghai is legendarily pliable. He traces the tip-off and arranges to meet the dime-dropper, but it never happens. The French Garde find a dead Eurasian answering to the man's description, a horn-handled knife in his back, on some wasteland close by French Park on Route Voyron. The *flics* give big Gallic shrugs and mutter 'Greeks probably, Corsicans possibly, gypsies potentially, Macanese maybe'. Once more Little Nicky hits a dead end and sits in his office sweltering and getting nowhere.

It's now late summer 1936, and the Velvet Sweet Shop heroin factory sideline has swelled Jack Riley's coffers considerably. Little Nicky's hunch about his digs was correct; he's got a nice Frenchtown pad in the Route des Soeurs and is hunkered down in there with Nazedha. She wants to make it all cosy and Russian-style; Jack's left it bare, stark—like an orphan's dormitory, a sailor's bunk, a prisoner's cell. Nazedha tries to soften the edges of Jack Riley somewhat, but she doesn't get much further than a bowl or two of potpourri. Still, it's close by the Canidrome for the fights and the dogs, and right by a couple of decent restaurants with private rooms for discreet meetings. It's also opposite a hole in the wall called the Manila Bar, a jukeboxy little joint where Babe hangs out these days drinking gin and French, off the dope again after the scare of the Moon Palace raid and a night in the cells, chewing gum cadged from the sailor clientele, betting on the bronzed Argentine boys at the jai alai over the road, and picking up moneyed tourists to refresh her purse.

She tipped Jack to the new apartment and sorts out the rent to keep Jack incognito. For a good weekly tip the White Russian concierge looks the other way. The apartment is rented by Mr. and Mrs. Lawrence, who run some kind of import–export gig. Anyone needs Jack urgently, they call the Manila on Shanghai-76772 and Babe answers, Astaire singing 'Cheek to Cheek' in the background. Jack figures it's best the city's standover men as well as Little Nicky, the U.S. marshals and the SMP don't know where he bunks.

13

Little Nicky wants to let Shanghai know D.C. isn't going to tolerate the flood of dope into America. Yasha's got his Green Gang associates in Shanghai not just shipping opium but manufacturing Cadillacs and morphine ampoules on a massive scale. 'Shanghai is now both a distribution and a manufacturing center,' Nicky tells the *North-China Daily News*. 'Morphine and heroin are speedily taking the place of opium as the main narcotics being smuggled to the United States . . . There's dope coming in, in large quantities, to organised crime in New York City and as much now suddenly flooding into the ports of Los Angeles and San Francisco. I'm here to end that.' Those in the know raise an eyebrow. New York, sure, and a little to L.A., but who's shifting large quantities of Shanghai dope to San Francisco?

Sunday night, the day before New Year's Eve 1936—there's smoke at the back of the Red Rose at four a.m. Some local Chinese call the police, and the cops from Hongkew station bust in the back door to find Sammy Wiengarten starting to roast in the back office. A fire's raging, the safe door's swinging open, and the Christmas takings are gone. Sammy is cooking in his captain's chair with his head back, but not so much the cops don't notice that someone kindly staved in the back of his skull before they set fire to the place and walked out with nine thousand bucks (according to his brother, Al, who'd totted it up earlier that night). Another ten minutes and Sammy would have been cinders, the whole thing put down to a burglary gone wrong or old Sammy falling asleep at his desk with a lit cigarette. The cops drag out what is left of Sammy Wiengarten and then stand back, watching the Red Rose incinerate, vodka bottles popping, the timbers cracking like the castanets of its White Russian faux-jazz *manouche* band.

Every kind of rumour swirls around the Sammy Wiengarten murder. Sammy was trying to cut the Portuguese out of the whore-for-Macao-visas action in Hongkew; Sammy had screwed the Corsicans on a Frenchtown deal; Sammy cheated at cards and scammed the high-stakes Russian card games at the Broadway Mansions for plenty of gelt; Sammy didn't pay the SMP enough protection money; got on the wrong wide of Jack Riley's Friends by rigging their slots to pay him plenty and leave Jack a smidgeon; barred a lushhead marine who took it really personally; raped his Chinese chef's daughter and was righteously revenged by the old man. What nobody says is that New York decided Sammy must have fucked over Yasha and Lepke by setting up his own San Francisco routes and they, seriously pissed, got Du's Green Gang boys to sort him out. It makes sense at their end—there's dope coming in from Shanghai to the west coast that they don't know about. They figure their Shanghai connections are fucking them over. Maybe, but that's loose talk. Implicate Big-Eared Du and you'll get hatcheted and burned too if you get loose-lipped.

Little Nicky asks around and gets . . . bupkes. He appeals to the SMP for any information—veteran Detective Sub-Inspector John Crighton, who heads up the SMP Crime Squad, is keen to co-operate. He taps his legendarily extensive list of informers in the Shanghai underworld. Crighton's snouts say Sammy's killing was dope-related but that he wasn't cheating the New York mob. They say someone else is running dope out of Shanghai in competition with the Hongkew mob—but they don't know, or won't say, who. John Crighton hits a wall; Little Nicky knows the feeling.

Still, the SMP has to explain it somehow to keep the newspapers off their backs; the pushy hacks like rangy, chain-smoking J. B. Powell over at the *China Weekly Review* editorialise that the SMP can't control a dope-related crime wave. So the SMP got a yarn from their opposite numbers in the Frenchtown Sûreté that seemed to explain Sammy's murder. The Sûreté's theory cooked up in their Route Stanislas Chevalier HQ? The Portuguese mob were looking to muscle in on Sammy's action and sent over an ex-Frenchtown flic who'd been fired for selling guns to *lieu-maung* out the back door of French police headquarters to apply some pressure on Sammy. The rotten flic was crazy sweet on a Russian hostess over at the Metropole Gardens Ballroom on Gordon Road. The Natasha was costing him serious money in furs, jewellery, and good steak, and he needed extra cash just to keep her attention. The theory was plausible; he'd been in the Red Rose earlier that night complaining he needed cash and looking desperate. The SMP and Sûreté scoured the Settlement and Frenchtown, but the supposedly lovestruck ex-flic conveniently turned up OD'd soon after in a Chapei flophouse; the Sûreté closed the file. It was a tale anybody who knew Shanghai could easily believe.

Whatever . . . Sammy Wiengarten was out of the dope business. In fact all business was over for Sammy, after fifty years of running the Jukong Alley. His brother Al takes the hint, sells up at a knock-down price, and skedaddles to Tientsin for a quiet life running a small dive bar, never to speak of his Shanghai days again. Most of Shanghai forgets the Wiengartens in a weekend and moves on. But Joe mourns Sammy. He'd been a good friend. Joe and Nellie see him buried and tell each other that Sammy was a mensch; he'd never have betrayed Yasha, never have crossed Lansky, and DSI Crighton's Crime Squad theory courtesy of the Frenchtown flics' imagination was junk. Someone else was moving dope out of Shanghai to the States.

Still nobody looks in the direction of the Slots King.

14

Jack's side project is getting harder to hide. Crawley is shipping heroin out, but not before he has personally consumed a fair amount of it. Jack's got enough cash to seriously sit down and talk with Joe about buying a stake in his planned nightclub and becoming pit boss. They agree in principle over dinner at the Venus, subject to Jack accruing the necessary front money.

After Sammy is murdered, Jack thinks it's time to shut down the Velvet Sweet Shop operation, but Crawley and Ah Lee aren't interested, and so the sideline rolls on. Jack continues to bring in more slot machines from the Philippines and Macao with his Velvet Sweet Shop proceeds, and Crawley works out a deal to stuff the machines with black market guns too. They come courtesy of U.S. marines in Manila with gambling and dope debts who've traded their service firearms to pay off the vig after the super-high interest rates the casinos charged left them high and dry. It's good money, but risky—Riley knows better than most that U.S. Army–issue firearms showing up all over Shanghai at armed robberies and kidnappings, or on the hips of self-appointed warlords, will push U.S. authorities in China to act. He's not happy, but Crawley's addicted to his own product now and not listening to sense anymore.

Then Crawley, getting ever more greedy, gets a slots contact of his own and starts smuggling machines into Shanghai, selling them to joints that didn't truck with Riley and the Friends. Dope's one thing, but the Slots King isn't about to let anyone else in on the one-armed bandit action. Jack makes a call, and Schmidt and some Friends go out with sledgehammers to smash up Crawley's bogus slots and anyone they find installing them. Partnership over.

But how to deal with Crawley himself? The man is getting in deeper and deeper, injecting more of the product, stewed nightly to the hilt, increasingly desperate to get more cash and send out more dope via the marines and nurses. Jack insists they need to cool things or get roasted like Sammy. Ah Lee agrees it's got too crazy, but Crawley's not listening; he's dope-brave and not fearing anyone including Lepke, Lansky, and Big-Eared Du. The man is heading off the rails—walking round Hongkew clubs with a serious-looking Mauser C96 sticking out his belt, scaring the swells, and embarrassing everyone by beating the shit out of his White Russian wife in public. Then he starts turning up in Frenchtown bars where business gets done smooching his seventeen-year-old secretary. Riley knows he has to distance himself from Crawley fast and calm things down.

Then Crawley goes totally off the reservation. He rapes his Chinese maid, touches up his Russian squeeze's eleven-year-old daughter—molests his own stepdaughter and laughs about it. He's an angry drunk who pulls his gun in one too many nightclubs. When he does it at DD's a couple weeks into January, just days after Sammy's funeral, Joe is at the bar and tells Crawley to quit it. Crawley's drunk, he's high, he's up in Nellie's face, leering and asking her how she'd like to mule dope for him to San Fran in her Russky snatch. Jack heads over and sucker-punches Crawley before Mickey bundles him away from the gawping punters. But it's too late: Crawley's smutty suggestions have let the cat out of the bag, and Joe sees it all clearly now.

Joe sends Nellie home in the Canidrome Buick and goes back

to DD's angrier than anyone has ever seen him. He finds Jack sitting round after-hours with his crew and tells them all he needs to talk to Jack personally and privately. Joe doesn't shout, he doesn't argue, he doesn't get aggressive—that's not Gentleman Joe's way. He tells Jack he knows he's been side-dealing to San Francisco with Crawley, and that he's responsible for Sammy Wiengarten getting bludgeoned and burnt to a crisp. He's fucked up the good thing they all had. Jack can forget running a casino at any Farren's joint; any understandings they might have had are off. Joe'll keep schtum to avoid a war, but that's that—the two of them are finished. And Jack should make no mistake: if the boys in Hongkew and New York worked this out there would be one hell of a war in Shanghai. Everybody, except Little Nicky and the SMP, will lose if that happens, so Joe will bite his tongue. But Joe and Jack are finished. Joe gets up and leaves; Jack sits there and fumes.

But Jack doesn't forget Crawley. The next day Schmidt rousts him from his opium dreams and escorts him to the docks while Mickey packs his bags. Jack tells Crawley he needs to go lie low for a while back in California, clean himself up. When he's straightened out they can restart the business. Crawley knows he's gotten seriously out of line and jumps at the ticket home. He steps off the boat in San Francisco a few weeks later for his R and R and is met at the bottom of the gangplank by customs officers, courtesy of a Little Nicky telegram from Shanghai. They find a large stash of heroin in his luggage alongside some stolen U.S. Army guns. Paul Crawley disappears into a federal penitentiary for a mighty long time.

Just how Little Nicky knows Crawley's coming home, not to mention the contents of his luggage, is anyone's guess. The U.S. Treasury agent's Shanghai office is in the phone book; Little Nicky himself takes the calls.

It's the dames who eventually lead to the fall of Lepke Buchalter and the East Coast drop-offs—those swell-looking gals travelling solo. Nicky had been looking at the liners out of Shanghai to the States. But he eventually cast the net wider and started to check the sailings to Europe via Suez. Girls, travelling alone, plenty of luggage, some with newly minted husbands carrying passports from every banana republic south of Texas. Showgirls, cabaret hoofers, students who'd never seen the inside of a lecture hall, 'secretaries' who hadn't been gainfully employed for some time, if ever, and had never touched a typewriter in their lives. Shanghai to Marseilles; Cherbourg to New York. Girls born in Russia, girls born in Harbin but travelling on Portuguese, Cuban, Peruvian, Venezuelan, Greek passports to ease their access out of Shanghai, into Europe, on to the States, always taking roundabout routes to Manhattan. Girls who shouldn't have money for a steerage crossing going first class on P&O, with a suite on the Messageries Maritimes, or reclining on a deck lounger on Norddeutscher. It smells bad; the whisper is Hongkew Jewish nightlife connections to Louis Buchalter and Yasha Katzenberg. Little Nicky tracks the girls, has his agents meet them in Manhattan to search their bags and scoops up plenty of dope from under their lingerie and dresses. They carve up their luggage trunks and find untold riches. He follows the trail backwards and breaks the ring, busts the bent customs officers. He teams up with the French Brigade des Stupéfiants, and they pick up more showgirls from Shanghai arriving in Marseilles with heroin-stuffed trunk cases for onward passage to New York. The girls go to prison, but not one of them squawks—they don't know anything anyhow, because the Hongkew boys used too many cutouts to track back to them easily.

The whole business starts falling apart throughout early 1937. Every ship docking up and down the East and West Coasts of the United States is met by Little Nicky's U.S. Treasury agents. And not just the U.S.; it's the earlier stops too, to prevent the couriers getting off early and travelling overland: Marseille, Cairo, Port Said, Alexandria, Genoa. They rigorously check manifests in Cherbourg, Trieste, Hamburg, and Southampton for anyone whose journey originated in Shanghai or any other China Coast port from Weihaiwei down to Hong Kong. It works; the shipments getting through slow to a trickle. Word quickly gets back to Shanghai, and few are willing to be couriers anymore. Joe and the Hongkew boys figure it's time to shut it down; it will only be a matter of time before Nicky tracks the girls back to them. They'd kept quiet so far, the cutouts had worked in obscuring their involvement, but that wouldn't last forever. It'd been a good thing while it lasted; everyone had banked some serious cash and, Sammy excepted, was alive to spend it.

By autumn '37, Louis Buchalter has a five-thousand-dollar bounty on his head and an indictment against him, in absentia, in federal court on conspiracy to smuggle heroin into the United States. But Katzenberg disappears after Nicky gets too close—back to Romania, the smart money says. Little Nicky wants to arrest the Shanghai end of the routes too. He tracks the trail back to the Shanghai Docks, downriver at Woosung and the landing stages at Wayside and Yangtszepoo Roads in Hongkew, but there it goes stone cold dead. But best not jump too far ahead . . .

15

In February 1937, with the demise of his dope routes and the fallout with Joe, Jack is hitting the bennies hard as Chinese Shanghai gets ready for its own new year. He's cracking drunks' heads a little too much on Blood Alley; bouncing bad debts at the Bamboo Hut a little too vigorously, losing it a little too regularly with Nazedha. The casino with Joe was Jack's shot at the major leagues, to rise up from bar owner and Slots King to rank with the likes of Garcia, to own the town. Now that dream is a bust.

The Chinese New Year party for 1937 is a big, big deal at the Canidrome Ballroom—goodbye to the year of the rat, welcome to the year of the ox. Tonight, Jack T. Riley has taken a table right on the edge of the dance floor, a slightly glass-eyed Babe on one side of him, a surly Natasha on the other. He's wearing a tux, sipping ginger ale from a crystal champagne glass, but up close he's jagged—fingers drumming the table, knees jerking; eyes darting about incessantly. He's rubbing his forehead till it's cherry red, chewing his bottom lip till it bleeds, grinding his teeth. Jack's not thinking straight, and those in the know see he's out for trouble. Everyone knows Joe and Jack have fought over something and that their casino deal is off. Now Jack's here to disrupt, pure and simple: to ruin everyone's night. Babe and the Natasha are suitably over-lubricated and underfed, ready to cheer old Riley on. But Joe and Nellie aren't there. Jack could have sent some Friends down to sort this out, but he enjoys taking care of this sort of business. When he'd got a call out of the blue at the Manhattan from Tung and Vong saying they needed a favour and did he still want to piss Joe off, it had made his day. Let the fun begin . . .

Buck Clayton, his Harlem Gentlemen, and the beautiful Derby are still a smash at the Canidrome, leaving takings down at other night-clubs all over Shanghai. But, uniquely for any foreign act in the city, Buck and the boys are being paid American-level salaries in genuine American dollars. Shanghai's got inflation jitters bad and, with China's national currency collapsing due to ever-present fears of Japanese invasion, Messrs. Tung and Vong are feeling resentful at paying out real American greenbacks, costing them more every month. They've got a solution, but it involves the Slots King and some Jack Riley–inspired mayhem.

Jack sits right up front and stares down Buck on the bandstand, unnerving him. Buck is teeing up the band for the introduction of the Hollywood Blondes. The girls come out of the wings from the right-hand side and start their routine. It's eleven p.m. and Jack is still staring; Buck is staring back now; neither man blinking. Then Jack is on his feet, neck all twisted up, pointing, telling him, 'Turn your eyes the other way', and when Buck doesn't, Jack calls him a 'black son of a bitch'. Buck walks over to confront him, but Jack doesn't wait and swings wide on the surprised Buck. He knocks him down on the dance floor, jumps on him, and rains blows to his head. The Hollywood Blondes are screaming and scattering while the Harlem Gentlemen ditch their instruments, pour off the stage, and pile on. There are several dozen tables of gussied-up and tuxedoed swells watching with their mouths wide open. Seems Blood Alley just came to the Canidrome for the night.

Jack is tough; he's Navy prizefighter good, but he's overwhelmed. He gets in a few punches, but the boys swarm him and beat the living shit out of him, sitting on his chest, banging his head on the dance floor, delivering some kicks to his ribs. Derby, soft and sultry, all café crème, now shows her wild side to protect her man. She jumps in for a swipe at Jack, ripping red fingernails down his face—part varnish, part Riley's blood. Her nails hurt more than Clayton's solid punches to the face. Jack is losing badly, even with Babe on Derby's back like a doped-up banshee.

Eventually the fight gets broken up and Riley is kicked out, bloodied, with a smashed-up nose, cut lips, and a cracked rib, but laughing out loud. Bloody and bowed himself, Buck makes it back onto the stage—Derby, torn dress still just about hanging together, breathes deeply and then wows the stunned audience with a deep and throaty 'Stormy Weather' like nothing just happened. But the job's done. Doesn't matter what everyone in the crowd knows and says, that mad Jack Riley started the scrap and Buck was the innocent party—Tung and Vong exercise the clause in Buck's contract that says he's out if there's any trouble. The next night Tung and Vong bring in a Manilamen band that costs a fraction of what Buck and the Harlem Gentlemen do and they take Chinese dollars as pay. The Canidrome never did such good business again.

Joe finds out and goes crazy, but stubborn Tung and Vong won't budge. Jack's revenge is sweet. Joe feels bad for Buck and gets the boys a new gig with Sol Greenberg over at the Casanova. But the good times are over, and Buck can see the Japanese asserting themselves on the streets more and more. The band plays the Casanova till they've scraped together their fares back to California, and then they jump on a steamship and head for home.

16

By July 1937, tensions are rising across the country. Manchuria wasn't enough for the rapacious Japanese, and they moved south, towards the old imperial capital that had been won and lost by so many warlords in the previous two decades. At the Marco Polo Bridge, just outside the ancient city's walls, they engineered an 'incident', a supposedly kidnapped Japanese soldier, and used it as a pretext to invade. The Japanese soldier wandered back to camp a few days later after sleeping off his hangover, but by then the Imperial Army had captured Peking, occupied the Forbidden City, patrolled the ancient city walls, marched through the crowded *hutongs*. They moved swiftly on to take the treaty port city of Tientsin. Most people think they'll come for Shanghai next as they move south. Tokyo will want to control the Yangtze trade.

Joe is run ragged. Every night he crisscrosses town in the chauffeured Buick sorting out problems, soothing frayed nerves, calming angry punters, making sure everything stays nice on the dance floor. The dope cash has dried up, and he needs to build his stash from running floor shows to try to keep his nightclub dream alive. He starts his evening at the Canidrome, making sure the swells are seated and fed and the band is playing the sweet tunes with Teddy Weatherford. The place is not the same since Riley smashed the joint up, but it's still pulling in plenty of punters—the Hollywood Blondes and the Manilamen band aren't too bad. He and Nellie don't talk so much these days; Joe's still an errant husband too regularly. But they might take a turn, cut a waltz for the early-evening crowd. Gentleman Joe and Sweet Dusky Nell are still a draw, even if they're staring daggers at each other as they slide across the ballroom floor.

From Frenchtown it's across to the Settlement, where he drops into the Elite Bar. He's got a floor show running there that warms up for Viennese chanteuse Lily Flohr, and it still needs tinkering. Then the Paramount—a long, long chorus line where the turnover is rapid. Nellie kicks the girls to the curb for the slightest infraction and then expects the new ones to know the moves swiftly. The Paramount has a couple of dozen girls, and Joe needs to spruce and spice up the routines regularly. Then it's back to Frenchtown and the Canidrome for the second set. The late-night crowd is in and Dapper Joe Farren has to cruise the booths and the front tables, acknowledge the taipans, schmooze the big-shot Chinese. Finally, Joe returns to the Paramount for the end of the show to make sure Nellie's okay and not throwing a tantrum at the girls. He has to get the taxi dancing right for the after-show crowd, and make sure the Natashas are sticking to ginger ale and apple juice and not hitting the booze and the powders. Maybe later, past three a.m., he might head out to Jukong Alley and the clubs to gab with the boys and cruise the joints before ham and eggs at the Venus Café with Sam Levy. There's always the possibility of a little liaison with a chorus girl. Those girls haven't really ever meant anything to Joe, just distractions and conquests, at least until Larissa.

She walks into the Paramount with a friend. It's summertime, and the girls are wearing last year's fashions, with home-stitched blouses and moth-eaten stoles from a wardrobe in St. Petersburg. She's young, twenty-one tops. She gets a job as a coat-check girl. Joe catches a look at her behind the counter, and he's smitten. He can't help himself. He tells her she should be a dancer, she should be spotlit; she says she's been taking tap classes. He tells her to work at it and he'll give her a tryout for the Peaches, put her in the chorus line, the best one in town. She wants that; it's better money, and the after-show dinners and the dance hostessing beat the cloakroom tip jar hands down. Joe auditions her one afternoon after rehearsals, when Nellie's not around. She dances barefoot on the stage, her red polka-dot dress swirling. She's amateur, with no training to speak of, but she's got that thing Joe likes, that innate sexiness that draws the punter's eye along the chorus line to one girl and fixes it, keeping them hooked. It's how he met Nellie, after all. Joe spins a chair round on the stage and straddles it, shirtsleeves rolled up, as the girl catches her breath. What's her story?

Larissa Andersen is the Khabarovsk-born, Harbin-raised daughter of a Tsarist Army father who couldn't stay when the Reds took over. Joe says Andersen doesn't sound Russian, and she says there's some Swedish ancestry back there somewhere. She's a deep, dark brunette—hair parted down the middle schoolgirl-style. Big, dark eyes, full lips, pert nose—Joe has fallen hard and doesn't even stop to realise she's Nellie with a decade shaved off.

Nellie finds out she's got a new chorus girl who's not up to scratch, and she's mad as hell. She sees Joe eyeballing her. She puts up with it, whips the girl into shape—she never blames the girls. She knows the type. Larissa's pretty enough, but her manicure's home done, her shoes cheap leather, and her clothes are threadbare, lace added to detract from the moth holes. Still, Joe is all over her like a cheap serge suit, making a fool of himself. One day Nellie casts her eye over the trays of the postcard sellers on Yu Yuen Road, the driftwood who hawk cheap penny postcards of the acts on the Paramount bill. Top of the pile is Larissa, the newest girl in the show, in black-and-white, lit well. It's a decent studio shot of the girl looking sultry in a lush black sable fur with obviously not much on underneath.

Nellie knows that coat—Joe bought it for her at the Siberian Fur Store, down in Little Russia on the Avenue Joffre. They were in love the day he bought it; they didn't eat anything but rice and pickled vegetables for several months afterwards as that coat cleaned them out. But they hadn't cared back then. The tears roll, her kohl runs; she grabs the postcards and tears them up, flinging the pieces in the gutter. While Joe is on his nightly run she fires Larissa and tells her to never come back.

Joe finds out, and now he's mad as hell. But Nellie's madder. She screams and shouts in their uptown apartment, breaks the china, overturns the furniture, throws the framed photographs around. Joe pleads innocence. But it's not that he probably screwed her. He'd screwed plenty before. Those postcards shame her, make her look like a fool, and she's had it—had it with the Paramount, the Peaches, the Blondes, the Canidrome, had it with Gentleman Fucking Joe, with the dapper Ziegfeld schtick, had it with Shanghai. He moves to console her, but she slaps him, breaks his glasses, and leaves him scrambling for them on the carpet in a myopic rage. He storms out.

Nellie calls up Joe's chauffeur, packs her bags, takes her jewellery and her savings, some mementoes and four trunks of clothes, loading them into the Buick. She gets to the docks with no particular destination in mind, but the boats are all full, there's not a bunk to spare—not first class or steerage; Europe via Suez or America via Kobe; no amount of squeeze will get you a cabin tonight. Peking and Tientsin have already fallen to the Japanese army and they're approaching south, towards the Yangtze. Those who can read the writing on the wall are pulling up sticks and lighting out before the hurricane hits, and Nellie Farren is stuck on the dock. There's nothing to do but go home.

17

Looking back, it all turned to shit on August 14, 1937. Tokyo had eyed China possessively, taken Manchuria in '32, edged down towards Peking, across to Mongolia. The Japanese had then engineered an excuse to take Peking and the international treaty port of Tientsin before rolling south towards the Yangtze. If they were to cut off the Nationalist government and take China, they had to capture Shanghai—the country's major money centre and entrepôt. The Japanese repeated their trick in Shanghai—they engineered an excuse, invented a supposed provocation, to justify attacks on the Chinese portions of Shanghai to the north of Soochow Creek—Chapei, Paoshan, and Kiangwan. They established a command centre in Hongkew Park, close by the district's Little Tokyo section that was home to the majority of Japanese in Shanghai, and began shelling into the packed streets. The Chinese Army mobilized and rushed reinforcements to Shanghai, including the elite Eighty-Seventh Division from Nanking, to join the supposedly crack Eighty-Eighth already in the city—the two best-trained divisions Chiang Kai-shek had at his disposal. The Chinese hunkered down at the North Railway Station and faced the Imperial Japanese Army. The barrage of shelling set fires raging in Chapei and Paoshan, their ferocity increased by the strong winds hitting the city as a typhoon passed close by. All Shanghailanders were ordered to leave the Chinese portions of the city by order of their consulates. Chinese refugees from Hongkew crowded the Garden Bridge trying desperately to reach the safety of the Bund and the central portions of the Settlement; snipers faced off against each other across the rookery rooftops. The Chinese administration imposed a curfew in the areas it controlled and enforced a blackout.

The Shanghai Volunteer Corps was called up to protect the Settlement, all SMP and *Garde Municipal* leave was cancelled, while French troops guarded the borders of Frenchtown. British soldiers set up anti-aircraft batteries on the racecourse while the U.S. Fourth Marines patrolled the length of the southern bank of the Soochow Creek. August in Shanghai—you could fry eggs on the sidewalks. At the Manhattan on Blood Alley, Jack and Mickey lined up beers on the counter for any Marine that wanted one—gratis. As the Japanese shelled Chinese Shanghai, wild fires raged across the Soochow Creek. Shanghailanders crowded onto rooftops, held war parties, drank 'explosive' cocktails, and watched the show. It didn't feel real; it didn't seem as if the skirmishing over in the Chinese quarters could actually cross the creek and impact on the lives of the 400 and Shanghai's nonstop party. But it did—dramatically and horrifically.

Saturday, August 14 was the day the bombs fell on Shanghai, a day the newspapers soon dubbed 'Bloody Saturday'. The Japanese fleet was moored provocatively in the Whangpoo opposite the Japanese consulate in Hongkew. The mighty guns of its flagship, *Idzumo*, repeatedly pounded shells into Chapei and Paoshan. In the capital, 190 miles away from Shanghai in Nanking, Chiang Kai-shek called a council of war. It was decided to use the Chinese Air Force to attack the *Idzumo*. The job of sinking the Japanese flagship was delegated to a square-jawed Texan who had recently retired from the United States Air Force and gone to China: Claire Lee Chennault. He knew it was an almost impossible mission: the pilots were not vastly experienced, the typhoon passing Shanghai meant cloud cover was low and visibility poor, and the *Idzumo* was a large target, but dangerously close to the packed streets of the foreign concessions.

The mission was a disaster. The Chinese pilots aiming for the *Idzumo* pounded the International Settlement by mistake. The first bomb, all two thousand pounds of it, sailed down towards the Settlement, the Nanking Road, and the Palace and Cathay Hotels, which stood opposite each other at the junction with the Bund. The initial bomb ripped through the roof of the Palace Hotel. The hotel's tea lounge, restaurant, lobby, and bar were all destroyed. Many of the dead and injured were only found later, still in their rooms. Part of the Palace's façade had been blown away and had begun to collapse. One man, blown out of his room on the fourth floor, clung perilously to the edge of the building. Nobody could reach him, and he eventually plummeted to the ground, smashing through the glass awning of the hotel entranceway and onto the pavement.

Seconds later another bomb glanced off the side of the Cathay Hotel's ferroconcrete structure, cracked the canopy covering the entranceway, and exploded into the tarmac. Shrapnel hit the clock on the front of the Cathay, which stopped at 4:27 p.m. exactly. The bomb left a gaping crater right outside the front doors. Always a busy intersection, the street instantly became a mass of burnt-out cars. Flames licked from a gutted Lincoln Zephyr parked near the hotel's entrance. The Bund end of Nanking Road was carnage. Dead and dismembered bodies littered the street. Charred corpses had been flung by the blast as far as the waterfront, landing on the dead who moments before had been clustered together watching the skies above. Seven hundred overwhelmingly Chinese refugees had been crowded around the waterfront junction, seeking shelter from the rain and winds. Many died instantly; others were horribly injured. Nanking Road became a corridor of mismatched limbs with blood on the shop windows, burnt-out taxis, and screaming amahs looking for lost babies.

Fifteen minutes later, two more bombs fell close by, this time just over the border and in Frenchtown, on the crowd milling around the Great World Amusement Palace, where acrobats, kinescopes, streetwalkers, and opera singers attracted passersby. It was the French Concession's busiest junction, and that day it was even busier than usual as the first floor of the Great World had been turned into a refugee reception centre for those escaping the Japanese shelling north of the Soochow Creek. The first bomb detonated shortly before hitting the ground, sending out a spray of deadly eviscerating shrapnel that killed people more than seven hundred yards away. The second bomb hit the asphalt street and created a huge crater, ten feet by six, adjacent to a traffic control tower. Dozens, perhaps hundreds, of Chinese refugees queuing for soup at the base of the building were killed on impact. Many injuries were rendered fatal by the intense gas pressure from the explosions; some bodies simply evaporated. At both blast sites perhaps as many as five thousand died, with thousands more wounded, Shanghailanders as well as Chinese. Bloody Saturday was the worst aerial bombing of a civilian city in history.

But the worst of it was reserved for Chinese Shanghai: Paoshan was flattened, northern Hongkew firebombed, Chapei set aflame. Japanese marines poured ashore from the *Idzumo,* which, remarkably, managed to avoid taking a single hit the whole day. They set up camp in Hongkew Park and patrolled the district in Midget tanks. From there they started moving street by street through Little Tokyo and then towards Shanghai's strategic North Railway Station. China fought back, in hand-to-hand combat on the northern edges of the Settlement; Hongkew and Chapei streets became sniper alleys.

Eventually only the devasting firepower of the Japanese Navy cannons from the *Idzumo* on the Whangpoo saved the Japanese lines and routed the Chinese Nationalist Army, ordered to advance into the northern districts by Generalíssimo Chiang Kai-shek. Shanghailanders, protected by reinforcements rushed from Hong Kong and landed ashore by the United States Asiatic Fleet, watched from rooftops, looking to the north and east. That Saturday evening the rose-tinted sky across the Soochow Creek was like a second sunset, the filthy water refracted into a tepid piss-yellow, the sky alive with sparks and cinders. You could feel the heat from the raging fires two, three miles away in the heart of the Settlement; you could smell the stench of the unburied dead wafting over the creek.

The firestorms raged up north of Hongkew's Little Tokyo, and crowds of flag-waving Japanese civilians stopped the fire engines getting through to douse the flames eviscerating Chinese homes. Seventeen Japanese Imperial Navy battle cruisers, stuffed to the gills with bluejacket reinforcements, docked to defend the thirty thousand Japanese in Little Tokyo. Mitsubishi 'Claude' fighter planes and Nakajimas dive-bombed northern Shanghai, and dog-fought Chinese Nationalist fighters. The Rokusan Restaurant burned; Hongkew High School burned; the Shanghai South Railway Station burned; and a photograph of a filthy, crying baby in the rubble made the front page of every newspaper in America and Europe.

The Trenches bar strip was now the frontline of sorts—Jukong Alley mostly rubble, the Venus gutted by flames, Riley's Bamboo Hut bombed out, the Scott Road Trenches brothel shacks ignited as their dry planking walls and roofs sparked. A steady stream of silent Chinese refugees continually poured over the Garden Bridge into the safety of the International Settlement; uncounted thousands more poured into Frenchown. The prostitutes, pimps, and ne'er-do-wells of the Trenches crossed the Settlement and found their way to the Western Roads, just outside the Settlement's jurisdiction, left largely unpoliced and a no-man's-land. It became their new home; the newspapers soon dubbed it 'the Badlands'.

The Chinese refugees who flooded the Settlement and Frenchtown slept on floors, in corridors, empty godowns, the municipal parks, the grounds of the city's temples. They brought with them cholera and disease; British and American troops were inoculated, and Shanghailanders flocked to hospitals to get their shots too. The Settlement's population shot up from one and a half million to four million in a matter of weeks. The city gates clanged shut by Municipal Council order: the Settlement, Frenchtown, Nantao Old Town, and all surrounding Chinese areas were within the now termed *Gudao*, the Solitary Island. All rice shops and food stores closed and were under heavy guard; rice supplies were now controlled exclusively by the Japanese. Food prices spiralled upwards, canned milk stocks sold out, strict fuel rationing was imposed, and the queues started early. The Avenue Eddy, the border between the Settlement and Frenchtown, was reduced from seven to two lanes, and barricaded with barbed wire. Long traffic jams ensued; Shanghailander tempers flared.

The following week, the heat broke, and more rain fell from dirt-black skies than in any previous year on record. The ash, dust, and debris created by the bombing of Chinese Shanghai fell from the clouds in black globules onto the heads of Settlement and Frenchtown residents. Cholera, typhoid, and smallpox moved through the city, taking the weakest. The dead were overwhelmingly Chinese. They died on the edges of the Settlement, beyond the Western Roads, in semi-rural Hungjao. They were thrown into the fields and buried in mass graves close by mansions where taipans had once lived in splendour on the edges of the Settlement.

In the farthest Northern Roads and on the pavements of the Trenches, Chinese and vagabond foreigners alike were deposited on the curbside for collection. Across the Whangpoo, in Pootung, the authorities built a fenced-in camp for the sick, surrounded by barbed wire to prevent contamination. They were corralled, penned in at bayonet point, not given medicine. They were buried by masked prisoners in mass pits in the marshes, filled with coal tar and pitch to prevent the germs spreading. The Municipal Council recorded that by year's end their carts had collected more than a hundred thousand corpses from the streets, lanes, and alleyways of the Settlement.

To the north of the Settlement, Chapei and Paoshan continued to burn bright for weeks while Zero fighters and the Yank-crewed Flying Tigers dogfought over the skies. Shanghailanders watched the free show from the roof of the Cathay Hotel with binoculars—white dames in sheer satin and pearls sipping black market champagne as hell raged overhead and planes spiralled down into the Pootung marshes. It was a mixed bunch reflecting Shanghailander society—the *China Weekly Review*'s editor J. B. Powell sucked hard on one cigarette after another, pausing only to scrupulously tally the number of planes shot down; Alice Daisy Simmons stopped by to catch the aerial show after visiting her father's bullion dealing office on the Bund; sojourners in town from the still-arriving steamships; taipans after a days dealmaking watched the dogfights with stengahs brought to their tables. They raucously cheered the brave Nationalist fighters and booed the Japs; they carried on dancing while burnt ash from Hongkew wafted gently into their punch bowls.

The Japanese stopped short of invading the International Settlement; they stayed out of Frenchtown to appease Paris. Invasion would have meant war with the British and French Empires as well as the United States of America; Japanese Marine bluejackets against the U.S. Fourth Marines and Scottish Seaforth Highlanders, Welsh Fusiliers, and the Royal Ulsters stationed in the Settlement. Tokyo's fight, for now, was with China and Chiang Kai-shek in what was now dubbed 'Free China'. That would change, but until then, life, of a sort, went on in the Solitary Island.

The city was divided. The SMP effectively retreated from north of the Soochow Creek, closed their stations, and turned into a skeleton force in the Eastern District—Hongkew, Y'Poo, and the Northern External Roads were all now Japanese gendarme and Kempeitai territory. Soldiers bunkered down and faced each other through sandbags, barbed wire and machine-gun nests; American M1903 Springfields faced Japanese Type .38s. The Japanese soldiers got confident and transgressed the long-established racial dividing lines of the Settlement. White women got their faces slapped by Jap police as they tried to cross the Garden Bridge over the Soochow Creek from the European Bund to refugee Hongkew. Those same Japanese forces would go on to capture Soochow, rape Nanking, and conquer almost all of China's vast hinterlands by the end of the year.

But elsewhere on the Solitary Island, new opportunities rose up, new chances for the taking for men and women with nowhere else to go.

The wild beasts of the mountain have a king who rules over the wolves. This king comes from the east and commands the wolves to eat all human beings they meet, leaving the bones for their cubs to gnaw and sharpen their fangs upon. Now the wild men from the lands to the east have come again to the Yangtze, ordered by their king-emperor—they are Japanese and the wolves their obedient soldiers. The Japanese place loudspeakers near the Garden Bridge over the Soochow Creek separating Hongkew from the Central District, calling on Shanghai and all China to surrender. They demand the foreign devils leave the Settlement, they urge the Shanghainese to turn their backs on their Occidental masters as well as their corrupt Generalíssimo Chiang Kai-shek, and to follow Wang Ching-wei, their new leader, Tokyo's friend and puppet. They are commanded to recognise and submit to the supremacy of the Greater Japanese Empire—Dai Nippon. The alternative is described in the Sanko Seisaku, *the 'Three Alls' Policy: Kill All, Burn All, Loot All.*

As the killing and the burning and the looting takes place, mangy, half-starved wolves have been driven from their lairs in Kiangsu and Chekiang. Wolves—ch'ai—are reportedly feasting on the mutilated dead in the streets of Nanking and tearing at the flesh of Chinese corpses on the banks of the Yangtze. They are rumoured to be roaming the abandoned temples of the Purple Mountains outside Peking, running along the shores of Hangchow Lake and even seeking victims in the hills of Sheshan, just to the west of Shanghai.

Pootung farmers say wolves are mauling their chickens and desecrating fresh-dug graves, ravenous for human flesh. They are digging up the bodies and feasting on corpses. Farmers with land left to farm now light bonfires at night to keep them away, standing ready with shotguns, sharpened hoes, and spades to protect their remaining livestock. Mothers keep their babies close, and small children are confined. The wolves are never sated.

The Japanese worship wolves at their shrines, where they bow before okami gods. The wolves comprehend Japanese speech. The wolves will be upon us soon and devour us all, tearing flesh from our limbs as we scream.

This, people believed . . .

PART TWO

The Lords of Misrule

Shanghai is full of Jews, Japs, and gunmen and it's a
toss-up which are worse. Law and order have gone
with the winds and gambling joints and opium dives have
taken their place. Shanghai has gone mad; everybody
hippity-hoppin down the primrose path . . .

—Hilaire du Berrier, 1939

Shanghai is not a town at all; Shanghai is a poison.
Man-eaters live here, naked cannibalism rules here.
This town is the world's refuse heap. Whoever comes
here, white or Chinese, has cracked up somewhere
before and Shanghai does the rest.

—Vicki Baum, *Shanghai '37*, 1939

It was like living on the rim of a volcano.

—American journalist J. B. Powell
on life in Shanghai in the 1930s

SHOPPING NEWS
—'BREVITIES'—
MONDAY, OCTOBER 19, 1937

These are extraordinary times and some pretty extraordinary things are occurring that do not speak well of our elected Municipal Council at this moment of crisis. So the bureaucrats of the Shanghai Municipal Council, and their opposite numbers in Frenchtown, have been doing everything in their power to curb rice profiteering and relieve the desperate plight of the masses. As a result of these *strenuous efforts* (hah!!) on the part of our esteemed authorities, local rice prices have increased only THREE HUNDRED PER CENT. It looks almost as though rice profiteers had received assurance from high places that the track was being cleared for them and the sky was the limit. Recently we at *Shopping News* called them rice profiteers and their political protectors vultures . . . today we extend our apologies to all vultures.

Which reminds us that, with the full permission of our elected representatives, the gougers at the Shanghai Telephone Company have been permitted to raise prices to astronomical levels, all at a time when the necessity of making calls to loved ones has never been greater. How much more blatant must the Settlement's profiteering become before the ratepayers rise up in revolt? Call the Municipal Council now—if you can afford it!!—and tell them they're doing the enemy's work for them!!

Radio Station X.H.M.A. has made a catch—Carroll Alcott will start broadcasting for them 'toot suite and pronto', according to Station Manager Jack Horton. Quite how the bloated newspaper columnist will sound to his legion of fans we do not know, but Alcott has sworn that he'll 'tell it like it is' in Shanghai and 'anyone who don't like it can go jump'. We wonder what the boys over at the Japanese Consulate will make of that!! Alcott's show will be at 8 p.m. daily and sponsored by FLIT, the World's Leading Insecticide. FLIT ALWAYS KILLS.

Can the recent spate of murders of foreigners in Hongkew be divorced from the fighting between rival dope gangs that's ongoing? *Shopping News* thinks not. The Brains Trust at Municipal Police H.Q., headed by Commissioner Bourne, may be scratching their heads, but surely the current flurry of nighttime arson attacks north of the Soochow Creek are narcotics related? Does anyone honestly think different? And why does our police force appear so ineffectual?

It's high time the Settlement smelt sweet again, don't you think? And that's why readers can claim a 15% discount against any purchase at SUZETTE'S, 133 Yuen Ming Yuen Road. Right now Suzette has fresh stocks of Potter & Moore's Old English Mitcham Lavender—quietens tired nerves and soothes you into a refreshing sleep.

Something on your mind? Editorial: Rm 540, 233 Nanking Rd. Tel: Shanghai—10695

18

The dead haunted Shanghai that autumn and winter of 1937. Since Bloody Saturday at least three hundred thousand had been killed, predominately Chinese: bombed, shot, strafed, burnt, diseased, frozen, and starved. Their relatives demanded they be interred, buried, returned to their ancestral villages, but these privileges would be only for the wealthy. In the Northern External Roads, to the west in Hungjao, in far eastern Y'Poo and across the Whangpoo in Pootung, the corpses were gathered on giant funeral pyres, both humans and the dead mules and horses left behind by the retreating Chinese army. In one day more than a thousand bodies were burned.

The crematorium smell hung over the city, and the ash of the dead turned to grey slush in the gutters when it rained. Living Shanghai literally waded through the remains of the city's dead. Those whose families or clan guilds could pay were embalmed in coffins and stacked one upon another in hastily erected bamboo godowns along the city's western fringes. Yet with Shanghai surrounded by marauding Japanese soldiers, the dead could not be transported to their home villages. These hundreds of coffins, many piled up along the banks of the Siccawei Creek, were gradually covered with rubbish and, eventually, forgotten, as they and their contents were slowly absorbed into the sodden banksides.

Walk quickly, step lightly, past the junction of Avenue Haig and Edinburgh Road. Pay attention to your stride, look down, and avoid the building that stands on the corner, its windows blacked out. This place is the Vien Coffin Storage Company, a giant repository for the dead. The Municipal Council collects the dead left unclaimed in the Settlement and deposits many of them at Vien's. In the Western External Roads, just beyond the jurisdiction of the SMP and the Frenchtown authorities, the job is left to devout Buddhist volunteers. The numbers rise and so, people say, do the ghosts of those unable to settle. The coffins are filled, nailed down, and sealed with wax. Alongside the dead sit hundreds, perhaps thousands of empty coffins, hurriedly produced by carpenters for the future. Shanghai has become a city of the dead, and Vien's holds sixty thousand coffins in readiness in their Edinburgh Road repository. When Vien's is full, the Buddhists put up yet more bamboo shacks nearby to store the bodies, and hope burial spots are found before the spring comes and the corpses thaw.

In November the last dregs of the Chinese Nationalist Army withdraws from the very far reaches of Shanghai in defeat and humiliation under the thunder of Japanese cannon. They have been totally routed throughout the Yangtze River delta. The city's crime boss, Big-Eared Du, follows shortly afterwards, leaving Shanghai for Hong Kong. Thus ends the Green Gang's fifteen years of absolute control of the city's underworld. Green Gang thugs disappear or are absorbed into Wang Ching-wei's puppet thug gangs. The Western Roads, undefended, are left to their fate.

Before the Chinese collaborators took control, before the old gangs fled, the city's Western Roads District was where the wealthy lived, where they relaxed. It was beyond the frenetic fringes of the

International Settlement and the French Concession, far from Hong-kew, with its cluster of raucous honky-tonk bars, refugees and sailors; safely beyond the forbidding slum of Nantao; the old city of Shanghai, with its smells of peanut oil and camphor; and the far-flung Chinese quarters of Chapei and Paoshan. The air was cleaner, the sky bluer—or so it seemed. The cigar-smoking foreign taipans, money-obsessed bankers, share hawkers, and bullion sharks of Shanghai's giant *hongs* lounged by the pool of the Columbia Country Club sipping cocktails, congratulating themselves on their privilege. Couples danced sedately to White Russian jazz bands performing tepid versions of the latest standards: foxtrots at a reg-ulation seventy beats per minute; a waltz every fourth tune. Hot, humid, airless Shanghai summer nights. Sometimes they journeyed out to the Avenue Haig for dinner and the floorshow at Del Mon-te's nightclub; otherwise they dined in their palatial homes with soft-slippered servants at their elbows.

After the Japanese invasion, the Western Roads District changes overnight. Speculative construction firms erect barnlike prem-ises on the wasteland along the Great Western Road, Edinburgh Road, and the Avenue Haig, on the very edge of the Settlement and Frenchtown's jurisdiction. Two floors, three floors, four, five . . . it's all jerry-built, but with a lick of paint and muted lighting they can become atmospheric dance halls. Despite prohi-bitions the new venues soon morph into gambling dens—roulette wheels are spinning again, alongside baccarat tables, craps, *fan-tan*. Where once the Del Monte had stood on its own, out on the western fringes of the city with its lawns, Versailles-inspired statuary, and naphtha-lit driveway, comes a cluster of palaces of sin, stretching from Siccawei in the south to Jessfield Park in the north. In the alleyways and lanes between them bamboo shacks become brothels, dope dens, grind shops for low-end gamblers, *shabu* methamphetamine merchant stations, and Hwa-Wei lottery parlours.

19

The Badlands becomes a lawless no-man's-land, encircled by Japanese-manned barbed-wire barricades that rise or fall depending on the quality of your papers and the cumshaw tip you profer. The genteel Shanghailanders, shocked by the assault on their citadel, rapidly depart China on evacuation ships or retreat into the fragile safety of the foreign settlements, hoping in vain that the Japanese will be vanquished.

The Kempeitai form a collaborationist Chinese police force and put it under the control of Wang Ching-wei. Wang had once been Generalíssimo Chiang's closest ally but now, as Wang sided with Tokyo against his own people and became China's very own Marshal Pétain, they have become deadly enemies. Wang's thugs are reinforced by the remnants of Big-Eared Du's hoodlums, supplemented by corralled hungry and desperate peasant boys under orders from the Japanese military police. General Kenji Doihara, a legend to be feared in Manchukuo where he personally oversaw the implementation of the 'Three Alls' policy, comes south to Shanghai. He sits down with Wang Ching-wei and gives him titular authority over the Western Roads, along with the operation of number 76 Jessfield Road, a gothic mansion in the heart of the district. Number 76 will go on to become one of the most feared buildings in Shanghai—a twenty-four-hour bordello, dirty money-counting house, and torture chamber. Wang takes his orders directly from the universally feared Kempeitai.

Doihara uses his contacts to distribute narcotics from depots in the Western Roads. There's opium, both pure and refined into heroin and morphine, as well as specially manufactured sixteen-ounce vials of cocaine from patriotic Tokyo businessman-controlled factories on the Japanese-occupied island of Formosa, flooding in on Imperial Army and Navy transport ships. More is brought in by entrepreneurial ronin who stuff suitcases, army kit bags, funeral urns, and Korean prostitutes' vaginas with even more dope to sell in Shanghai. Doihara makes the Badlands truly bad—awash with opium as well as philopon methamphetamine, an Imperial Army mass-manufactured specialty. Philopon is a so-called 'murder drug'; it makes men killers, and Tokyo needs hundreds of thousand of cold-blooded murderers if it is to subjugate all of China. It is addictive, strips men of their consciences, allows them to Kill All, Burn All, Loot All with impunity and no moral sanction.

Dope prices fall below those of rice, *shabu* prices even lower, and addiction rates subsequently skyrocket. Doihara deliberately pumps narcotics through every channel he can to sap the will to resist. Low-rent whores are paid in opium; drug runners, mules, and dealers are all paid in dope. The market is flooded with Golden Bat cigarettes, the mouthpiece of which contains a small dose of heroin. Doihara creates addicts by the thousands as tobacco smokers find themselves slaves to a darker drug. And he knows just how easy it is to succumb: Doihara himself is an opium addict with a massive habit formed in Manchukuo.

The Japanese Army establishes the Shanghai Amusement Supervision Department, which 'taxes' the grind shops, dope dens, and lottery parlours on their daily take. The Hwa-Wei lottery, so beloved of Shanghai's Chinese underclass, is rigged to high heaven. The taxes are phenomenal: fifteen thousand Chinese dollars a day to stay open at the largest casinos. The Kempeitai bosses enforce the taxes—no pay, no play.

Cabbage Moh, a Cantonese smuggler and drug dealer from triad-controlled Shumchun on the Hong Kong border, sees an opportunity to the north and opens dens supplying dope and philopon ferried up the Soochow Creek and distributed out of Fah Wah Village, adjacent to the new sin strip. Refugee peasants turned *lieumaung* loafers patronise the Fah Wah alleyway brothel shacks, getting mean with the girls. Tuberculosis is quickly endemic among Chinese and Shanghailanders with a taste for the pipe, the pill, the needle. The Japanese bomb the Chengzong Sanatoria, the city's major tuberculosis clinic for the poor and indigent. The patients are scattered to the winds and mostly end up begging in the Badlands. These unlucky sufferers die in the streets as pedestrians swiftly side-step them and pull their scarves over their mouths.

The Japanese military presence in Shanghai is funded almost entirely by the Western Roads Badlands—dope, coke, morphine, philopon, girls, gambling, and Golden Bat. Wang Ching-wei's coffers bulge despite much of the profits going to the Kempeitai to fund the war on China. Doihara gets a congratulatory telegram from Tokyo and is made a member of Japan's Supreme War Council. To celebrate, he opens a tatami-matted Japanese officers' bordello in Frenchtown on Route Dupleix, staffed by coerced Shanghai movie starlets. Regular soldiers file into 'comfort houses' in Nantao old town and on Menghua Jie, where Chinese women dressed in cheap kimonos are compelled to service the victors by the score.

The Green Gang gone, the foreigners step in to play. These are the men with nowhere else to go, who are wanted pretty much everywhere, who have no letters of transit, passports, or exit visas. The exiled White Russians, the Jewish refugees, the desperate and the bad, those on the lam or AWOL marines now find the city's vast empire of rackets dumped in their laps, gratis. No evacuation ships for these people. Jack Riley, with his false name, fingertips, and a long-expired Chilean passport, cannot leave; Joe Farren has no desire to return to Nazi-controlled Jew-hating Vienna; Nellie, Nazedha, Sasha Vertinsky and all the rest of the White Russians fear Stalin's gulags even more than the Kempeitai. These men and women will stay come what may—there are no visas for them, no refugee ships, no new homelands to welcome them.

This is where Joe Farren and Jack Riley will choose to stake their claim . . . to become the lords of misrule in Shanghai. Eternal outsiders both, they choose no-man's land as their kingdom.

20

Jack and Nazedha have been to the Grand on Bubbling Well Road to see *Way Out West*. By May 1938 it's already been out a year, but Laurel and Hardy just crack Nazedha up. It's been a rocky romance; Nazedha is disgusted by Jack's fracas at the Canidrome, and pissed off with his jangly nerves and quick temper courtesy of Doc Borovika's Benzedrine supplies. But perhaps a new spring will change things. Jack races through the Settlement in his newly imported red MG Brit roadster with Nazedha by his side, mink coat ruffling in the wind. He jumps red lights, fishtails the intersections, and laughs in his rearview mirror at the tall khaki-turbaned Sikh traffic cops waving their bamboo lathis impotently in his wake. Jack loves speed, loves machines, loves scaring Nazedha in the passenger seat. She screams delightedly, gripping his thigh. On the corner of Gordon and Bubbling Well, marines hang about shooting the shit. When they see Jack, they line up and salute. Jack returns their salute with a tip of his hat while Nazedha gives a royal Russian wave to the Slots King's ever-loyal leathernecks.

Cashed up and hungry for action, Jack is a millionaire now and doesn't care who knows it. The newspapers claim Jack is earning more than twelve thousand American dollars every month, just in Frenchtown. The SMP have estimated that the total annual income from slot machines in the Settlement is in excess of a million Chinese bucks. Jack owns them all, plus more up in Chinese Chapei and now, of course, in the Badlands. He's personally pulling in twice what the SMP think, and then there's the Manhattan, the hastily rebuilt Bamboo Hut with a whiff of smoke mixed in with the fresh paint job, the DD's chain, of course—and don't forget what's left of the Velvet Sweet Shop dope cash. Nazedha has taken the DD's business in hand and upped the profits at the other branches—DD's Russian Restaurant on Bubbling Well Road is pushing out blini and zakuski, DD's Cafe nearby is a popular after-work cocktails joint, while DD's Downtown gets the bachelor crowd as the Russian barmaids shake dice with the griffins for drinks. Jack's a rich, rich man and dresses like it in tailor-made suits and imported leather shoes. He calls a fancy plum-voiced English broker in an office on the Bund and tells him to buy more Shanghai Power Company shares, telephone company, gas too. Why not? The bourse is just gambling for the 400. DD's is legit money, so he can spend it legit too, on the stock exchange. Don't look too long, and the Slots King might seem kind of respectable these days.

Of course, he's still Lucky Jack, solid bucko mate, beloved of the Fourth Marines. These are the same men who feed his slots and play in the local league against his Town baseball team of Friends and nightlife diehards. The Town team is captained by Demon Hyde from the Del Monte, who played a mean game back in his San Joaquin Valley days, with Mickey O'Brien as their slugger. Jack loves to bat, and he'll take shortstop if required, but mostly he likes to pitch, and the Lucky Jack legend grows thanks to his jackrabbit ball. It's brought out when things look bad, and whizzes past the stunned batters unprepared for a freakily good pitch. The marines laugh at the Town team—men in 'Shanghai' embroidered shirts, with nightclub pallor, thick waists, and slicked-back hair, longtime expats, still woozy after a night running the myriad clubs and bars of Shanghai. But thanks to Demon, Mickey, and Jack's rabbit ball, the marines lose as many games as they win.

Since the Japanese invasion and the subsequent U.S. and British troop reinforcements, Blood Alley is packed, the Settlement is hopping, the Marines Club overflowing with new arrivals. Securing the Settlement from Japanese attack means lots more leathernecks shipped in from Manila and squaddies brought up from Hong Kong. The Badlands is off-limits to soldier boys, it's outside the SMP and Little Nicky's turf, beyond their jurisdiction, and it's where the big gambling action is, less than a mile from DD's on the Avenue Joffre. Jack can't stop thinking about how that strip would be perfect for a joint with class acts and well-greased roulette wheels.

Jack still wants serious wheels action from the swells; he wants Badlands coin too—moving up from copper and brass to silver and gold. Shanghai may be surrounded by killing and war, but the SMP, on point of long established principle, is determined to never allow roulette wheels in the Settlement, and only the most clandestine will survive the Anti-Gambling Squad raids. But the Kempeitai and their Chinese puppets in the Badlands couldn't give a shit as long as they extract their taxes. Jack needs a Badlands in, a swank venue. There's no getting around it for him—that means Joe Farren. Dapper Joe still runs the best floor shows, with queues round the block for the Canidrome and the Paramount—repeat that trick with roulette wheels and 'gold mine' doesn't even come close: it's more like a mint, and you've got a licence to print money. But he and Joe are still mad as hell at each other. The air needs to be cleared, and Jack knows he has to do the clearing.

The Municipal Council has announced a ten p.m. curfew on all nightlife due to the 'emergency', and the Frenchtown bosses have followed suit. Joe's day starts early now, with 'tea dances' from five-thirty to nine-thirty p.m. to cater to the straights who need to scramble home before curfew hour. But plenty want more—Jack has moved his floor show to ten at DD's, as has Victor Sassoon at Ciro's. Joe moves the Canidrome and Paramount floor shows to ten to lock in the after-curfew crowd. The Canidrome has moved the dog races earlier and the boxing's gone early too, so you don't have to miss anything. Tea-dance away your afternoon, catch the dogs or the fights late afternoon/early evening, and then move on to a nightclub and stay settled till morning and curfew's end around sunup.

Chapei and the Badlands offer the best deal of all—no curfew and no closing till dawn, with the Del Monte still firing on till long after the sun has risen. But it's getting tough running dance halls. Before Bloody Saturday the foreign places charged a dollar for two, maybe three dances; then overnight it went to a buck for seven twirls. Go to the predominately Chinese joints, like the Flying Swallow or the Moon Palace, and it's a dollar for eight, nine, sometimes ten taxi dance turns a night. Profits are slashed. The money's now in gambling . . . and gambling in the new Shanghai of the Badlands means roulette. The spinning wheel is the real big earner.

Joe is still running nightly between the Canidrome, the Del Monte, and the Paramount—Frenchtown to Siccawei to Settlement. The Follies, the Peaches, the Blondes, and the Natasha chorus lines up in smouldering Hongkew all require his magic touch too. And now he's got to help out Sam Levy, who's relocated his firebombed Venus Café to Frenchtown's border with the Badlands. Sam has persuaded Joe to run a chorus line in the new place. It's a stretch, but it's tough saying no to a man whose place got bombed to shit.

Joe's got a stash, thanks to the Red Rose dope ring, and knows the all-night, no-rules Badlands is the place to invest—Chinese developers are throwing up big wooden shacks that, if draped in neon at night, might be mighty swell joints. Joe knows that where he goes the punters will follow. Nellie's not so sure; the Badlands means bad people and bad alliances, and she's deadset against any involvement with Jack Riley. But any Badlands joint would need a casino, and Joe knows nobody else has got the gelt and the know-how to fund one right now except Riley. The Portuguese won't work with any but their own; Russians are the same way; the old-time criminals like Stuart Price, who ran casinos before the Great War, are wise counsel but out of the game these days. Veteran clandestine roulette-wheel operator Bill Hawkins up at the Burlington Hotel is solid, but too old-fashioned in his ways to pull in the level of punters Joe wants. And Joe's not working with the Japanese, so it's Jack or nobody. Truth is, Jack's got the flair and, despite being a loose cannon, people love the slippery gonef. Joe tells Nellie it's a new era and that means new deals; it's time to let bygones be bygones. Nellie says Jack's crazy, it'll end badly. Joe just shrugs and says he can handle it.

Still, nobody here's an idiot. Nellie's right—Joe knows you can't trust Jack, but it's Shanghai—you can't trust anyone! Sure, Jack is combustible, explosive, ready with his fists—Yang Pat prizefight champ, cellblock bruiser, Venus door muscle. That shit Jack pulled with Buck and the Harlem Gentlemen at the Canidrome was a royal pain in the arse. But Jack has sent apologies, got Nazedha to reach out to Nellie, and, at the end of the day, it was Tung and Vong trying to cut the wage bill and extract maximum profit from the joint that started all the bullshit. Jack knows that in the Badlands he's outside his comfort zone of Fourth Marine Friends and Blood Alley buddies. Joe's got more pull—Louis Bouvier and Carlos Garcia are backing him, there are Al Israel and Demon down the road at the Del Monte, and Albert Rosenbaum as Joe's right-hand man.

Nellie meets up with Nazedha for *kaffee und kuchen* at the Astoria Bakery in a booth right next to an E. T. Riley slot machine. Nazedha says Jack is serious these days—it can all be copacetic as long as the money rolls in. Nellie doubts that, but stays schtum. Joe heads over to the Del Monte and sits in Al Israel's office sipping stengahs and getting advice. Al reminds Joe that Jack needs him more than Joe needs Jack. Albert Rosenbaum shrugs and says, 'Let the American run the wheels, and if he starts trouble we'll dump the cocksucker in the Soochow Creek and start over.'

21

Courtesy of Gallic banker and Frenchtown fixer Louis Bouvier's connections, Joe's still got a shot at the joint on the Great Western Road he had his eye on before the bust-up with Jack. It's a big warehouse of a place with three floors, on the boulevard that runs straight out of the Settlement into the Badlands, a ten-minute drive from Bubbling Well. Joe is legit, never been busted, never been in a courtroom. Now he's got a licence from the Municipal Council; it says 'entertainment only' and no gambling, but that's something to worry about later, or maybe never. But he still needs someone to bank the wheels and run the casino, someone who's got pull with the Japs and puppets and can finesse the taxes and other associated bribes to manageable limits. Jack is the only candidate.

Nellie and Nazedha set up a double date for all to make nice officially at the Canidrome Gardens for the boxing. Jack tells Joe to bet on the Russian boy, with a grin, wink, and flick of the thumb on the side of his nose. It's an offering, an apology, a new start.

The Monday night fights at the Canidrome consist of four bouts, starting at five-thirty p.m. The first three are warm-ups for the main event, which tonight, August 1, 1938, is Harbin-born, Shanghai-based Andre Shelaeff, the ladies' favourite. He's got movie-star looks, he's the Welterweight Champion of the Orient, and he's defending his championship belt against the Filipino Lucio 'Young' Alde. It's a grudge match, and Shanghai is betting right down the middle—the KO champ the 'Russian Hammer' versus the more experienced Manilaman carrying an additional nine pounds in punching power. Alde is still smarting from his last fight with Shelaeff in Singapore a few months back, when he got booed out of the stadium accused of taking a dive. Those allegations of fight rigging didn't go away, and Alde got a three-month suspension. Then he demanded a rematch, a final fight before retiring and a last big purse. The Canidrome was it.

Back in the blinding arc lights of the Canidrome, Riley, Farren, and their respective crews are in attendance. Jack has block-booked a stand to give them some space. He's got Mickey in tow, Nazedha on one arm and Babe on the other. But tonight that's it—no Friends or hanger-on Marines, no intimation of a gang fight. Joe is in the stand with Nellie. She's looking relaxed in the evening heat in wide-bottomed blue linen trousers, a white mess jacket, and a red kerchief. Albert Rosenbaum fans himself with a newspaper, eyeing Jack warily. Nellie and Rosenbaum are on board for Joe's sake, but they still both advise against this joint venture.

Outside their stand the stadium is packed: plenty of chain-smoking local hoods from Frenchtown and the Badlands are betting heavily on their boy Shelaeff; not so many would have gambled on Joe and Jack's happy reunion. Seemingly every White Russian in town has scraped up a few dollars to put on the Hammer. The White Russian drinking dens—Sasha Vertinsky's Gardenia, the Hungaria, Yar—are all empty tonight. Look around, and it's a rogues' gallery—Fat Tony Perpetuo of the 37427 gambling joint on Bubbling Well Road; José Bothelo and his Portuguese mob, who run the Silver Palace casino; old Bill Hawkins and Stuart Price, who've operated floating roulette wheels across the Settlement since the turn of the century; Swiss thief Elly Widler and his crew; Al Israel and Demon Hyde from the Del Monte sitting with Sam Levy and the Venus Café girls; Sasha Vertinsky and his squeeze Boobee taking a night off from the Gardenia; the Russians who run high-end, high-stakes card games at the Broadway Mansions, the Route Voyron gypsy clan huddling tight. And Shanghai's Filipino community of musicians, gigolos, and croupiers is out in strength to see their boy take his belt, and his reputation, back.

Nine p.m. on the dot and the two men enter the ring with their seconds. Shelaeff's manager, Harry Seelig, is ringside as ever, and nodding to Jack. A thousand wolf whistles greet a Natasha in a tight dress who walks round the ring holding up a big card with a number one on it. The ref brings the two men to the centre of the canvas and makes them touch gloves for a clean fight. The bell rings, and round one is on. Unsurprisingly, Alde puts up a tough fight and doesn't back away from the punch, landing a series of thunderous left jabs that send the Manilamen contingent in the Canidrome wild. Shelaeff is clearly still feeling the bruises and the aches from his fight with the big Shanghai-based Ukrainian hitter George Levchenko two weeks before. Levchenko had gone down, but not before landing some painful jabs to Shelaeff's upper body that left dark black-and-blue marks.

Alde can go the ten rounds, but Shelaeff is younger, hungrier, faster. Both boxers are soon drained—the hot, humid August night leaves them gasping in the sultry air, their chests heaving, the perspiration running into their eyes, a salty, stinging tang. The floor of the ring is stained dark with their sweat and blood, and both men take a lot of punishment.

Shelaeff is forced to use precious energy blocking Alde's trademark swings. Alde misses and puts himself momentarily off balance, open to the legendary Shelaeff hammer punch, but the Harbin boy fails to land one sufficient to put his opponent down. His senses are off, maybe, or his tired arms too sluggish for the final blow. Uncharacteristically, Shelaeff has to go in and work two-handed barrages to Alde's body, gruelling up-close work that leads to some inevitable head-butting. Fierce, repetitive jabs are aimed at Alde's kidneys, but they're never quite enough to force him back onto the ropes to finish him off with that famous right hook.

Shelaeff takes a tough punch to the solar plexus, between his exposed diaphragm and his navel, which debilitates him momentarily, and Alde puts him on the ropes. But Shelaeff fights back. The crowd screams itself hoarse. Nazedha and Nellie laugh loudly as Babe jumps on the wooden benches and screams at the Russian to hit harder, hit fucking harder!

In the final round both men are exhausted. Alde pushes Shelaeff onto the ropes, scrapping, holding, and pushing again, fully using his nine-pound weight advantage. Shelaeff battles out of his grip, looking for space to swing, but Alde moves back in quickly, head down to avoid a lethal chin shot, for successive body blows. Shelaeff keeps working to avoid head butts that could open up an eyebrow, leaving him blood-blind and vulnerable. The crowd is now on its feet, willing a KO from one or the other fighter, Frenchtown fixated on what just might be the greatest night's boxing the Canidrome has ever seen. Shelaeff, who has only ever had a few fights go to the second round, has a real opponent for once. Both men collapse in their corners as the bell clangs and it finally ends.

Perspiring profusely, the white-shirted referee takes the microphone and announces a draw to slow handclapping, boos, and hisses. Bottles and coins rain down from the stands into the ring, and the ref has to duck for cover. Joe starts to stand up, looks at Jack and shrugs a *What the fuck?* Jack winks and motions for him to sit back down, mouthing *Trust me*. More booing, more hissing, more coins and EWO beer bottle caps rain down into the ring.

Two minutes later and the ref is back as the crowd start to file out. He mumbles into the mic that he's added up the numbers wrong; Shelaeff has won on points, and the championship belt stays his. The partisan Canidrome crowd goes wild and floods back to the bookies to get their winnings—the surge nearly tips over the bookies' stands. Shelaeff is cheered to the rafters, the Manilamen in the crowd booing loudly but drowned out by the local roar. An exhausted Shelaeff is carried out of the ring suspended above the arms of his fans; Alde looks devastated and confused by what's just happened. Joe and Jack walk back to collect their winnings. By the bookies' stand Joe passes half to Nellie, the other half to Rosenbaum, and shakes Jack Riley's hand. The deal is on.

Jack and Joe make their way up to the members' bar in the tower overlooking the dog track and the boxing arena. Carlos Garcia welcomes them and shows the party to a table right up front by the window, pulling out chairs for Nellie and Nazedha, chilled champagne at the ready. Carlos puts his arms round Joe's and Jack's shoulders and wishes them both luck; he bends down and kisses the girls on the cheeks. Louis Bouvier moves in with the paperwork for Farren's Inc.—registration, licence, all signed and sealed. Albert Rosenbaum and Mickey O'Brien start talking logistics, getting this show on the road. Joe and Jack shake on it again, and Joe leans in to Jack's ear as they hug for the onlookers—no sidelines this time, Jack. Jack nods like he really means it. And just like that the Badlands gets Farren's, the biggest, fanciest, richest nightclub and casino Shanghai has ever seen.

From the top of the Canidrome Shanghai looks staggering. You can see clear downtown, across Frenchtown to the river and the line of grey battleships—British, American, Japanese, French— moored along the Whangpoo; across to the Avenue Eddy and the skyscrapers of the International Settlement; back behind them to their new home, the money-making machine of the Badlands. Lights twinkle, a thousand wisps of smoke rise from the chimneys of the laneways, army searchlights sweep the skies north towards Hongkew and Chapei. The men look like kings; the women like queens. Jack and Joe think it's the start of something beautiful. The deal is done, for better or worse.

22

It's five a.m., two days after the Farren's deal. Al Israel's in his office above the dance floor at the Del Monte stashing the take in his strongbox. Al's wife, Bertha, is sleeping in their apartment on the top floor. Demon is downstairs in the casino supervising the early-morning cleanup of the joint after a busy night. Demon hears two shots from upstairs, grabs his pistol from behind the bar and heads up to Al's office. Bertha, asleep, is woken by the shots, and runs down to Al's office in her nightdress. Together they find Al slumped over his desk in his Chinese dressing gown, the office trashed, signs of a struggle, the strongbox emptied. Al has been shot through the back of the head, execution-style; the bullets exited through, and just above, his right eye and lodged in the teak wood of his desk. The SMP investigate, and they even arrest Demon, thinking he might have shot Al over control of the club. But that's a nonstarter. They kick him loose; the investigation goes nowhere fast. Little Nicky digs around, thinking maybe this is still dope-related business being sorted out eighteen months after the Wiengarten killing, but the assassins are long gone.

Al Israel, Joe's old mentor at the Del Monte, saw the Badlands mushroom around him, and the transition left him feeling exhausted. What had been a sweet thing became a world of extortion, violence, and gang war. As the Western Roads District became the Badlands, Al was confronted with a never-ending queue of those offering protection and wanting taxes—the Chinese puppet collaborators at their number 76 Jessfield Road fortress, the Kempeitai, rogue ronin, local *lieu-maung* on the make, and *pi-seh* chancers. He told them all to fuck off. He wasn't paying. When the loafers and thugs associated with Cabbage Moh and the Fah Wah triad drug gangs wanted to sell dope in his joint, he slammed the door in their face; when the white-armband wearing representatives of the Kempeitai came demanding taxes, he refused to pay; when gangsters associated with number 76 wanted to run his roulette wheels for themselves, he laughed at them. Al was kicking sixty, but he hadn't mellowed any. He was adamant and stubborn; Al Israel had run the Del Monte before any of these thugs came to town. He hadn't paid the Green Gang when they put the squeeze on him, he'd sent the Corsican mob's bogus Sûreté detectives packing, and he wasn't paying any arriviste lowlife now. Al got Demon to beef up the protection on the door, put ex-SMP Sikh heavies on the street gates to allow in only genuine punters, and moved himself and Bertha into an apartment on the top floor to guard his nightly take. The demands got more vocal; every night troublemakers tried to bust in, tear the place up, destroy business, scare the customers, force Al to sell to them. He saw them all off, till that August night.

They bury Al at the Jewish cemetery run by the Shanghai Chevra Kadisha, up on Baikal Road in Y'Poo. The great and the good of the Shanghai rackets travel north across the Soochow Creek, motoring slowly through Hongkew in black suits, to see him off. Bertha stands over the grave while Al's legions of friends and customers crowd round the turned earth: fellow members of Jack's Town baseball team, the old-time Portuguese and American gangsters who've known him from the start, the high hats of the Canidrome where he hung out before work sipping champagne.

The Natashas who'd danced in his Del Monte chorus lines hang back so as not to annoy Bertha, who has eyed them warily over the years. Joe is a pallbearer, as is Demon, now running the Del Monte solo. Swiss thief Elly Widler, Sam Levy from the Venus, Mickey O'Brien, and Jack Riley make up the numbers and help them carry the coffin.

All the old-school Shanghai Jewish nightlife crew follow behind—Al Wiengarten, who came down from Tientsin, Sol Greenberg from the Casanova, Fred Stern and Joe Klein who ran the Elite, Monte Berg from the Little Club, Berlin refugee Freddy Kaufmann from the Cathay Tower nightclub, every *Yiddisher* bar and cabaret owner from Wayside and Broadway to Frenchtown and the Western Roads. Graveside, Bertha is distraught; she has to be held up and supported to stop her from sinking at the knees in grief into the Y'Poo dirt. But canny Al had invested thirty years of Avenue Haig profits in diamonds, kept in a bank vault in California; she can return home grieving but rich, and needs nothing except the safebox number.

Just two days after the Farren–Riley deal is struck, here is a stark reminder to any who thought Shanghai's Western Roads would be easy money: the foreign joints of the Badlands all pay their taxes, no exceptions. Any attempts to avoid payment to the Badlands powers that be, to bar the drug dealers they sanction to trade in the Badlands, would be met with a deadly response.

At the end of September, Demon sees Bertha off at the docks on an evacuation ship back Stateside; the boys have made sure she travels first class. Sam Levy arranges for the Manila Rhythm Boys to form up dockside and play Al's favourite tunes for her as the ship slips its moorings and heads downriver to the East China Sea. Back on the Avenue Haig, Al's murder proves to be just the start of a downward spiral. Al, the longtime survivor, was the first victim of the Badlands, but far from the last.

The war for China continues. Generalíssimo Chiang Kai-shek organizes the Free China resistance from the wartime capital of Chungking at the head of the Yangtze. The Japanese Air Force bombs the city nightly, but it's a natural fortress of rock. In the run-up to the 'Double Ten'—October 10, Free China's National Day—Generalíssimo-loyal guerillas ramp up their activites. A puppet official is shot dead by an unknown sniper as part of the covert battle across the city. Criminals take advantage of the chaos, and on Frenchtown's Rue du Consulat two employees of an import-export firm that refused to pay protection money are horrifically injured by bombs lobbed through the front door. Three days later hand grenades are tossed into a crowd on the Szechuen Road Bridge, wounding a dozen civilians. Why? Nobody knows. On September 30, 1938, Free China scores a major victory with the assassination of Tang Shao-yi, whom General Doihara of Japan had hoped would become China's compliant puppet president. Tang is gunned down in his Frenchtown living room by Free China hit-men posing as antique sellers and offering him looted treasure.

SMP and puppet thugs trade shots on Jessfield Road, killing two cops. Commissioner Bourne orders all SMP men in the Western Roads District to patrol in groups, with safety catches off. The puppets squat in several big houses along Jessfield Road on either side of number 76, fill them with newly deputised and armed thugs, and build sandbagged machine-gun emplacements on the street. On the other side of the Badlands, they occupy a Formosan Islander–run gambling joint near the Del Monte, install more number 76 guns-for-hire, and put an additional squeeze on the Hwa-Wei lottery parlours and dope dens.

The violence drags on through the winter. Another hit man narrowly misses killing puppet Shanghai mayor Fu Xiao'an, titular Chinese bossman of the Western Roads casinos and dope dens, a fat seventy-year-old traitor transplanted south after loyal service in Manchukuo. The gunman kills Fu's bodyguard. The Kempeitai give chase and corner the hit man, who shoots himself in the head rather than face interrogation. Japanese soldiers cut out his heart and liver and place them before the dead Japanese bodyguard as a sacrifice. It ratchets up the stakes spectacularly. Two dozen puppet officials are assassinated across the city by Free China hit squads—Japanese police, wives and children of puppet officials, innocent bystanders, taxi dancers going home all get hit in the crossfire. And it's just the beginning as the fight for the Badlands melds into the war for Shanghai and becomes an inseparable part of the overarching struggle for survival by China herself.

SHOPPING NEWS
—'BREVITIES'—
MONDAY, NOVEMBER 21, 1938

So the Shanghai Municipal Council has again granted the American-controlled Shanghai Power Company permission to put Settlement users of electricity thru' the wringers . . . this time for a surcharge of 150 per cent. In other words, this so-called public utility is to be allowed to collect its charges upon what amounts practically to a gold dollar basis. INTERESTING IS THAT THE FRENCH-TOWN POWER COMPANY WHO HAVE THE SAME GENERAL OPERATING COSTS TO MEET (BUT DON'T HAVE TO FEED GOLD DOLLARS TO THE NEW YORK FATCATS) HAVE INCREASED TO DATE ONLY FIFTEEN PER CENT!!!! WHAT GIVES GRANDEES OF THE MUNICIPAL COUNCIL? WE KNOW YOU'D ALL LIKE TO KNOW.

The police in the Western District—that's the Badlands to most of us now—have been ordered by our wistful Willies to look the other way if they notice any trouble, fill their ears with cotton wool so the sound of shooting will sound like peas popping, and if they're actually shot at to stand perfectly still so as not to spoil the dear, darling *pi-seh* gunman's aim. Darn if we wouldn't like to put Commissioner Bourne and his sidekick DSI Crighton on a Badlands patrol . . . at 26 shillings a week. We'll bet a million those gentry would scram so fast you could play checkers on their shirttails.

Looking desperately for that extra special birthday gift for the taipan or tycoon in your life? Problem solved, if you visit Alexander Clark's at Sassoon House (Tel: Shanghai—10719) where a new range of the famous Rolex Oyster timepieces are now in stock—waterproof and with chronometer precision because, as we all know, time is money in Shanghai. Take this issue of *Shopping News* with you for a 10 per cent discount on any watch in stock.

Times are tight for everyone but those infamously rapacious Shanghai Gas Tycoons, it seems. They know winter's a'coming and they're planning yet another surcharge. The Municipal Council has to approve it, but since when did the Gas Fuhrers not have enough Council members in their pockets? They'll vote it through, that is when they come back from their summer recess at the Columbia Country Club, or filling their lungs with fresh air up at the Mokanshan resorts. But they'll be back next week and we urge our four thousand subscribers to hit the phones and shout PHOOEY!

What's the bee in your bonnet? Editorial: Rm 540, 233 Nanking Rd. Tel: Shanghai—10695

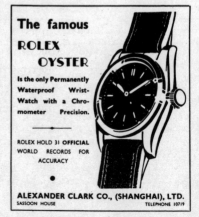

23

From tiger to rabbit—Chinese New Year 1939, and Shanghai's buzzing with the news that a Riley–Farren joint is in progress, and it'll be the biggest casino in the Badlands. On the Great Western Road the painters are in, and Nellie is auditioning dancers. Jack and Mickey head down to the docks and meet an incoming U.S. Navy transport that found room for three Manila-made teak roulette tables with Bakelite wheels, American-style double-zero felt lay-out. Things of great beauty. There are more tables for baccarat and dice, and Joe has ordered a red carpet to be rolled out on opening night.

It's taking longer than Joe and Jack might have hoped. Both of them needed to raise money to grease the endless palms—number 76, the Kempeitai, Chinese cops, the guys who deliver the coal, connect the water, plug in the electricity, and those who collect the trash. Squeeze, cumshaw, kickback. Work is stopped by thugs claiming to be from the unions, then by more thugs claiming to be strikebreakers and wanting money to break strikers' heads on the flagstones. Pitched battles ensue between the two sides. Months drag frustratingly by. Joe has laid out for air-conditioning and a dehydrator to chill the place so he can keep the windows closed and the mosquitoes out along with the less pleasant smells of the

Badlands gutters. But that doesn't come cheap—they need to pay to boost electricity from the Frenchtown grid. Joe figured it would be a while before they could open the doors—hell, it'd be a while until the joint had doors. Still, they were on their way at last.

But first, Joe needs a crew. The Nazis, Japanese artillery strikes, and a little providence provide. With so many Chapei and Hongkew joints bombed out, their enforcement teams are looking for new employment. Walter Lunzer was the contact, a big bear of a mensch who'd tended the bar and watched the door of more than a couple Jewish-owned Hongkew joints, always with a twelve-gauge under the till. He'd been a low-level gangster in Vienna's Jewish ghetto till the Germans rolled in, and then he and his crew had decided to sail for Shanghai and pastures new and Nazi free.

Wally Lunzer comes down to the Western Roads from Chapei with his crew of good-looking boychiks, all slicked-back hair and sharp suits, to a man in total fucking awe of Dapper Joe. Lunzer packs a Mauser Red 9 under his meaty armpit while the boys keep knuckledusters and rubber coshs about their person, ball bearing–filled saps in their trouser pockets, and Bengal razors in their breast pockets. The boychiks don't need to be taught how to smile wide for tips, 'ma'am' the married dames, kick the hopheads to the curb, recognise a nasty drunk who is about to start swinging, and a bad debt at a hundred yards, scan the crowd for dips and purse snatchers and give gentle reminders to regulars whose chits were due. Joe snaps up the team to run security for Farren's. Nellie was right when she said better them than the Friends of Riley.

Back at the Manhattan, Jack guzzles hot-plate coffee to make it till first light. He's getting older; the routine gets tougher. Coffee and Benzedrine leave his nerves jagged, but hell, they beat the sleepy eye. He gets night sweats, he gets fearsome comedowns, his moods swing erratically, and Nazedha gets the worst of it. He shoots Navy nostalgia bullshit with Mickey while the coin is counted, and Schmidt watches the door with his Mauser on the bar and the safety off.

The deal with Farren is a seriously hefty investment, but it'll pay back fast, even with the Kempeitai taxes to pay. The slots still pour cash nightly, thanks to the ever-faithful marines. The soldiers stay out of the Badlands by order of the MPs and have their fun in the Settlement, where Jack's slots are dominant. DD's is still selling dance tickets and booze to the Shanghailander and Chinese swells crazy for high-octane cocktails, like DD's house special: equal parts brandy and Italian vermouth, a dash of absinthe, another of Angostura bitters, well shaken with a cherry and a squeeze of lemon peel on top. Double up the measures for the regulars and go heavy on the absinthe.

Jack is moving in the direction he wants to, towards the wide-open Badlands of infinite possibility. But it's taking a serious toll on his legendarily short fuse, and there are nightly rows with Nazedha. Still, it comes like a bolt. Mickey O'Brien tugs his sleeve outside the door of DD's, pulls him to one side, and whispers in his ear that she's gone, Jack, taken off with some Dutchie. Took the S.S. *Potsdam* to Sumatra, married the guy on the ship, going to be a planter's wife in Medan. Jack slugs Mickey right there on the Avenue Joffre, outside DD's, swells gawping, and lays in to him till Schmidt, who's waiting in the Packard, pulls him off.

Fuck it. Fuck her. There's too much else to think about; too much else in Jack's benny-fried brain. The war is the bad news now. It looks like Free China is finished. They can assassinate the odd puppet official in Hongkew, but they're on the retreat and Tokyo's on the advance. Soochow, Nanking, and right up the Yangtze; Amoy, Foochow, Canton down to the border with British Hong Kong—all Jap territory now. D.C. is now thinking maybe

Shanghai is indefensible and the coming fight is between the U.S. and Japan. They're preparing. Marines are to be shipped out, not shipped in; soon there will barely be a thousand left in Shanghai to liberate from their wages. Jack locks himself in the Manhattan for two days, stares at a bottle of Johnnie Walker and considers taking his first swig since 1924. Then an old memory shows up, with what some might suggest is perfect timing. She's no regular, that's for sure. She looks like she took a wrong turn somewhere on the Avenue Eddy and hit Blood Alley rather than the Cathay Hotel. She walks in the door unannounced in a cloud of chypre, and he knows her straight off—Evelyn Something Russian, but she's got a Brit accent? Oleaga, that's it—she's still using that name, though the Russian gent's long gone. She looks good, though she's the wrong side of forty in a young dame's town. He remembers that night in Manila—punching out Paco, taking Evelyn back to his room, seeing her off at the docks the next day, her perfume trace on his sheets for a week. Evelyn tells Jack she's been floating between Manila and up and down the China Coast; Tientsin, Weihaiwei, Amoy down to Hong Kong. She's pitched up permanently in Shanghai now and is looking to do some business. She's read about the Farren tie-up, heard about Jack's girl trouble. Maybe she's got something else that might interest Jack? It's time to return the favour for his having sorted the nasty Paco problem way back when. Jack says he's always interested in a proposition, runs his eye up and down her long legs, but remembers they used to call her Evil Evelyn. He takes her home.

Jack drinks coffee the next morning with Evelyn, pours out his woes, shoots some old-time nostalgia shit about Manila. They reminisce on the early-morning breakfasts back with Ed Mitchell at the Rhonda Grill, the Navy dances at the Metro. Seems an age ago to Jack, who is, as usual, wired and jangly from not having slept. Evil Evelyn lays out her proposition: she's looking to set up a brothel on the Avenue Joffre, in the heart of Little Russia where nobody ever calls the flics—she's got contacts who will sort it with the Garde Municipal and put up half the cash; Riley can stake her the other half. It'll make a mint and pay back the investment real fast. It's a brothel with a difference—gigolos for bored white Shanghailander women—and it'll pay twice for all concerned, once on the day and once more for the clients to keep their afternoon activities from their husbands. It's a gigolo whorehouse turned blackmail sting. Jack knew the evil in Evelyn wouldn't take long to show itself. But you know what? It's Shanghai—it might just pan out. After all, Don Chisholm drives a brand-new German Mercedes up and down the Bubbling Well Road like some kind of Shanghailander Gauleiter on his own blackmail earnings from the *Shopping News*.

But he remembers his promise to Joe—no more sidelines—and he passes; brothels aren't his thing anyway and queering his Badlands pitch would be crazy now it's got this far. Evelyn smooths down her dress, puts on her lipstick, heads for the door, and says, 'Well, Jack, dear, if you ever reconsider . . .'

The Chinese army has retreated from Shanghai back to Soochow, to Nanking, to Hankow—defeated each time by the Japanese Imperial Army. They evacuate from the Solitary Island up the mighty Yangtze to the fortress city of Chungking, now capital of Free China. There they regroup in the caves and wait for the Mitsubishi bombers of the Japanese Air Force. Chungking is blitzed, bombed, firestormed nightly . . . but after the bombers retreat to refuel and rearm, the city emerges once more into the mists that regularly cloud the final Nationalist metropolis.

North of the Soochow Creek fires still smoulder. Endless blocks of sprawling ruins stretch as far as the eye can see, where once were mills, filatures, factories, tenements, schools, shops, temples, homes; where two million Chinese lived, worked, procreated, hoped. Now, come nightfall, across most of this district, the streets are deserted. Chinese who have to pass through move swiftly, believing the ghosts of the dead hover above their former residences. Japanese sentries seldom venture abroad in these quarters after sundown. The clanging of gongs is heard from one bombed-out and deserted terrace; devils innumerable are believed to gather at the firestormed North Railway Station terminus at night seeking reunification with their dead relatives.

On certain nights, so it is said, when the moon is especially bright, kuei huo, devils' fireballs, can be seen bounding chaotically down the broken streets and passageways. The Japanese call them rin-kwa or kin-kwa—gold fire; the foreigners know them as will-o'-the-wisps. Japanese soldiers foolish enough to follow these ghost lights do not return and are found dead in the morning, in alleys and laneways, their eyes wide open and reddened by fire. The Japanese say that the phosphorescent lights are Chinese Hitodama, 'soul flames', found on battlefields and summoned by fox demons, the demons of fire. The Chinese say the kuei huo are a force summoned by the legion of Shanghai's dead to take revenge on the Japanese. The kuei huo retreat, as the soldiers seek to capture them, and then engulf and consume them in fire.

They are manifestations of the Whangpoo's marsh gas, seeping through the cracks of the city to expel the unwanted, poison them, destroy them.

This, people believed . . .

24

Plum rains; gold fever. The annual plum rains, the *meiyu*, hammer Shanghai in July 1939, steaming off the sidewalks as the newly arrived humidity evaporates the rainwater to a fine mist. Settlement streets become unpassable and Frenchtown basements swiftly flood, drowning Chinese refugee families caught by surprise. In Hongkew, the Sawgin Creek overflows, the drains back up, sewage spills into the streets. Flooding in the Soochow Creek washes dead bodies downriver and deposits them in the alluvial mud flats of the Whangpoo by the Bund, to be fished out by the marine police using long bamboo poles with boat hooks on the end before the taipans in the offices overlooking the river have their luncheons disturbed by them. Riverside godowns flood in a matter of minutes; legions of rats swarm out of their trapdoors into the surrounding alleys.

On Shanghai's streets Chinese shroffs and bookkeepers hold sodden newspapers over their Kobe felt hats; Shanghailanders sweating in worsted wool suits still—linen is in short supply this year—turn up their collars despite the newly humid air. Office ladies, shop girls, and off-duty taxi dancers raise their oiled paper umbrellas as they hurry along the Bubbling Well Road up near the Paramount, skip the puddles in Frenchtown on the Avenue Joffre, seek sanctuary in the cafés of Little Russia, and huddle under the awning outside DD's till the worst passes. It's not cold, though the plum rains do bring the temperature down to a more comfortable level; it's simply damp. And then the rains stop as suddenly as they come. The people sheltering in the doorways of the Settlement and under the plane trees of Frenchtown resume their journeys. Rickshaw pullers wipe off their seat cushions and look for the richest pickings from among the crowd of pedestrians. Pedicab drivers push down on their pedals to get moving, stiff limbs responding to their efforts, and look once again for fares. Shanghai is temporarily cleansed.

But the queues outside the bullion dealers on the Bund never move during the plum rain downpours. The isolated and surrounded city has slumped into massive stagflation: the value of notes and coins changes daily, and the exchange rates leave people dizzy. The expectant have risen early to join the line at the Shanghai Gold Exchange, behind people who have spent all night on the pavement to be first in the doors. Others queue by the brokers' offices—a line two hundred long waits patiently, soaked, snaking round the corner from the offices of Simmons, the Settlement's largest bullion brokers. Wealthier Shanghainese pay peasants to sleep out in the queue and hold their place till morning. Gold becomes an obsession, and rumours swell: only gold is safe, only gold will survive and increase in value. The exchanges see prices rise sky-high; brokers like Simmons see their profits surge on the fears of the populace. Prices swell for everything. Bread that was twenty cents before the Japanese came is now $1.20 Chinese; coal that was a ten-spot a tonne is now 250 Chinese bucks and largely dust. Rice dealers, accused of hoarding and profiteering, are attacked by mobs of hungry, inflation-ruined peasants.

The end of year two of the war, the first twenty-four months of *Gudao* is approaching, and Shanghai has gold fever bad. Bullion sharks—inflation millionaires, speculators—are the new symbol of the city's venality, and everyone wants to be one. More rumours swirl: the yuan will be devalued overnight; the puppets will refuse to recognise Free China currency, wiping savings out instantly; the Japanese will destroy all currency and replace it with their own 'invasion money'. The Japanese cannot abide the yuan—it's still a Nationalist currency and gives Free China a financial foothold in encircled Shanghai.

All fears are realised as the value of yuan collapses even further under the onslaught of stagflation. Talk of war in Europe throughout the summer only accentuates Shanghai's financial panic. Alice Daisy Simmons and her father deal more bullion than ever: bullion is transportable; bullion is dependable. The moneychangers along the Bund do a roaring business; it's said they can tell a bad dollar by blowing on the edge of coin and listening. But over in the Badlands, any money—gold; silver; dollars American, Chinese, or Mexican; yen; yuan; taels—rolls and rolls . . .

On September 1, 1939, those European war jitters become reality. Germany invades Poland—and two days later London and Paris declare war on Berlin. Priorities change. Already the Solitary Island, Shanghai becomes even more isolated, and with the British now at war for their own island's survival, the Settlement will be barely defended as the Royal Navy and any remaining soldiers head elsewhere. The news from Chungking is almost as bad, as the dreaded Mitsubishi bombers pound the Nationalist citadel nightly. But in the midst of this, there's no alternative for Shanghai, no other option for Joe and Jack but to carry on: Farren's opens on the twenty-first with a Riley-backed casino upstairs and Joe's name in neon, shining out over the Great Western Road.

25

Finally: opening night—Farren's. Inside, a full house—bar, restaurant, and floor show, with three more floors of gambling upstairs. The master of ceremonies? Joe Farren, the dapper Ziegfeld of Shanghai. Want to play the wheels? Then talk to the casino's pit boss, the man who'll sign your marker or have you escorted to the door sans jewellery, watch, wallet, and wedding ring: Jack T. Riley.

Joe and Jack's new joint can hold six hundred at full capacity, seat two hundred for dinner and the floor show, with the gambling up on the floors above to cater to the rest—roulette, chemin de fer, craps, dice, and, naturally, slots. Reassuringly heavy security is provided courtesy of Wally Lunzer and the boychiks—recent bomb attacks by Free China hit squads on Jap-friendly gambling and dance venues are fresh in the mind. Still . . . it's opening night. The Great Western Road is arc-lit like a Hollywood premier outside Grauman's Chinese Theater. Let no one say Joe Farren ever lacked ambition—a decade in Shanghai and now he's ruling the nightclub roost with a vengeance, just like he said he would.

The swells—or what's left of them after the evacuation ships have departed—start to arrive at ten p.m. It's still a pretty swank crowd for a still just-about swank town—a cavalcade of the great and the good of the sin capital of the Orient, tripping down in limos and taxis from the Settlement to see what Dapper Joe's got for them. At its more reputable end, a few uptight taipans or stuckup Brits, swinging loose for one night with the wives sent to safety in Hong Kong, Australia, or back to Blighty; catch them on the red carpet with their secretaries on their arms and a pack of ambitious griffins not far behind. Those that make money even in the worst of times, the traders and go-betweens; the compradors and brokers. Al Rosenbaum personally escorts the bullion broker's daughter, Alice Daisy Simmons, up the stairs to the roulette tables. She's exactly the kind of high roller Farren's wants. Later, Jack will make sure Alice and her friends are comped drinks and smokes all night to make sure they don't stray too far from the tables.

Here's the honorary Cuban consul, a man with his hand permanently out for cumshaw; the slimeball Portuguese commercial attaché, talking up Macao's neutrality with his arm round the honorary Brazilian consul—the Portuguese mobs paid both men three times as much as their government salaries in squeeze every month. Here also is the nest-feathering brigade of officials from swamps like Venezuela, Mexico, Chile, all with passports for sale and letters of transit falling like confetti, now worth more than gold. A Portuguese visa had been a few hundred dollars' cumshaw to a corrupt official a year before; now the price is treble, quadruple. Still they mingle—Portuguese bossman Fat Tony Perpetuo, Macassared hair slicked back with some simmering *señorita* on his arm, trades gossip with fellow countryman José Bothelo, while the consuls in white linen suits hover near and smile through nicotine-stained teeth.

Badlands faces. Slots King Jack, Evil Evelyn on his arm, signs markers; Mickey O'Brien, in his first tux, keeps a wary eye on the croupiers and feels the itchy starch on his neck. Albert Rosenbaum bites the silver dollars to ensure their genuine Mexican provenance. Babe, back from yet another Jack-funded dope cure with the

German hypnotist, wafts in looking like a million dollars in an apple-green cheongsam to wish Jack luck. The DD's crew, with their trademark blondes on their arms.

Less welcome these days is Don Chisholm, who's decided he thinks Berlin and Tokyo are the future. He's got a nightly gig broadcasting anti-American, anti-Allied crap on Kempeitai-funded XGRS radio. Joe's quite clear—he can't stand Chisholm or his claptrap on the wireless, but tonight isn't the night for a ruckus. Everyone's favourite Shanghai crook, Elly Widler—gun runner, conman, grifter, purveyor of rare Tibetan furs, gambler and thief— arrives with his new squeeze on his arm. Elly's pushing fifty; she's not yet twenty. Elly kvetches as ever with Sam Levy; his girl-friend looks bored and eyes the Basque jai alai stars in their tight pongee suits. His all-Swiss crew mingles with the Russian boys from the Broadway Mansions card games, keen to see how Jack runs his wheels. Elly moves on to chat with old timers Bill Hawkins and Stuart Price, muse over the old days, grabbing drinks off passing trays to toast the memory of poor old Al Israel. Elly proposes the toast: *alav ha-sholom*, may he rest in peace. At the front tables the 'reserved' signs are whipped away as Shanghai's number one fixer, Carlos Garcia, and his French moneyman, Louis Bouvier, arrive with their wives dripping diamonds. Joe makes sure they get what they want when they want it.

The local celebrities turn up to give the gawkers a gawk—here's Farren's boyhood favourite, Viennese chanteuse and former silent-movie star Lily Flohr. In exile from the Nazis now, she's still a star in Shanghai. The boychiks clear a path for George 'Lewko' Levchenko, their welterweight hero now that Andre Shelaeff's gone to find fame in the golden boxing rings of California. Lewko is straining the seams of his suit with a silky blonde Harbintsy babe on his arm, while his manager grabs the press boys for pics and col-umn inches. Here are all the Paramount Peaches, of course, com-ing to say hi to their old boss, Follies mingling; the Hollywood

Blondes, who've just finished at the Canidrome, have pedicabbed it over. Here's Sasha Vertinsky from the Gardenia round the corner, with his trademark silver-tipped cane, top hat, tails, and monocle, and the gorgeous Boobee in satin, sniffing the last dabs of coke up her beautiful aquiline nose.

Vertinsky and Boobee are White Russian Badlands royalty. He was a genuine star of the pre-revolutionary Russian stage who moved through the Russian émigré communities of Constantinople, Berlin, Paris, and America before ending up in Shanghai. He entertains nightly at the Gardenia, and the crowd always applauds before he sings 'Dorogoi dlinnoyu'—'Those Were the Days'—'Kokainetka,' and 'Tango Magnolia'. Boobee, with dresses that barely conceal her porcelain skin, manages the Gardenia for him. She is the queen of the Settlement's army of Natashas. Her cleavage is deep, her back exposed from sharp shoulder blades to arse, a place only those wanting a hard slap would ever dare put their hand. When Boobee hops on a bar stool, lights an opium-tipped cigarette, and crosses her long legs, the sound of a dozen tensed-up male necks swinging round is like the report of a gunshot across the floor of the Gardenia. Boobee and Vertinsky have quick-fire tempers: they argue at the club and throw glasses; the punters duck for cover, but it never keeps them away. She calls him *ublyudok*, bastard, which he is, technically; he called her *shlyukha*, whore, which she isn't quite. Both have fearsomely bad cocaine habits.

These days, the natives get some Badlands action too—there's not enough foreign money to go round in these times of war and repatriation. The Badlands welcomes all . . . and their wallets. Here are some playboy Chinese with their Cambridge accents and Oxford brogues—none of them have ever worked a day in their lives, and certainly never set foot in daddy's stinking sweatshop in Chapei. Here too are the hack-pack regulars who've squeezed and begged their way onto Farren's guest list: the whoremongering Ralph Shaw from the *North-China Daily News*, that fruit from the *Shanghai Times* said to have a taste for young Japanese boys, the Associated Press guy with his White Russian princess, who's about as royal as Joe's hairy Jewish *tukhes*. Shura Giraldi, the hermaphrodite boss of the Peking Badlands, is in town for the opening, with his dance troupe girls done up like ersatz Dietrichs. Frenchtown flics come over the border for a complimentary pastis or three: district Sûreté captains check out the action and the girls. The local contingents of Corsican dope runners and Maltese pimps attend, of course, looking to get some grease from Farren. Even a couple of Manila-based silver smugglers come to see how Shanghai swings. And finally, there's a special long table for the old Red Rose gang—Monte Berg, Sol Greenberg, Freddy Kaufmann, Fred Stern, Joe Klein, Demon Hyde, and Al Wiengarten—the veteran wise rabbis of Shanghai's rackets with their plump, attentive wives in attendance. Joe passes out cigars and brandies, Jack comps each wife a pile of chips for upstairs to go and lose.

You wanna spend? Farren's got eight craps tables, each with its own sticksman; sixteen blackjack, fifty slots, and three roulette wheels. You suggest they're rigged, and Farren's head of security, Wally Lunzer, will come over and acquaint your head with the Great Western Road flagstones. You want a marker? See Jack Riley. Short on cash and want to turn that emerald necklace into chips? Albert Rosenbaum will quote you a price. And here's the floor show: the Dani sisters looking all dark-eyed and lovely, harmonising while the entrées are served. Joe and Nellie take to the floor and glide like old times, their disagreements put aside momentarily, Joe's cheating temporarily forgotten. The crowd roars when they bow, the men stand and applaud, the old Red Rose wives dab their eyes. Nellie still looking as fabulous as she did at the Majestic in '29. Then dancing, the band—Mike's Music Masters of Swing, fresh in from playing at the Oost Java Club in Batavia, exclusive now to Farren's. It's everything Joe ever wanted.

Outside, the beggars of the Badlands congregate as the cars and rickshaws pull up, shaking their Craven A cigarette tins for coins. There are country children with twisted limbs, women in rags thrusting forward near-dead babies; others display evidence of leprosy or syphilis or gangrene; limbs lost to the deadly shuttles of the silk filatures that power the Settlement's riches; horrific burns on show. Opium ghosts stagger through the crowds, heads down, noses running, hands outstretched. Bad joss, some say, to not throw coppers into their open palms.

Wally Lunzer's boychiks know the beggars' tricks and move them on, roughly, with kicks, flicking lit Camels in their faces, cursing them in Yiddish, then pidgin—*no wantchee, no wantchee*. If they're allowed to congregate, they'll stand still, hands out, begging. If coins come, they move on; if a Shanghailander tries to shove one aside, the beggar will collapse to the pavement, writhing, rolling around, yelling. The other beggars will swarm and raise an outcry until only a pocketful of change flung high into the air will disperse them as they fight each other for copper coins.

Ignore the rest of the Badlands—Farren's is bringing high-class Shanghai back for the first time since Bloody Saturday. It's like the old days of the Plaza or the Majestic, the early days of the Paramount, and the heyday of the Canidrome all over again. And Joe loves his crowd. They've followed him from the Settlement via Frenchtown, up to Hongkew, down to Siccawei, and now to the Badlands. They hail from England, France, *Mitteleuropa*, the moneyed *latifundia* of the Argentine and Brazilian rubber plantations, Mediterranean ports, and White Russian émigré communities.

With Farren's, Joe got all the trimmings he'd read about in American magazines. The two great arc lights are 'borrowed' from the Fourth Marines for the night and jerry-rigged into the Settlement's electricity to scan the heavens. He's got the velvet rope, the boychiks in monkey suits, that impressive neon sign, *Farren's: the House of Surprises*. It's all complemented by the stainless steel cutlery (he'd have preferred silver but knew it would go missing in the punters' pockets if the staff didn't get it first), good Irish linen on the tables, and red-lacquered lamps of Ningpo cheval glass. Dinner is tender beef steak from Hongkew Market cooked by chefs poached from the Canidrome (Tung and Vong were pissed at that stunt), the bar stocked by Egal & Cie and, just before sunup and curfew's end, good hot coffee and fresh pastries from Bianchi's on the Nanking Road.

Joe stands at the bar, watches the punters dance, the gigolos eye up the single women, watches the gamblers move on to the upper floors and knows that the casino upstairs is packed. It's been a struggle: Shanghai being the Solitary Island means paying off multiple smuggling rings for just about everything—decent steak, branded liquor, acceptable wines. But Shanghai is still a town where just about anything is possible at a price. Japanese barricade guards still just about look the other way for a cut.

Jack leans on the bar next to Joe, scribbling down the night's rough take so far on a napkin. Joe's eyes open wide behind his glasses; Jack shrugs and says, 'Told you it'd be taxes plus five.' The world is going to hell in a handcart, China is being ravaged by war just a few miles from Farren's, but never have two men made more money in one place in all of Shanghai.

Dawn, the grey light of an early Shanghai morning, the neon on the Great Western Road turning pinkish against the first light. There are reminders of the times: armoured vehicles covered in the Rising Sun flag trundle outside on the strip, heading for the shift change at the barbed-wire barricades at the boundary of the Badlands. The last stragglers leave Farren's. Sasha Vertinsky supports a giggly Boobee out to the street, dragging her cashmere cape with fox fur trim on the pavement. He hails a rickshaw to take them to the YMCA soda shop, where Boobee loves the iced coffee and scores coke off the Ningpoese waiters. The rickshaw pullers crowd round shouting 'Mr. V., Mr. V.', knowing Vertinsky goes everywhere by rickshaw, likes to gab in Shanghainese, and always tips big for a Russian.

Parties are moving on—Fat Tony Perpetuo and the Brazilian consul are arm-in-arm; Elly and the Swiss are heading back for some early-morning cards at the Broadway Mansions; Alice Simmons and the bright young things of the remaining Shanghailander 400 head back to her penthouse for early-morning eggs and bacon; Babe is with some big shot she's picked up, suggesting they get comfy on a divan just big enough for two up back of the Moon Palace; Sam Levy and the old Red Rose crew are trying to persuade the Dani sisters to take a cab with them, to see how the Jukong Alley swings, and get slapped by their wives for the cheek of it. The crew laughs, the Dani sisters shrug like they could care about these old boys, the wives mock huff and puff—it's all good-natured. The kitchen staff loiters out back, palming smokes in the alley by the grind joints and Hwa-Wei lottery shacks. Mike's Music Masters try to pick up the hatcheck and cigarette girls, get a party going back at their digs in Frenchtown. Then everyone's gone but the help. Joe tells his boychik chauffeur to drive Nellie home; he needs to catch up with Jack.

Wally Lunzer bolts the door behind the last of them. Faint shafts of sunlight presage another humid day before Shanghai's long summer finally slumps into autumn and the temperatures start to drop sharply. Lunzer sends a boychik over the road to the *you-tiao* seller deep-frying dough sticks on the corner to get breakfast for all. A Chinese ayah sweeps up the night's cigarette butts, discarded taxi dance stubs, and other detritus, snaffling up a couple of dropped gambling chips. Then Joe Farren, Wally Lunzer, and the Vienna boychiks pull up chairs and a table in the centre of the now deserted dance floor. The boys loosen the collars on their flannel shirts, roll up their sleeves, trade gossip, talk girls, bets, Nazis, Europe . . . Chairs are flipped round, smokes lit, minesweeping the dregs left on the bar. The boychiks stay trim, work out during the day, but can't shake the 'nightclub tan', the ghostly pallor that comes with too little daylight. Joe brings over a tray—tea, sugar, lemon slices. He peels notes off a wad for the boys while the Manilamen band that plays sets between Mike and his Music Masters finishes packing up their instruments and leave. Lunzer unstrips his shoulder holster and hangs his clunky Red 9 over the back of the chair. Several of the boychiks clean their fingernails with cocktail sticks—working for Joe, they've begun to imitate his fastidiousness. Joe raises a glass, and the boys do likewise—lemon tea with Johnnie Walker tipped in to give it a kick—mazeltov.

And there's one more toast to make. Jack is upstairs in the office with the door locked. Joe knocks, and Mickey O'Brien lets him in. Jack is licking his calloused fingertips and counting notes, putting them into piles—Chinese dollars, American bucks, Japanese yen, British pounds, Dutch East Indies gulden, Filipino pesos, Straits dollars, Mexican silver dollars, Bombay rupees, the multifarious currencies of Shanghai—checking them all for phonies. Albert Rosenbaum is noting down the night's chits, who owes what for calling in later.

Jack hands over the night's figures to a soft *oy vey* from the proprietor. They both look at the safe stuffed with rolls of notes. Jack loosens his collar, kicks the door closed, and spins the combination wheel. It's the taxes plus five . . . and then another five. Wally Lunzer and Mickey O'Brien, with their shotguns and accompanied by Schmidt and a boychik, will drive the take over to a Frenchtown stash house on Route Remi that Rosenbaum has arranged for just such a purpose till the bank opens in a couple of hours. Doesn't do to leave cash on the premises in the Badlands; Al Israel is still on everyone's minds. They toast—Joe pours a whisky, Jack knocks back the last of his chicory roast. Farren's is open for business.

SHOPPING NEWS
—'BREVITIES'—
MONDAY, DECEMBER 17, 1939

Troubles aplenty but still merry Christmas from all at *Shopping News* . . . and don't forget to resubscribe for 1940!

After our recent survey of local police conditions, we find that more than forty foreign officers have tendered their resignations, while another seventy intend doing so. Store detectives, night watchmen and bank security guards make the same money with far less risk to life and limb. There are probably many more members of our once brilliantly organized international police force who, fed up with the disgraceful treatment dished out to them by the Municipal Council, intend resigning.

Mr. Peacock of the BLUE RIBBON DAIRY on Tunsin Road wishes to let hard pressed Shanghai mothers of young nippers know that, despite the so-called 'Emergency', Blue Ribbon STILL has supplies of milk available. However, orders must be made in person and there is a waiting list. Meanwhile we can report, after a weary trek across the Settlement and Frenchtown, that not a single can of condensed milk remains on any store shelf. We have to ask why the authorities are not prioritizing vital milk supplies when stocks are so low?

GROSVENOR GOWNS wish all *Shopping News* subscribers to know that they're opening a new salon this June at 249 Route Cardinal Mercier (Tel: 76058). Grosvenor are 'Modistes' in Ladies' dresses, coats, costumes and hats. All work is performed under the direct personal supervision of a guaranteed European cutter. *Shopping News* subscribers are welcome to the opening and will receive a 15 per cent discount on all purchases, orders and any alterations for two weeks after the store's grand opening.

Got a secret you just have to share? Editorial: Rm 540, 233 Nanking Rd. Tel: Shanghai—10695

26

The Caddies, Studebakers, Chryslers, and Packards line up nightly on the Great Western Road to deposit their occupants at the front door of Farren's. The men are in tuxedos, cashmere coats, and white silk scarves; the women in low-necked chiffon dresses and furs. The band plays, the dance floor hops, the waiters career in and out of the kitchens with trays piled high, the champagne corks pop. Joe is turning over the floor show acts to keep attracting the right crowd and get plenty of free newspaper space—Mike's Music Masters are getting rave reviews, but on their night off Joe pulls in Harry Fisher, an old Red Rose mensch, and his swing band from the Roxy. He's rigged wires in the roof and brought in an aerialist who soars over the heads of the late-night diners—it's a gimmick, but the punters love it. Jack tells him to make sure the girl is svelte or the roof will come down and rain silver dollars on the diners below. The Aristocrats of Harmony sing pre-dinner melodies. Joe books the magician from the Park Hotel's show after he's finished and the Svetlanoff Duo exhibition dancers to waltz for the early crowd. He's also brought in an Aussie couple called the Hartnells who've been based in London, fresh from headlining at all the best Mayfair nightspots. Joe bills them as 'Patter, Chatter, and Dancing'—Sandra and Frederic tumble and mug for the dinner crowd. All the while Jack watches the Manilamen croupiers spin the wheels upstairs and fire the cards at the punters.

The *North-China Daily News*, the *China Press*, the *Shanghai Evening Mercury*, the *Shopping News,* and the Chinese papers too, send photographers to jostle on the Great Western Road and snap the crowd. Sasha Vertinsky pops in nightly, chin held high, monocle in place (hush, there's no lens, it's an affectation); Lily Flohr comes by after her show at the Elite wrapped in furs and with bouquets of flowers for Joe's bar. Now and again she sings torch songs for the crowd and the Yiddish lover's lament 'Bei Mir Bistu Shein', 'To Me You're Beautiful', first in Yiddish, then once more in English. It never fails to tear Joe up. Then she doubles up with Gerhard Gottschalk, another Berlin exile running the Tabarin cabaret in Hongkew up near the Jewish refugee–heavy district of Tilanqiao, and they do comedy numbers, Gottschalk goosing Lily's rear, mugging for the crowd.

The photographers snap sexy Sandra Hartnell; they catch Babe with a good-looking Basque boy on each arm. The flashbulbs pop and catch Joe, followed by Jack and Evelyn. They pop some more and snap Shanghai Bund gold-bullion heiress Alice Daisy Simmons, still single and a high-ranking catch, on the arm of glamorous flyer Hal du Berrier (she'll end up paying Don Chisholm dearly to keep that picture out of the *Shopping News* and spare her poor daddy heart palpitations). Here's Mickey Hahn, *New Yorker* correspondent and nightlife maven, with her pet gibbon Mr. Mills done up in a tux on her shoulder; here's Clara Ivanoff, the most beautiful of the Paramount Peaches, with her handsome boyfriend, Vasia, who plays clarinet in the Paramount's White Russian house band. Nellie never shows after opening night; her dancing days are over and she hates Jack's guts. She can't help feeling that all this will go bad, sometime, sooner or later. Joe makes the most of her absence with a Dani sister or a Peach. He's hardly ever home; Nellie sits and fumes. Inside Farren's is a place to forget the war, the barbed-wire barricades, the checkpoints, the shakedowns, the in-flation eroding your savings, the newsreels showing Europe going down in flames, the bar stool gossip that maybe that was the last evacuation ship and now your fate is entwined with Shanghai's, like it or not.

The only catch is the Badlands itself, which is still bad—and vio-lence is ultimately bad for business. J. B. Powell at the *China Weekly Review* sums up the assassinations and shootings, the robberies and kidnappings as Shanghai's 'carnival of crime'.

It starts with sanctioned theft; licenced extortion. Number 76 thugs loot a gambling den on Connaught Road, hijack cars full of foreigners returning to the Settlement from the now nearly ma-rooned Columbia Country Club, and shoot up a Chinese wedding, grabbing the fat red envelopes stuffed with lucky money for the bride and groom. Two guests are gunned down, seven others wounded; no arrests are made. It moves on to street warfare: more number 76 gangsters on stolen motorbikes strafe an SMP patrol with machine-gun fire and lob two grenades towards their ar-moured patrol car. The SMP return fire and take down two of the motorcyclists, dead on the pavement.

The stock market spirals out of control; speculators hawk 'War Baby' shares in gun companies at crazy prices, promising fast and big returns claiming fake contracts with the British and German armies. It's a scam. The dividends don't materialize, and the gullible swallow opium to end their shame as their families are bankrupted. Rumours fly round, the market bounces up and down, hoarders stash cotton supplies in godowns—bought at a thousand Chinese bucks a bale, they boost the price to two grand. Those who sell profit; those who hold too long will see the market collapse completely. Fifty cotton trading import–export companies go bankrupt in one day; a half dozen Shanghai cotton merchants leap from their office windows, several of whom leave markers unpaid at Farren's. But when one racket collapses, another rises—calico, Saigon rice, sorghum, silk, and always, always in Shanghai, opium.

Decent dope is in short supply in the Badlands because Soochow Creek is silting up and Cabbage Moh's junks can't get through with the uncut stuff. Cabbage is supplementing the Badlands' narcotics diet with opium black pills and heroin red pills—'reds or blacks?' is the new cry of the street dealers. Little Nicky is back in the *North-China Daily News* estimating that the city has twenty-five hundred street dealers, many of them moonlighting cops, selling to an ever growing three hundred thousand addicts—and why wouldn't they swap law enforcement for drug dealing, as inflation wipes out their wages daily? Official black Nash cars cruise the strip bordering the Badlands with the SMP high honchos, armed bodyguards on the running boards, checking up on their sergeants, now clad in thick blue winter uniforms to keep out the bitter Shanghai winds.

Little Nicky heads to the Badlands to see the show for himself. The Western Roads are outside his remit as a U.S. Treasury agent, but he knows the men he wants are its denizens. Standing on the corner of the Great Western and Edinburgh Roads, a sideshow, a carnival of the doped, the beaten, and the crazed. He walks round to the Avenue Haig strip and encounters the playground of Shanghai's crackpots, cranks, *gondoos,* and lunatics. He's accosted constantly: casino touts, hustling pimps, dope dealers; monkeys on chains, dancing dogs, kids turning tumbles, Chinese 'look see' boys offering to watch your car. Their numbers rise as the Japs turn the screws on Shanghai ever tighter. Half-crazy American missionaries try to sell him Bibles printed on rice paper—saving souls in the Badlands is one tough beat. The Chinese hawkers do no better with their porno cards of naked dyed blondes, Disney characters in lewd poses, and bare-arsed Chinese girls, all underage. Barkers for the strip shows and porno flicks up the alleyways guarantee genuine French celluloid of the filthiest kind. Beggars abound, near the dealers and bootleggers in the shadows, selling fake heroin pills and bootleg *samogon* Russian vodka, distilled in alleyways, that just might leave you blind.

Off the Avenue Haig, Nicky, making sure of his gun in its shoulder holster, ventures up the side streets and narrow laneways that buzz with the purveyors of cure-all tonics, hawkers of appetite suppressants, male pick-me-ups promising endless virility. Everything is for sale—back-street abortions and unwanted baby girls alongside corn and callus removers, street barbers, and earwax pickers. The stalls of the letter writers for the illiterate are next to the sellers of pills to cure opium addiction. He sees desperate refugees offered spurious Nansen passports, dubious visas for neutral Macao, well-forged letters of transit for Brazil. He could have his fortune told twenty times over (gypsy tarot cards or Chinese bone chuckers? Your choice). He could eat his fill—grilled meat and rice stalls—or he could start a whole new life: end-of-the-worlders and Korean propagandists offer cheap land in Mongolia and Manchukuo.

Nicky wanders the thoroughfares and the back alleys of the Western Roads and sees life, such as it is lived in the Shanghai Badlands, on the eve of 1940.

27

Things remain tense after the New Year. Puppet mayor Fu Xiao'an launches a 'Badlands Cleanup' campaign, ordering the gambling joints to close but, beyond switching off their gate lights, nothing happens; behind the doors the roulette wheels keep spinning. It's not only the puppet authorities who are keen to impose order; the Municipal Council wants to look like it's getting tough on the Western Roads District. Tall, lanky, very English Godfrey Phillips, the Shanghai Municipal Council commissioner-general and the Settlement's top civil servant, opens talks with Mayor Fu on a joint SMP–Japanese police force for the Badlands to be called the Western Shanghai Area Special Police. Within the hour they're nicknamed the WASPs.

Days later, at nine a.m. on January 6, Phillips is driven down the Avenue Haig with Crime Squad boss John Crighton to see the now-notorious strip of sin for himself. Crighton is an SMP veteran, no stranger to raids, violent crime, and deadly shootouts with gangsters who would never surrender alive. He's a family man, but the law comes first. Famously, he had once been off duty and out shopping with his wife, Julia, when he noticed some men acting susupiciously. They began to rob a pedestrian. John Crighton pulled his gun and faced the robbers down. They ran. He left his wife on the street and chased them down a laneway. She heard shots fired and feared the worst. He arrested the men, finding that their pistol was linked to twenty-six recent robberies and a murder. He then took his wife to finish their shopping trip and carried their parcels home—he's that kind of Shanghai cop. Crighton was awarded the SMP's Distinguished Conduct Medal. Few senior officers were more respected by the ranks of the SMP, or more feared by the city's criminal elements. Godfrey Phillips, a man who spent his life behind a desk signing chits, was fortunate to have John Crighton with him that day.

As the car moves down the Avenue Haig, three hijacked rickshaws block the road, forcing the SMP armoured Nash 400 sedan to stop; three gunmen open fire at point-blank range. That Saturday morning Godfrey Phillips is the luckiest man in Shanghai; a dozen Mauser Red 9 pistol shots rip by him, one missing his ear by a whisker, another passing between his legs. Not one hits him. Crighton pushes Phillips down on the floor of the Nash, covers him with bulletproof vests, and they hightail it out of there back into the Settlement.

Phillips and Mayor Fu agree on the formation of the WASPs. Phillips listens to Crighton and makes sure he gets what he wants in the deal. Crucially, the new force is tasked with investigating any cases involving foreign nationals and suppressing all forms of vice and crime in the Badlands. Phillips, echoing Crighton, wants the new force to serve notice on the foreign gangs of Shanghai, with immediate effect. In reality it won't be that fast, but the gangs will have no choice but to defend their interests—no matter their nationality. And that includes Joe and Jack.

The first few months of 1940 have been decent for Joe and Jack—the tables at Farren's are raking it in. The casino makes good money even with the increasing Kempeitai and number 76 tax demands, which involve Jack having to break bread with his Japanese contacts in Hongkew to try to keep the demands from spiraling ever upwards. But by the beginning of summer, Jack's major troubles are in Frenchtown rather than Little Tokyo.

The French Concession authorities finally decide to get tough on slot machines—upping taxes in the hope that the raft of small bars and holes-in-the-wall that exist solely on their slots take will go out of business. It hits Jackpot Riley's pocket hard—fifty one-armed bandits are confiscated and smashed up overnight, with more gone from Blood Alley, including those in the Manhattan. Paris has fallen to the Axis powers, and the Japanese are effectively running the Frenchtown police now, with pro-Vichy officials' compliance. Their ronin cronies install their own slots in the bars and boîtes of the Concession; Jack can't do a thing about it.

The Municipal Council and the SMP are pressing harder than ever for the Badlands casinos to be shuttered. They're mostly foreign-run, and the SMP is obsessed with maintaining the fiction that the foreign powers are all good and that Shanghai is not a haven for white gangsters and ne'er-do-wells. The Badlands makes that position hard to maintain. The Japanese issue an order to eight Badlands joints to close, but it soon becomes clear the order is cover for a hostile takeover by the Kempeitai themselves with their Chinese puppet pals out of number 76. Thirty or forty number 76 goons raid the Broadway Club, occupy it, and reopen it as the New Asia Club, with collaborators managing it. Rumour has it the new managers paid a stone-cold hundred grand in Chinese dollars to number 76 for the right to take it over. The Hollywood reopens as the 1238 Club, with roulette wheels and opium-smoking divans just where they'd been the day before. The Monte Carlo reopens as the 99 Shanghai Club. It's whispered those clubs that reopened paid a ten grand 'special tax' to the Japanese.

And Farren's? Joe and Jack have greased the wheels with suit-cases stuffed with cash to Jack's Japanese contacts, and they're pull-ing in the Settlement elite, which means they slip down the list of those joints to be busted . . . but Jack can only restrain the demands so much, and those excessive taxes are starting to bite into the prof-its. They need to make more. Joe's clever idea to lure in those wor-ried about the bullets over in the Badlands? A *Gone with the Wind* night. The flick is on at the Roxy on the Bubbling Well Road, and the whole town has seen it. Lay it out—an old-fashioned waltzing competition with a hundred bucks prize money for the best couple. The Aristocrats of Harmony will play Southern songs; the Hart-nells will demonstrate how to waltz with West End class. Joe takes out half-page advertisements in the *North-China Daily News*, the *China Press*, and the *Shanghai Mercury and Evening Post*—but not the *Shopping News*. The idea of giving any gelt to openly Nazi-loving Don Chisholm sticks in his craw, and he point-blank refuses.

On the night, plenty of Scarletts turn up, but Nellie steals the show in hoops and crinolines—'Fiddle-dee-dee, this war talk's spoiling all the fun'. Joe had begged her to come, and eventually she agreed. The boychiks are kitted out in Union blue, the bartenders in Confederate grey. The Aristocrats don blackface with straw boaters, minstrel-style. Vertinsky shows up in Rhett Butler duds, Boobee as a super-sexy Southern belle. Sandra Hartnell is sweet, sweet Olivia de Havilland, and Frederic's got up as Leslie Howard. The cigarette girls, trays piled high amid complimentary Farren's matchbooks, are dressed tonight as saloon bar sweeties, the Chinese staff in cowboy gear. The chorus girls twirl their hoops to flash lacy drawers, and Sandra Hartnell sings 'Pennies from Heaven' for the crowd. Even Jack Riley, looking over the balcony from the roulette tables, is all gussied up as Robert E. Lee with Evelyn on his arm in a tight, tight corset looking like the sexiest of camp followers. The band drowns out the gunfire popping outside the front door.

But there's a war on . . . right outside the door, just across the Soochow Creek, and in Europe too. With Paris fallen and the old marshal establishing his Vichy regime across France's empire, collaborationist gendarmes are patrolling Frenchtown virtually arm-in-arm with the Japanese, and half the Sûreté has skipped town to Hong Kong to join up with de Gaulle's Free French. Everyone knows that the war will come to the Settlement soon enough. Tokyo knows it best of all.

SHOPPING NEWS
—'BREVITIES'—
MONDAY, JULY 16, 1940

All of Shanghai is preparing to raise a toast and wish fare-ye-well to the brave lads of the Seaforth Highlanders as they prepare to depart our fair Settlement. We're sad to see them go, but are they needed any more? London believes they will be better stationed in their colony of Hong Kong. Perhaps it is not us who should be weeping, but rather them, swapping the Paris of the Orient for the Barren Rock?

As rice prices spiral so there have been disturbances at shops and distribution centres. These disturbances—let's call them what they are: 'riots'—seem to us to be created by the SMP themselves through their actions of firing above the heads of the crowd, despite Commissioner Bourne's optimistic warning to the Chinese public to 'seek shelter in such cases'. This is the height of stupidity, for how are the hundreds of Chinese shoppers seeking food to know when the police are to start shooting and, even if they knew, where are they to go to avoid police bullets? These actions show the antiquated policing methods that prevail in the Settlement and are reminiscent of the old 'SHOOT TO KILL' orders of the 1920s.

It is no secret that a serious feud has existed for many months between the police and the gangs of desperadoes who have selected the Western reaches of our Settlement for their activities. Scarcely a week goes by but that some policeman is killed or wounded and while we do not wish to give the impression of tenderheartedness toward armed desperadoes we cannot seem to see how society is the gainer if from one to a half-dozen law-abiding citizens have to be sacrificed for every desperado that is bagged!

Taking in the new plethora of nightlife in the Western District will require some fine dresses ladies, and JOSEPHINE'S on the Yuen Ming Yuen Road is the place to buy. Take this issue along this week and receive a 25 per cent discount on all gowns, shoes and accessories. Proprietor Mr. Henry H. Cohen awaits you for a personal fitting on the second floor.

Know something we don't? Call up and whisper in our ear. Editorial: Rm 540, 233 Nanking Rd. Tel: Shanghai—10695

"Josephine's Gowns. (Registered.)

HENRY H. COHEN, Ltd.
Wholesale and Retail
19 Yuen Ming Yuen Road

**2nd Floor Only
Please take Lift**

28

Foreign gangs are running the biggest casinos in direct violation of all laws, and the Japanese aren't serious about clamping down on them—WASPs or no WASPs. The scenes on the Avenue Haig appear as if from Hieronymous Bosch, the killings and beatings too much, the attack on Godfrey Phillips a step too far. The China Coast newspaper editorials ask where the long-promised WASP patrols are. The public is outraged, so the papers say—Shanghai is 'agog' at the audacity of the foreign criminals at loose in the city. Anti-rackets campaigner J. B. Powell at the *China Weekly Review* characteristically doesn't hold back and declares the Badlands to be a 'Monte Carlo Regime'. The wags respond that it's more like the French Riviera, just without the sun or the sand, but with all the chancers, gold diggers, fake Russian aristocracy, and call girls.

The SMP is pushing hard for action, and Commissioner Bourne's career is on the line. Crime Squad boss John Crighton is dispatched to turn the city's underbelly upside down and declares 'war on the Badlands, war on the foreign rackets and the foreign casino operators'. You can expect Thompsons, you can expect Mausers, you can expect the Riot Squad's Red Maria and armoured cars backed by baton-wielding Chinese constables and sharp-shooting Sikhs. Commissioner Bourne vows that 'this scourge on Shanghai's good name will be ended'.

Meanwhile, the American Court for China that provides justice for American citizens in Shanghai announces plans to appoint a new U.S. marshal with powers of arrest to support Little Nicky and other Treasury agents in ending the embarrassment of their citizens' criminality in Shanghai. Yes, he'll be armed; yes, he'll take down any American gambling kingpin in the city who dares raise his head above the Soochow Creek's stagnant water. They hold back from actually naming Jack Riley—but only just. The Honourable Judge Milton J. Helmick of the U.S. Court for China, a thin man with a jutting chin on the end of a long neck, declares, 'We will have no Chicago on the Whangpoo'. Word of Shanghai's lawlessness spreads: *Time* magazine calls Western Shanghai the city's 'Little Sicily'. Shanghai's war on crime has just ratcheted up a notch, and the gauntlet has been thrown down—by Shanghai's newspapers, by Shanghai's police, by Shanghai's justice system. They intend to end the good times for the rogue foreign gangsters in the Badlands.

A call requires a response. Things are getting too crazy. The Japanese and number 76 want their taxes; refusal is unacceptable. The police and the courts are arming up; the press is castigating the Badlands and its nightlife proprietors. A united front is called for. Peace is paramount if the Badlands is to continue to profit.

Carlos Garcia is perhaps the one man who knows everyone in the foreign gangs of *Gudao* Shanghai and whom everyone in the rackets respects. Garcia calls a meeting; he declares the urgent need for talks. The mutually agreeable and neutral place for a sitdown is Sasha Vertinsky's joint, the Gardenia on the Great Western Road.

Garcia says when crackdowns come, it's the gangs who go to war with each other and do the police's work for them—he saw it in '29 when he did a year in Ward Road Gaol, thanks to an SMP crackdown.

On the night of September 5, 1940, the Kempeitai order the barriers lifted for the long line of Caddies, Packards, and Studebakers with number 76–issued laissez passers to ease access to these Badlands bosses. They arrive at the Gardenia and park right alongside Jack Riley's low-slung MG roadster. A car thief would have a dream haul tonight; a car thief would be dead and dumped in Soochow Creek if he even thought about it.

The Gardenia is all blue satin walls and avant-garde art Sasha Vertinsky picked up someplace on his travels, a giant samovar behind the counter. There's an open bar with Boobee mixing and pouring while waving her cigarette holder about; hors d'oeuvres and caviar with vodka shots for any who want the delicacies. The hatcheck girls and the cigarette sellers are sent home, the Russian boys from the Broadway Mansions are hired to man the doors back and front and the street outside, Red 9s bulging, saps and coshes ready—'*Izvinite*, so sorry, closed tonight.' The men who run the rackets of foreign Shanghai will not be disturbed.

Vertinsky mixes with the gangs. Gossip is the Russian vice, and Vertinsky's specialty. He makes everybody laugh, breaking the tension. His breath is like pure battery acid when he whispers in your ear, his eyes usually bloodshot. His daily diet? Champagne and cocaine exclusively. The joke was nobody had ever seen Vertinsky eat—ever, not one solitary bliny, not even a lowly bowl of kasha. Joe Farren's boychiks called him Nosferatu, with his fishing-hook nose, heavy-lidded eyes, his English tangled in Russian vowels, his growling Ukrainian *r*'s. He blinked noticeably slower than most people, the languid eyelid flicker of the cokehead. It was disconcerting all the same, along with his propensity to let his head droop forward and then suddenly snap back up and stare straight at you.

He rouged his lips, powdered his face—Count Dracula, the master of ceremonies for the evening.

The gangs assemble, a gathering of the high-crime milieu of Shanghai come to talk. The puppets are installed in number 76, just yards from the Gardenia, the Japs on the border of the Settlement, and now Bourne and the WASPs are looking to interfere with business. There can be no fighting over the spoils up and down the Great Western Road, along the Avenue Haig, the Edinburgh Road, and across the Badlands. Demarcation is needed—separate spheres of influence.

Carlos Garcia, running to fat in his beige suit, holds court with tall and gaunt Stuart Price, the legendary old man of the Shanghai rackets. Both men are respected; both men are wealthy almost beyond measure. Their judgments will be considered fair; their decisions just. Jack Riley is backslapping and handing out complimentary Farren's chips, sipping seltzer courtesy of Boobee, who knows he's mean as a coot but doesn't drink or smoke. Boobee has one of the boys nip out back and get Jack a pot of coffee you can stand a spoon in, just how Lucky Jack likes it. Joe Farren is close by, showing the unity with Riley most said couldn't happen; Joe's *consigliere*, Albert Rosenbaum, is also on hand. It's not quite a gathering of friends, but at least of men with mutual interests.

Fat Tony is there, still running high-stakes baccarat and illicit wheels at the 37427; so is José Bothelo, who runs Macao visas and letters of transit from his base at the Silver Palace Casino. Veteran Brit casino organiser Bill Hawkins and Vertinsky sit at a table with the Route Voyron gypsy clan who chain Lucky Strikes and don't say much. Evil Evelyn arrives and toasts Jack for the old times in Manila. She's tonight's only female, excepting Boobee. Word has it she's actually going to open a joint with Axis protection on the Edinburgh Road. The Gardenia is, tonight only, a Badlands sanctuary for the white racketeers of the city.

What is agreed? Peace among the gangs, a united front against the WASPs. Any arguments will be mediated by Garcia and Price, the longest-serving bad hats of Shanghai. There will be no more feuding, no more stunts like Jack rolling round the floor of the Canidrome with Buck Clayton. Riley waves his hands in the air—'Okay, okay!' A standard ten grand a day tax per venue to the Japanese—everyone would pay; everyone could afford it; Jack could sell it to the Japs as good business all round. The Kempeitai would be guaranteed their profits and could ease off the enforcement. Everyone would combine to share roulette tables with any joint that had its tables smashed or confiscated by the WASPs or the SMP, so business could carry on as quickly as possible. Call it what it was: a syndicate, like the American gangs had formed at Atlantic City back in '29. Those legendary names all in one room—Luciano, Capone, Lansky, Lepke Buchalter and others—each supporting the other for maximum profit and survival. This sitdown was the Shanghai version. The Badlands would be stitched up, the transition complete from the old world of Big-Eared Du as emperor and the Green Gang, where the foreigners existed on the fringes, to a new world, one where the Badlands was theirs, all theirs, and ruled by their syndicate.

Truce on, all to play for now in the Badlands. The men and women who'd come to Shanghai—from Mexico City, the Marseille Panier, London's East End, the slums of Lisbon, the American Midwest, New York's Lower East Side, across the Russian steppes from Bolshevism, the Jewish ghetto of Vienna and all points in between—create a gangster's paradise, sanctioned by the Japanese Imperial Army. They toast, they drink; Vertinsky entertains, Boobee pours. Peace reigns, roulette wheels spin unhindered, profits are maintained, taxes paid. From now on, to go against any member of the Shanghai Badlands syndicate is to go against them all.

29

There's a new mensch about town. He's spinning the wheels at Farren's, playing baccarat over at the Arizona, fan-tan at the Ali-Baba—anywhere anyone will give him a marker. He introduces himself to all and sundry as Sam Titlebaum, newly arrived from Chicago. There's a radio war going on—Chisholm and his new sidekick, Herbert Erasmus Moy, a New York–Chinese newly arrived in Shanghai and turned traitor, are ranting on pro-Nazi XGRS while former newspaper columnist Carroll Alcott is pushing the Allied cause on rival station XHMA. New boy Titlebaum is moonlighting on the radio at XHMA as Carroll Alcott's stand-in when the big guy needs a break. He's just as anti-Axis as Alcott and boasts he's going to get a U.S. marshal's badge along with a shiny Colt .45—fast-tracked, 'cause he's a righteous thief-taker.

Jack figures having a future U.S. marshal owe you is a worthwhile investment and lets him get in to the house deep. Titlebaum bets large and loses big as Jack and Joe listen to his all-American hero tales. He props up the bar at Farren's, ordering stengah after stengah. Everyone loves his gab. Born and raised on Chicago's South Side, ex-Chicago PD and served with honour. Doubt that? You might. Titlebaum claims a reputation as a big-mouth cop who swore holy hellfire on the city's gangsters. The legend, according to the man himself: he carries a bullet in the hip from a gun battle with one of Capone's goons out in some back alley. Incapacitated from active duty, he crossed over to the press, worked for the *Seattle Star* as their Chicago correspondent and became a bigtime columnist, syndicated in a couple dozen states, ripping into police corruption and connivance between cops and gangsters. Organised crime was a scourge smothering American democracy; rotten cops were gutting the heart out of the Stars and Stripes. America needed big men with big guns; men who could take back the country for the decent working stiff—Gary Cooper meets Walter Winchell, against a Depression-era backdrop of soup kitchens and hobo camps.

He claims things got hot: plenty of death threats from criminal elements and dirty cops equally, bullets in envelopes sent to his office, his name spelled out in newsprint cut out of the dailies— Tittlebaum, Titlebawm, Titebom—the spellings never much good. Slow-moving cars prowling around his pad in the early hours; guys looking at him strangely in taverns. So, Sam says, he hopped ship to China and pitched up in the Settlement. Jack dismisses him as a loudmouth, a self-aggrandising fantasist, and writes him another marker.

But things work out the way Sam said they would. The Honourable Judge Milton J. Helmick of the United States Court for China gets what he's been calling for: a righteous American marshal with a five-pointed star and a gun on his hip. In mid-September, Sam Titlebaum goes down to the U.S. Court and files the paperwork to get himself a badge and a gun, which is rushed through on the nod by the local district attorney, Charlie Richardson Jr. He's introduced to Little Nicky, who squares him on the priorities of American justice in Shanghai: no more nighttime forays to Farren's for Sam; no more shooting the shit with Jack and Joe.

The great and the good of the American colony turn out to

meet and greet. A banner across the room proclaims *SHANGHAI AMERICANS WELCOME OUR BRAVE NEW MARSHAL*. Sam Titlebaum—in blue serge suit, cowboy boots, and an emerald stickpin, with oiled-back hair—is seriously hungover but puts those perfect ivories on display; he got his teeth fixed up in return for advertising the skills of a Hungarian dentist with a place just off the Bund on XHMA. He puts his hand on the Bible and swears to uphold and defend all that is necessary. The formal oath of office over, Sam looks around for a stiff drink.

Pinch-faced Shanghai Moral Welfare Society wives look disapprovingly at his holster; dolled-up and bored businessmen's wives eye him hungrily. Judge Helmick takes the stand, chin jutting, and welcomes Titlebaum, before reminding the crowd of lawyers and worthy burghers of the topic of the day. 'We all know of the long-standing scourge among the American community of the ne'er-do-wells—the gamblers, the vice merchants, the sharks and buccaneers. It's time to clean them out, folks.' The room raises a toast to the man who's going to save them all. Sam grins large; Little Nicky shoves a tumbler in his fist—at last, hair of the dog. The *China Press* and the *Shanghai Mercury* snappers pop flashbulbs as Sam shakes hands with Judge Helmick.

The men have got a story prepped for the press: a strategy to bring errant America on the China Coast to heel. Judge Helmick declares one Edward T. 'Jack' Riley target number one for the U.S. Court for China—American-run slot machines and roulette wheels are a curse on our country's good name. Titlebaum leans in so the hacks can catch him, and he's got the playbook down pat in no time—'Riley is a bad man who threatens the solid reputation of this here International Settlement and the good name of the United States within it.' Judge Helmick gets the punchline, by now well tried and tested: 'We will have no Chicago on the Whangpoo.'

The press laps it up; Sam figures he'll never have to pay that marker to Riley or Farren now; he's badged up and untouchable.

The judge, the consul, the fed, the district attorney, and the new marshal all toast for the cameras. Sam throws back the long-awaited glass and gags on seltzer. Little Nicky whispers in his ear, 'No booze round the good judge, Sam. There's work to do.'

Shanghai's got Don Chisholm—he of the scandal-filled *Shopping News*—and his Führer-admiring partner Herbert Moy tuned in and loud on Nazi-funded XGRS. They call themselves 'Mack and Bill' and spew bile on the airwaves nightly. Moy usually kicks it off—who remembers if he's Mack or Bill? 'The Brits are finished, German bombers are destroying their lame morale . . . Buckingham Palace has been destroyed by the Luftwaffe. How much longer can they last? The French have turned tail and admitted defeat, the Swastika flies in Paris now; a new strength where before the Popular Front was weak and Jew-controlled. The Dutch have rolled over, the Belgian queen fled to the smoke-filled rathole of London and deserted her people. In Madrid a new day is dawning, the anarchists and the communists routed . . .'

Chisholm takes up the rant: 'America should stay out of Europe's business. America should concentrate on its own mess after the Jews created the Depression in '29 and got their patsy Bolshevik Feodorvich Roosevelt elected president to represent their money. Japan is fulfilling its destiny in the Orient . . .'

And then it's more from Moy: 'China's enemy is not Japan but rather her old foes, Britain, France. Did Tokyo forcibly spoonfeed opium to China? No, it was England. Generalíssimo Cash-My-Check takes American Jew money and feathers his own nest while his wife, with her own bloodstained hands, beds Washington politicians and siphons money to her own syphilitic family . . . The rising sun is just that—rising—and old Europe's day is done.'

Mack and Bill's hate-filled rants are the final straw for Joe. He bans Don Chisholm from Farren's. Jack does not demur—Chisholm vouched for heroin smuggler Paul Crawley as a stand-up guy, and we all know how that ended. There are always others lining up to play the Farren's tables. Let Dodgy Don and his SS-admiring side-kick go drink with the Hitler Youth and *sieg heil* all fucking night long, for all he cares.

Chinese families hide their daughters, lock them away in back rooms and attics. They dress them as boys, bind their breasts, cut their hair. They fear the Japanese emo, *their* akuma—*demons, fiends, devils—that capture young women and force them to prostitute themselves. When these* emo *are finished with them, sated, but without souls or reason, they devour the women whole, who are never seen again. Free China guerillas from Chungking secretly distribute rice paper perodicals containing the letters of a young woman, the supposed estranged daughter of a puppet traitor, to her lover, a brave warrior of the Free China resistance. She declares that she will not be eaten up by the Japanese* emo, *or be consumed by China's despised* hanjian *traitors, collaborators, literally 'evil-doers'. Raped by the Japanese, she vows to kill in return, to avenge herself and China.*

All Shanghai knows of Menghua Jie, Dream Flower Street, in the heart of the Nantao old town. Everyone knows that women are kidnapped and taken to a guarded mansion on that street occupied by the Japanese. Within, Shanghai's daughters are turned into living ghosts, dead though alive, their final devourment long and horrible. They are destined to reside in hell, or wander the wastelands outside the city forever. Menghua Jie is but one of many places in Shanghai where women are raped and eaten by the Japanese demons. There are other occupied mansions known as weiansuo—*comfort houses— where daughters disappear. Ziang Teh Road, Kungping Road, Route Dupleix. Many more exist in the lanes and alleys of Little Tokyo. People say there are more than 150 such places from Hungjao to Pootung, Hongkew to Siccawei, where the Japanese demons queue to devour the so-called* weianfu, *the comfort women, Shanghai's kidnapped daughters all.*

This, people believed . . .

PART THREE

The Hour between Dog and Wolf

L'heure entre chien et loup

A French saying referring to the moments after sunset when the sky darkens and one's vision becomes unclear, making it difficult to distinguish between dogs and wolves, friends and foe.

Everything in Shanghai is for sale. But for the city itself, there are no bidders . . . Shanghai is a city of fear.

— Frederic S. Marquardt, 1940

There always has to be some place where the world sweeps its dirt and refuse.

— Josef von Sternberg, on Shanghai

30

Everybody knows that eventually the U.S. Court for China at Shanghai will come for Jack. The Settlement's extraterritoriality laws mean you can only be tried by a court of your own country under your own nation's laws. The SMP has long been sick of Jack T. Riley but unable to do a damn thing. There's no law in Shanghai that says you can't gamble, just that you can't run a gambling joint featuring roulette wheels. But the court can't touch Jack for the roulette wheels at Farren's—the Badlands is Japanese-protected and way out of Judge Helmick's jurisdiction, which is limited to American citizens and their indiscretions in the Shanghai International Settlement. And there are no laws that say you can't operate or play a slot machine. But there is a United States law that bans gambling, and that applies on the Whangpoo to American citizens. Helmick thinks he can get an easy conviction.

The judge gives the Riley case to Charlie Richardson Jr., special assistant to the district attorney of the United States Court for China. The U.S. gambling laws will be the key to removing a man who's been a longtime irritant to Helmick's court—corrupting the Marine Corps with liquor and slots, rumours of more pernicious substances being traded, starting nightclub brawls in very public places, allegations of putting the fix in at the Canidrome boxing nights, doping greyhounds. Jack Riley is not Judge Helmick's ideal of a model American citizen on the China Coast. It's time to take down Jackpot Jack Riley, time to end his decade-long lucky streak. On Friday, September 20, 1940, the judge issues a warrant for the arrest of Edward T. 'Jack' Riley, on seventeen counts of violating U.S. legal statutes that 'prohibit engaging in the business of commercial gambling'.

The same day, John Crighton picks up Sam Titlebaum in his official SMP black Nash. Crighton's snitches tell him Jack is holding court at the Fourth Marines Club on the Bubbling Well Road, his MG parked outside. The men wait opposite until Jack comes out, ready to head down to Farren's for the night. They arrest him then and there, and take him to the holding cell at the American Court on Kiangse Road for arraignment—the Slots King with cuffs on for the first time in fifteen years. Titlebaum takes his wallet, tie, shoelaces, and loose change. They fingerprint him. Crighton and Titlebaum are shocked by Riley's acid-burned fingertips. Jack says it's an honour to be arrested by DSI John Crighton—congratulations on the Distinguished Service Medal. He stares straight through Titlebaum like he isn't there. Jack spends the night in the cell.

Early the next morning, Jack receives a number of special deliveries: ham and eggs, courtesy of Sam Levy; a freshly pressed grey-striped suit and suede shoes from Evelyn, with bulging pockets the warders don't notice because they're concentrating on her curves; bennies in a cigarette carton from Babe via Doc Borovika. Jack extracts the tabs and passes the cigarettes round the warders. Then it's up to the courtroom. Plenty of Friends are present, rounded up by Mickey O'Brien, laughing in the gallery. Jack's freshly pressed trouser and jacket pockets are stuffed with dollar bills. They poke out of his shirt pocket, his socks, Jack mugging all the while like a slimline Fatty Arbuckle for the crowd. He's got a high-dollar disreputable lawyer arguing a mile a minute for him like crazy, raising objections right, left, and centre.

There's a catch to the Shanghai justice system: the American court has jurisdiction over American citizens, but only if the U.S. Court can prove that you are, beyond a reasonable doubt, really a genuine American citizen. If they can't, then you walk free. The court clerk asks Jack how he pleads.

'Guilty. Provided you can prove I am a United States citizen.' And he winks at Judge Helmick.

Jack's lawyer tells the court Jack is a Chilean citizen. Here's his passport, admittedly out of date, but issued in Yokohama in 1932. He puts it to Helmick straight: if you can't prove Jack T. Riley is a U.S. citizen, then you have no authority over him. The judge pops a vein at the disrespect, orders fifty thousand Chinese dollars bail—that's a cool twenty-five Gs in American dollars, ten times more than the court has ever requested of anyone before. Helmick has decided to set an example amid pressure from the consul general, the Municipal Council big cheeses, and Commissioner Bourne.

Smarting, Special Assistant to the DA Charlie Richardson tells the court he will prove 'beyond a reasonable doubt' that Riley is an American. The lawyer is waving his arms, calling the bail amount a travesty. The judge is fuming, and Little Nicky is red-faced at the fact Jack's thrown a spanner in the works in less than two minutes in court. The public gallery is whooping, and Jack is licking his thumb and speed-counting bills with a big grin on his mug. He pulls fifty large ones out of here, there, and everywhere; Friends lean over the rails and hand him wads of notes Joe has pre-stashed from the Farren's safe for just such an eventuality. Jack mock bows, licks his thumb again, finishes the count, and hands the pile over to the court clerk. He tells him he'd better count it as you can't trust anyone these days, winks big for the crowd, and flips the Friends his trademark tip of the hat. It's pure theatre, Jackpot Jack style.

Jack steps down from the stand and tells Helmick there'll always be a drink for him behind the bar at DD's, and that his credit's good at Farren's if he fancies spinning a wheel or two. Helmick storms out of the courtoom, followed by his flunkies. Fifty Chinese Nationalist grand in big stacks on the court clerk's desk, and Riley walks free, leaving Mickey to grab the receipt. Just like back in '25 in Oklahoma, he leaves without looking back. Turning left onto Kiangse Road, he dodges the hacks and the snappers waiting on the steps round the corner at the court's main entrance on the Foochow Road. Evelyn has raced ahead and got the MG ready, and now she brings it over, slides across out of the the driver's seat for Jack, and they take off.

Jack is laughing like crazy and fishtailing the car through the traffic lights, down to the border with Frenchtown on the Avenue Eddy just south of the racecourse. Straight through—the *flics* know the red roadster and salute Jack as he flies past. Jack heads west straight down the long Avenue Joffre till it hits Avenue Haig, then he cuts across Edinburgh Road onto the Great Western Road. There's a chichi party waiting at Farren's, with all the familiar faces—Joe, Babe, Sam Levy, Elly Widler, Albert Rosenbaum, the doc, most of the old Red Rose gang, old Bill Hawkins and Stuart Price, the Town team guys, as well as various Friends. There's a buffet stacked with cold cuts and plates of more ham and eggs, done in the Venus Café style. The drinks are already pouring; Carlos Garcia is popping a bottle of genuine French champagne, and there's a steaming jug of Folgers coffee for Jack. To top it all off, the Fourth Marines band is up on stage and launches into 'Hail to the Chief'.

Later, it's time to go to work. Trucks fan out across the Settlement with white men driving and Chinese coolies hunched in back. Mickey O'Brien rides shotgun in one, Schmidt in another. They stop at Van's Dutch and the Santa Anna. They move on to the Handy Randy, the Lambeth Bar, the Jinx. At each stop they load slot machines onto the truck, one after another. Down Seymour

Road to Frank's, the New Clipper, and the Service Bar. To the Savoy and then Eddy's and Bruno's. Farther along they stop at Ma Jackson's Tavern, the Fourth Marines Club, and the Del Conte, a bar usually packed with marines from the Ferry Road barracks close by. They head north up to Hongkew, to the Astoria Bakery, the Magnet Café, and the Oceana Bar along Broadway, the Mascot bar and the Barcelona on Wayside. More slots, and more bars, taverns, nightclubs, cafés. By the end of the night there's not a slot machine left in the International Settlement of Shanghai. Jack and Mickey gather them all up and stash them in anonymous godowns in Y'poo. For the first time in years, the International Settlement of Shanghai is slots-free, and it's courtesy of the Slots King himself. An indictment on gambling charges for operating slots? What slots would those be, Your Honour?

31

September turns to October—the Blitz hits London; the RAF hits back, destroying Antwerp; the Luftwaffe can't get dominance of the skies over southern England and Hitler cancels his planned invasion. Closer to home, Japan invades French Indochina, and that means any pretence of Shanghai's Frenchtown as being under total Japanese dominance is well and truly over.

Regardless of world events, the wheels at Farren's continue to spin every night. Joe holds court at the bar, while three weeks out from his next appearance before the judge, Jack gets back to pit-bossing upstairs like old times. The regular crowd are glad to see him back—bullion-rich roulette addict Alice Daisy Simmons proffers a small bar of gold to Jack and Al that, in these gold-secure times, ensures she'll be spinning Farren's wheels for a fortnight without thinking about cashing in for more chips. Most of Shanghai is drowning under stagflation and watching their life's savings disappear, but Alice is in the gold business, and it's never been better. She can play the tables all night and not care. Jack and Al make sure she gets whatever she wants. But outside, the violence continues.

A top SMP cop investigating corruption in the force is shot at; he returns fire and the gunmen scatter. A *lieu-maung* gang bursts into the Paramount with guns and handcuffs, looking to kidnap four wealthy Chinese playboys inside for big ransoms. They fire shots when they can't find them; Nellie and the chorus line dive for cover. Nellie swears she's had just about enough of this shit. A puppet official leaves the Metropole Gardens Ballroom and hails a waiting taxi. He opens the back door and two gunmen inside, waiting, fire four shots into him, killing him instantly. A Yu Yuen Road café dealing dope and cocaine out the back door is firebombed with Molotov cocktails while the Johnson Garden ballroom, a new Chinese-run Badlands joint, is burnt to the ground. The *North-China Daily News* reports that it's all due to gang rivalries in the Badlands—and so it may be, but not foreign gangs. The syndicate holds.

The Kempeitai continue to assert their authority and now challenge the SMP overtly. Right on the border of Frenchtown, a gambling house and opium den of immense proportions now operates out of a mansion on tree-lined Route Courbet. The boss is a Mr. Kan, so tight with number 76 they are like Siamese twins. The Garde Municipal have been warned off by their new Kempeitai masters; Frenchtown police are a sham under Vichy collaborator control, the French Concession courts now administered by the Japanese. Across in the Settlement, the Japanese open the Asia Club on Gordon Road and turn that strip of the Sinza District into a new street of sin. Sinza becomes a Badlands in miniature, with all the trappings. The Japanese police patrol the area while the SMP keep out; Sinza Road Municipal Police Station becomes a ghost town, and Commissioner Bourne sits and simmers, having effectively surrendered that district without a fight.

Roadblocks go up around the Badlands in late November; it's an island within an island. The Japs pull rolls of barbed wire out from number 76 and place them across Yu Yuen Road, on Avenue Road, and along Jessfield Road, while also blocking off the Tsao Chia Tu Village food market. Cordons in place, bluejacket sentries commence checking everyone passing through. They manhandle foreign women, tip customers out of rickshaws and pedicabs, toss car trunks and upend shopping baskets onto the dirty street. The SMP complain, and are told it's in response to the shooting of a sentry on Yu Yuen Road. The sniper's bullet went clean through his jaw, blowing his face off—Wally Lunzer saw it all going past in a rickshaw. Strange thing is, as Wally told it, the soldier got sniped at in the afternoon, but the Japs had rolled out the barbed-wire barricades at lunchtime. It's a classic Imperial Army–engineered 'incident'—use an event to justify a reaction and forget the order those events came in.

The Kempeitai aren't crazy, though—they're not about to slaughter their golden egg–laying goose. Farren's and the Great Western Road are still just about outside the blockade, although getting there is now a pain—foreigners need passes to get past Tifeng and Edinburgh Roads. But Vertinsky's Gardenia club is in the blockade, and so are plenty of others—Madam Szirmay's Hungaria club, where the boychiks from Farren's hang out after hours, Jock's on Jessfield Road, where plenty of Friends line up for schooners of EWO, the Roxy with its turbaned Sikh security crew, the Ali-Baba . . . It's an all-out Kempeitai takeover of the area.

Cars line up at the blockade entrances and exits. Barbed wire covers all the laneways and roads leading off Yu Yuen, leaving residents penned in, unable to get to the market. Thousands of Chinese gather at the wire waiting to see if food supplies will come through, scared to leave the Badlands in case they can't get back to their homes. Number 76–authorised black marketeers set up stalls just inside the wire—a hundred bucks Chinese for a picul of rice; a dollar for a small catty of vegetables. It's profiteering on a grand scale, sanctioned by the collaborators.

The Japanese Kempeitai are getting brazen. They arrest five SMP men after they find one of their own beat cops with his head staved in in an alley up by Edinburgh and Kinnear Roads. The Kempeitai say they're rogue SMP, settling scores over cross-border firefights and skirmishes, and they torture the men at the gendarme station. Commissioner Bourne creates a stink; universally respected John Crighton negotiates, and the men are let go. They say the damn fool Jap fell off the running board of a gendarme Oldsmobile, and his philopon-hopped comrades inside didn't even notice.

All the talk is of war, and not much else. Evacuation ships, flights leaving for Hong Kong, out via Chungking, try the Burma Road, through to the British Raj. Ships to Lourenço Marques, wherever that is, Africa someplace. It gets to some: Demon Hyde calls it quits, sells the Del Monte to number 76 interests for a rumoured quarter of a million Chinese dollars, and ships home to California. Evacuate, evacuate . . . but where to? Australia, Hong Kong, America? For those with no papers, or for those—like Joe—who aren't welcome at their own consulate, those European Jews now subjects of the Third Reich, there is nowhere to go. Passports will not be renewed. The Portuguese have letters of transit for Macao and on to Lisbon—from there are possible routes to Britain or the United States. But word is thousands are waiting every day at the Lisbon docks for places that never become available. Touts scour the clubs and cafés offering false papers—identification inflation ensues as prices for a forged French passport start at a thousand francs.

The Blitz; the North African deserts; Paris filled with goose-stepping Gestapo sipping café au lait on the Champs-Élysées; London, Liverpool, and Southampton feeling the full force of Luftwaffe bombing raids nightly. Meanwhile, three or so years into the war in China, and the smoke from the ruins of Chapei still drifts across into the Badlands, smelling of sewage and leaking gas. The bluejackets on the cordons won't let the gas company trucks through, and the leaks just keep leaking.

But on the Great Western Road, the wheels are still spinning, and Jack Riley, seemingly untouchable, has got them greased up and earning nightly despite the Kempeitai's ever more rapacious tax demands he has to try to keep in check on behalf of the syndicate. The croupiers skim the wooden shoe across the felt, spewing cards for the baccarat crowd, and the dice roll. The Hartnells twist and tumble; Joe's aerialist flies above the heads of the crowd in a sequinned leotard; Mike's Music Masters are playing Artie Shaw's 'Nightmare', this week's favourite tune.

Even so, Nellie was right all along. She told Joe that Jack would be trouble. In the office upstairs one night, Joe tells Jack he needs to sort this thing with the U.S. Court, get Helmick off everyone's back, and concentrate on negotiating with the Japanese to limit the crippling taxes. He has to get Titlebaum and his crusade out of the way, and, incidentally, the guy owes us plenty and needs to pay, U.S. marshal or no U.S. marshal. Joe hears Little Nicky has sent Jack's seared partial dabs to Washington to see if they can make a match in their state-of-the-art crime lab. Joe is concerned, thinks Little Nicky has been aching to bust Jack for years now. But Jack's not worried—he holds up his hands and wiggles his gnarly fingertips. Helmick and Richardson have got no proof of citizenship, and without the slots they're stymied. He'll never take the rap. He assures Joe that if things go badly, the Kempeitai will spring him. They need to keep the channels open from the syndicate to Jap HQ in Hongkew and number 76; he says he's got understandings with the Japanese and the puppets.

Joe shrugs, says okay. Farren's needs to keep earning—tickets out of town and new boltholes will cost plenty. Nellie is pissed at Joe and says so: he needs to dump Jack Riley more than he needs to dump the showgirls. It's her final warning, although Joe doesn't know it.

32

The appointed date—December 4, 1940—and Jack is back in court. He showed bravado last time, ponying up the bail money like a carny barker, but that doesn't mean it's not serious cash. A no-show would mean he would forfeit the money, and that would leave Jack close to cash-broke, with all the rest tied up in his venues, Farren's, and power company stocks. With his slots out of action and stashed in Y'Poo, that old Chilean passport from way back when, and his seared dabs, Jack figures there's no case, or at worst a slap on the wrist and a fine. His ace in the hole is the Japs: as the main parley between the syndicate and the Kempeitai, he's worth a lot in kickbacks and connections. He's confident they'll spring him pretty quickly if Judge Helmick tries to stick a jail term on him. The future is Badlands wheels now anyway; the slots can go rust.

The public gallery is packed with Friends once again, and Jack is suited and booted, his pockets stuffed with U.S. currency once more just in case. It's showtime.

Charlie Richardson Jr. appears, a glint in his eyes. He brings out a file from the U.S. consulate in Shanghai from a decade ago. It seems good old Jack had once tried to register as a U.S. citizen— the file, signed by Riley, claimed he'd been born in San Francisco and that his birth certificate had been destroyed in the earthquake back in 1906. How very convenient.

Then Richardson calls Dr. Juan Marin, Chile's chargé d'affaires and consul general in Shanghai. Turns out the Chilean consul general in Yokohama back in '32 was recalled and jailed for corruption in Santiago. All passports issued at that time are null and void. Jack's lawyer argues that none of it matters, as Riley's not running slots anyway. The court doesn't care, they've got a hundred witnesses who'll say they saw the machines. There are photographs, E. T. Riley–embossed tokens; hell, there are advertisements in the marines' newspaper. The gambling charge stands. Riley starts to look antsy; his lawyer continues to object but is swiftly batted away by a determined Judge Helmick.

Next up is Little Nicky. Nicholson's a Treasury agent, so he can't make arrests in Shanghai—he needs the U.S. marshals for that or cooperation from the SMP. But what Nicky can do is go to the feds and get the FBI's attention and time. This access is the clincher, and he knows it. Joe had heard right; Nicky had indeed sent Riley's seared dabs from Shanghai to the feds in Washington. The feds seriously burned the midnight oil looking through thousands and thousands of records till they found a match—nine men had been on Jack's case twenty-four-seven for weeks. Here were records for Fahnie Albert Becker, formerly of the U.S. Navy Yangtze Patrol, 1917 to 1919, and also John Fonley Becker, back on the Yangtze again in 1921. Jack looks queasy up in the dock. A Treasury agent's arm is long and reaches into the United States Navy bureaucracy too. Little Nicky has even tracked down Becker's old paybooks and induction records, had them mimeographed and sent to Shanghai, and now presents them for the court's perusal. It's undeniable; Jack is looking seriously antsy now. But Nick has one more interesting point to make to Judge Helmick.

The FBI takes an interest in many things and has many responsibilities—anti-trust violations, bad banks, interstate shipment of stolen automobiles, illegal sales of contraband contraceptives, the prevention of prizefights, the seizure of stag films and smutty books, all crimes on Native Indian reservations and, most pertinently, in the U.S. Court for China at Shanghai that day, investigations and apprehensions of all escaped federal prisoners, wherever they may be.

And guess what? The FBI got the bit between their teeth, put in some extra hours of searching, and those prints from Little Nicky match those of one John Becker on file with the Oklahoma State Penitentiary at McAlester, where he'd been sent down for twenty-five years in May 1923 and escaped after just two. Jack had done his best to sear off those dabs with acid back in San Francisco, but prints go deep, and the feds managed to get enough matches despite the scarring to positively match Shanghai Jack Riley to McAlester John Becker.

Nicky can't resist pointing out that the Federal Bureau of Investigation and the Oklahoma State Penitentiary both still consider John Becker wanted and are looking forward to seeing him again upon his long-awaited return to the United States from the International Settlement of Shanghai.

There's always a paper trail. Charlie Richardson has done what he promised to do: prove beyond reasonable doubt that Jack Riley—John Becker to you—is an American citizen. Richardson, Nicky, and Judge Helmick look mighty pleased with themselves; Bourne and Crighton are on the public benches smiling at the U.S. court taking care of one of their errant own and likely to remove a major long-term irritant to the SMP too; Sam Titlebaum is checking himself in the mirror, slicking down his hair and getting ready to tell the assembled press that the U.S. marshals always get their man.

Then Helmick makes the biggest error of his otherwise spotless career: he recesses the court for tiffin before pronouncing the sentence. Seems he just couldn't resist drawing out his victory and savouring every last drop of it. The guards take Jack downstairs, and Mickey slips them a fat envelope on the way. They look the other way and act surprised as Riley walks out a side door away from the holding cell. A nondescript car is waiting; he hops in the back and disappears into the Shanghai traffic.

Jack is buzzing. He's just jumped bail on the largest sum ever demanded by a court in Shanghai. Back in the court, tiffin cancelled, it's mayhem. Helmick has ordered the bond forfeit; Titlebaum is questioning the guards; Little Nicky is demanding the SMP call in all officers on leave; Crighton has commandeered the courthouse telephone. Jack has now officially absconded and is on the run. Cue Shanghai's biggest ever manhunt.

Jack Riley is through the barricade at Yu Yuen Road and back in the Badlands. He's got Japanese friends who can ease his passage; his gendarme-issued laissez passer is still good for now. But it's not funny any more, not like back in September. Helmick gets to keep all that bail money now, and Jack's savings are set to dwindle, thanks to the exchange rates. It's bad—raising cash is hard in hyper-inflationary times, and life on the lam will be expensive. He's a fugitive and will have to sell his power company stocks to raise money. Selling the clubs and bars is problematic—it has to be through back-door means, and he'll no doubt take a major hit on it. Mickey is preparing to roll out the slots again, back into Chapei and the Badlands where the SMP can't confiscate them easily; back into Frenchtown where the Garde Municipal follows Imperial Army orders. But it'll be a trickle of coin compared to the old flood. Stagflation will kill what take there is.

He needs a place to stay, but Farren's is out. It's too obvious. There are already SMP men lining the bar waiting for Jack to show his face, scaring the punters; they stick out in their wide-cut suits, extra bulky to cover their shoulder holsters. For now he crashes in a back room at the Six Nations Casino under Elly Widler's protection, but the Six Nations may not be safe for long.

The December snows have come earlier than usual; the temperatures are the lowest since recordkeeping began. Shanghai appears to be freezing to a halt. The trolley cars push slowly along the Bubbling Well Road, lights barely penetrating the icy December fog, all the way to the border of the Settlement and the Badlands. The gongs clang; all change at Yu Yuen Road, barbed-wire barricades blocking the tracks. If you want to keep going, it's collars up, a never-say-die 'tramp' rickshaw, a taxi if you can find one, or head off on foot. The lines at the barricades are long, the bluejackets slapping anyone, man or woman, who smokes in their presence. Shanghailander men have stopped wearing hats at the barricades as the touchy Japanese Kempeitai sometimes take it as a slight, a sign of disrespect. They want it known that things have changed—Japan is top dog in the city now. Chinese are forced to bow to the bluejackets—several refuse and get themselves bayoneted, left to die on the pavement. Papers are checked by the brave sons of Nippon, who frisk you down for those hidden dollar bills that mean you're on your way with no comment, no slapped face, no questions. The barbed wire is pulled back and you're through. Number 76 thugs line up to pat you down for any leftovers on the Badlands side.

The snow covers all the sin and dirt of Shanghai and makes even the worst slum, the filthiest rookery or shadowy laneway, look clean and new and virginal, smoothing out the hard edges, coating the charred timbers, covering the city's cavities. But Badlands snow is flecked black, unlike the rest of Shanghai now. Number 76 and the gangsters have their own coal supply, and the smuts fly through the air like they do nowhere else in the shivering, beleaguered Solitary Island. By day the Badlands, snow or no snow, is filth, dirt, poverty. Yet it still comes alive at night, when the darkness hides most of the detritus and the neon reveals nothing but smudged red reflections in puddles of brackish melt.

One hundred years of old Shanghailander certainties are breaking down; the hierarchies are collapsing. The limey taipans and grey-haired Yankee potentates of the Far East are no longer the natural superiors of the stateless White Russian baker, the Jewish refugee tailor, the Romanian waiter, the Macanese bartender, Manilaman trumpet player, or gypsy troubadour. Shanghailanders of all stripes now look at each other with desperate eyes, the old Settlement deferences of a century gone. Money, and the getting of it, counts most now, and in a world of squeeze, corruption, cumshaw, double-dealing, and black marketeering, the once despised rise up. The dragon is the symbol of the city, but the rat is Shanghai's future.

What use social class, background, snobbishness, if it offers you no rewards? Like everyone else you're hungry, with holes in your shoes; you walk rather than taxi, or cram onto a previously unfamiliar trolley car; you count your smokes carefully, rationing them, then queue with God knows who for more, and pay double the price of last week. War brings a sort of equality, and yesterday's winners are rarely today's victors. The harlot wears tailored clothes and puts on new cosmetics; she's showered in black market perfume while the taipan's wife darns her stockings and wears the old fashions, the 1936 season eked out. Access is all; contacts are like gold dust. This is the time when another type thrives: the eternal survivors, those who know how to operate in the shadows, work the black market, think nothing of taking from those weaker than them. Still the foundation remains the teeming masses of China, the four hundred million 'black ants', ever and always at the bottom of the pile.

Joe cuts Jack off, sends word that he's not welcome on the Great Western Road. Crighton, Nicky, and Titlebaum would all love an excuse to shutter Farren's. Jack had said he'd sort it with the court and he hasn't—he's failed Joe. Jack expects what's his, though, and sends word back via Mickey. Joe tells Mickey there's nothing to give; with Jack on the lam the Japanese have taken the opportunity to tear up their verbal agreement with the syndicate, and now the Kempeitai are upping the taxes arbitrarily. There's no more negotiation over sticks of yakitori and glasses of Asahi beer up in Little Tokyo. Tell Jack to get out of town and stay gone, Joe says. Mickey knows Jack's not going to like that. Joe shrugs, throws his arms wide; there's nothing he can do for him.

But what if Jack gets crazy ideas? Joe shuts Farren's for a couple of nights, heads home for the first time in a month, and tells Nellie he's boltholing till the air clears and Riley has shot town. She tells him to bolthole for as long as he wants, because she's done. This isn't how it was supposed to be—hiding out from some lowlife American gangster; Joe still working his way through the chorus lines; theirs is the biggest casino in town, but paying all the money to the Japs. Joe begs and pleads, asks her for one last chance. She turns those dark eyes on him and says no more. She's out the door and down the stairs. He sees the Buick on the street with the engine running, smoke misting out the exhaust. He realises she's packed, loaded the car already, and she's not coming back.

Nellie heads to the docks once more; they're as crowded as ever. The Buick pushes through the crowds, the chauffeur leaning hard on the horn, scattering Chinese families clutching their belongings in bulging burlap sacks, children strapped to their backs, trying desperately to get on the already overcrowded steamers heading upriver—away from the Japanese. If they can make it back inland, back to their remote ancestral villages, then perhaps they can disappear, be safe, survive. The Buick, along with other Shanghailanders' cars, heads farther along the quayside to where evacuation and repatriation ships are moored, filled with the last of those who can afford to leave. Last time Nellie came here she was unprepared, she had no ticket and had to go back home to Joe. But this time she's ready. The Chinese chauffeur pulls up close to the gangplank, instructs the milling porters to take the lady's luggage from the trunk. He holds the door open for Nellie, and she steps out onto the quayside. She hands the chauffeur an envelope—a last token, a last gift. He tips his hat and nods, turns and drives away. The porters carry her bags up the gangplank while she shows her ticket to the purser. The small gate is opened, and Nellie walks up the steep gangplank. She has stepped off Chinese soil, off the terra firma of Shanghai into the comforting embrace of the ship. She is shown to her cabin, her trunk already there. She tips the porter, closes the door, slips the lock. She will unpack later, but for now, from her handbag, she takes out the Movado Pullman travel clock with the dark-red Morocco leather case Joe bought her back in the days when they still lived in that cold-water apartment on Woo Foo Lane and danced every night under the spotlight at the old, now long gone, Majestic Hotel. She places the clock on her bedside table, lies down, the freshly laundered pillow under her head, and gazes at its face, the second hand ticking the minutes by. She thinks back over the fifteen years since the Midnight Frolics, meeting Joe, dancing in Kobe, Batavia, Manila, Singapore. She remembers the Majestic and dancing with Douglas Fairbanks, Whitey's band, Woo Foo Lane early mornings when they didn't have much but were happy. The Follies tours and then the Paramount, the Canidrome . . . countless chorus lines recruited, rehearsed; her Aztec shimmy; those waltzes and tangoes with Joe. As Nellie feels the ship slip its moorings she chooses not to think of Joe's infidelities, the rows, the fights, the stupidity of doing business with Riley. Rather she thinks of the sprung floor of the Majestic, the cut of Joe's suit, the shine of his shoes, the flash of his smile as they moved effortlessly, knowing the eyes of the entire crowd were upon them. Shanghai had been good to them for longer than it was good to most. But Nellie knew that Shanghai always exacted her price in return for the good times and the profits, and Joe was now going to have to pay it.

As the ship steams away from the Bund, Nellie Farren doesn't even look out her porthole to watch the city pass by for the last time. She pulls the curtain and shuts out Shanghai for good.

33

Christmas Eve 1940. Snow is still whipping round the city, slushy in the Settlement, settling on the red-tiled rooftops of Frenchtown, leaking in through the jerry-built ceilings of the Badlands. Cast-iron buckets on the dance floor of Farren's catch the seepage during the day. On any previous Christmas Eve, from the roof of the Park Hotel on Bubbling Well Road, say, or the top of the Observatory at Siccawei, you'd see a skyline full of thin smoke trails from five thousand chimneys. Now the telltale wisps are few and far between. Little Tokyo is still warm thanks to preferential treatment, but even the take-what-it-wants Badlands is cold. The night sky shows nothing but stars.

It's the fourth winter since the Japanese invasion. The residents of Nantao old town shiver in their drafty shacks as Imperial Navy bluejackets tour the new comfort houses and hastily erected gambling sheds of the quarter. Council carts collect the frozen dead in the Settlement; the trucks of the Chinese Buddhist Benevolent Society pick up those of the Badlands. Six hundred fifty corpses are collected on one bitter December night; 450 of them are babies or small children. The public transport system is suspended as the electricity cuts out: trolley cars stall, and passengers get out and walk or slip up the Nanking Road. The few cars still with gasoline inch along Canton Road and down the Bund. The streets are uneasily empty as folks stay indoors and contemplate 1941, evacuation ships, and routes to Free China. It's Europe's second Christmas of war, and while the Luftwaffe set Piccadilly ablaze, Shanghai shivers on.

The syndicate is still holding, but without Jack to negotiate with his contacts, the Kempeitai are demanding higher taxes. There's been no sign of the SMP in the Badlands. You'd be forgiven for thinking Commissioner Bourne and the SMP were never going to act. Yet finally it begins, that Christmas Eve, but it's anticlimactic. The SMP Reserve Unit, aka the Riot Squad, backed up by armed Sikhs and Chinese constables, hits the Avenue Haig. They raid the Pai Loh, a number 76–controlled gambling joint. DSI John Crighton leads the charge into the large, square ballroom. The pit floor is covered with tables, around which mostly Chinese gamblers play fan-tan and roulette. The cops scatter the teacups and liquor glasses and crunch over the floor, which is covered in discarded melon seed shells spat out by those hunched around the tables. The Pai Loh isn't Farren's or the Arizona or the Ali-Baba; it's a Chinese joint that does things the Chinese way. SMP constables storm the balconies where Chinese businessmen sit with their mistresses—off-duty taxi dancers in cheongsams, Eurasian Macanese women in tight-fitting Western suits. Those up high usually place bets by lowering silver dollars in small baskets on strings to the pit bosses below, a veritable stream of baskets constantly moving up and down, an elaborate pulley system across the ceiling. To the side of each table a cashier makes the bet, biting each piece of silver to verify its authenticity. A shroff notes the bet in a ledger next to scales that can weigh jewellery or ingots to value them. The Crime Squad makes ninety-four arrests, confiscates the roulette wheels, fan-tan tables, and a sizeable quantity of opium and somewhat less of cocaine, heroin, and morphine. The Chinese cry foul, why just them raided, why not the foreign devil–run casinos too? Most assume this is just a test run, and more raids will follow.

Early hours of Christmas morning, snow falling still, the party rolls on, the raids don't come. Farren's, Eventail, the Argentina, Elly Widler's Six Nations, Perpetuo's 37427, the St. George's Garden, Bothelo's Silver Palace . . . the Badlands stays open, even though Jack's not haggling about the taxes anymore and they're screeching skywards. The man in question spends Christmas unknown to everyone but the closest of close Friends in a back room at the Six Nations. Elly Widler sends a turkey; Mickey brings bennies from the doc; Babe carves; Jack swears he'll get revenge on Joe for freezing him out.

Inside the barbed-wire encirclement, it's the Gardenia's last night. Vertinsky's debts are huge; he can't support his and Boobee's cocaine habits. He jokes in his last floor show that cocaine keeps out the freezing night—look at Boobee still in a backless chiffon dress; she doesn't feel the cold. But then, Russians don't, though God grant us Stalin freezes in the Kremlin tonight and his *khuy* drops off—Vertinsky cracking wise all night, eyeballs wide, the master MC, high as a fucking kite. He'll be reduced to peforming in the few remaining Russian clubs for tips and then hugging the bar at Farren's till dawn, drinking on Joe's tab. He'll eventually manage to kick the white powder. But Boobee will continue to trawl the Badlands in search of a score, until one time she won't come back.

Across the Badlands, barmen huddle by the radiogram listening to the BBC's Eastern Service that crackles and intermittently cuts out thanks to Jap blockers. Still Herbert Moy squawks on XGRS that all of China will soon be 'liberated', under a 'new order for a new Asia'. Don Chisholm rants that England will fall by next Chinese New Year, 'a new Europe united under the undefeatable Third Reich'. Sam Titlebaum is putting out feelers looking for Jack, but his rounds involve plenty of libations and Christmas merriment too. Little Nicky tells him to focus on Jack; they had him, and his absconding under their noses was a massive loss of face. At Farrens's Joe takes his meals in his office; the *boychiks* remain wary of an unscheduled Riley visitation that everyone knows could never end well. But he never shows.

Joe keeps things going, just about. He pays through the nose for coal from Hongay's on the North Szechuen Road. Hongay has stockpiles it pays Shantung strongarm guards to protect at night. Joe starts to feel that things are getting back to some kind of normality, even with Nellie gone. He never got to ask the chauffeur which boat she took—the Buick and the driver never showed again after dropping Nellie off dockside. He prays Jack has done the sensible thing for once, hopped a tramp steamer and is halfway to Batavia or Pago Pago by now. Nothing to do but keep on keeping on. Joe ensures his boilers are stoked and the joint warm, pushes the acts on stage and orders the band to keep playing. The Farren's chips are still swept up across the green felt of the gaming tables with Albert Rosenbaum now as pit boss, signing the markers in Jack's absence. The Filipino croupiers shiver in the cold; the swells keep gambling undaunted.

As dawn approaches the band continues to play—the Manila-men musicians figure it's better to stay on the stage in the warmth than head home through the cold to their garret flops. Joe insists on festive jolliness: Wally Lunzer roams the joint as a rock-solid Father Christmas, red suit covering his Red 9, fake beard and a suspiciously German-sounding 'Ho ho, *meine leibchen*'. The waitresses are dressed as elves with mistletoe pinned to their caps, cheek-pecking the swells. Joe Farren passes the punch bowl, as much the host as ever. He eyes the chorus girls dancing to jazzed-up carols and the Hartnells spinning to a high-speed 'Jingle Bells' as the aerialist soars over the diners in a Jack Frost costume. Whatever the season, however raucous the party, some keep to their chosen vices. Upstairs, Al makes sure Alice Daisy Simmons and the other hardcore gamblers are comped drinks, get cold plates of turkey and lights for their cigarettes. Those roulette wheels just keep on spinning.

34

Firecrackers and explosions across the Badlands welcome the Chinese New Year of 1941. It's the year of the snake—how very fitting. The dragon has departed but breathes fire till the last. Now the snake slides out of the ashes, through the muck of northern Shanghai, across the fetid, silted Soochow Creek into the Settlement and makes its way westwards down into the Badlands. Across the city, the January Spring Festival turns into a bloody month.

Chinese New Year is traditionally when all debts come due and Shanghai crime rates go sky high. This year does not disappoint. On the first day of the lunar new year, seven armed robberies are reported before noon, shots fired at every heist; a European Shanghailander is forced into a public toilet at gunpoint by thugs and relieved of his money, clothes, shoes, and watch. A bus is boarded by ten 'juveniles' on the Avenue Eddy, who rampage through the bus snatching necklaces and pulling rings from the passengers before jumping off and disappearing. Japanese police engage in a shootout with four ronin on the Bubbling Well Road, subdue them, and find them in possession of sixty packets of high-grade heroin, heading towards the Badlands.

In the days and weeks following, it continues. A Chinese sanitation worker is gunned down in broad daylight on the Nanking

DD's Bubbling
Well Road illustration
(*from the DD's Cocktail Guide, 1939*)

870 Bubbling Well Road

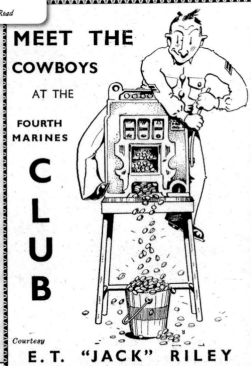

RIGHT:
An advert for Jack Riley's
slot machines in *Walla Walla*
(the newspaper of the 4th
Marines in Shanghai), 1940

BELOW:
DD's Avenue Joffre
Chinese New Year flyer, 1941
(*The China Press*)

MEET THE
COWBOYS
AT THE
FOURTH
MARINES
CLUB
Courtesy
E. T. "JACK" RILEY

ENJOY YOUR
LUNAR NEW YEAR'S EVE
AT
DD's Night Club
TINO AND HIS ORCHESTRA
815 Avenue Joffre   Telephone 71609

Slot machine at the Astoria Confectionary and Tea-Rooms
at No.7 Broadway (opposite the Astor House Hotel)
(Courtesy of Daphne Skillen)

Slot machines in the Russian restaurant and nightclub Arcadia
(291 Route Amiral Courbet), 1940
(Courtesy of Katya Knyazeva)

ABOVE AND BELOW:
Larissa Andersen promotional photographs, 1940
(Issued by the Tower Club)

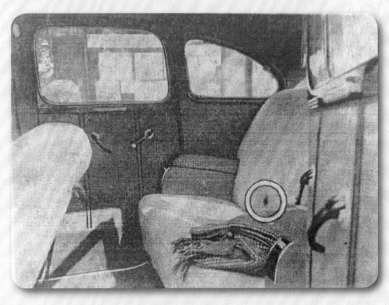

ABOVE AND BELOW:
Godfrey Phillips's gunshot-damaged car, 1940.
A bullet hole in the seat shows how close Phillips came to being hit.
(North-China Daily News)

ABOVE, RIGHT, BELOW:
Buck Clayton, Derby and
the Harlem Gentlemen
at the Canidrome
*(Courtesy of University of
Missouri–Kansas City, Miller
Nicholls Library, LaBudde
Special Collections)*

OPPOSITE PAGE:
Old Shanghai postcards
*(Courtesy of author's
collection)*

从和平纪念塔远望上海外滩的豪华高层建筑。

The Bund

摄于本世纪30年代的上海南京路。

Nanking Road

1934年建成的上海百老汇大厦,在外白渡桥北岸,是一座具有早期现代派风格的建筑。外观简洁,高22层。

Broadway Mansions and the Garden Bridge

THE CHINA WEEKLY
REVIEW

報論評氏勒密
A Weekly Newspaper Established in 1917

February 8, 1941

Puppet Gunmen Rub Another Name
off Nanking's Blacklist of Journalists

Gauss-Johnson Switch

Badlands Policing Fiasco

Axis Whispering Campaign

Shanghai Finance Faces Bitter Currency
Battle, Declares John Ahlers

VOLUME 95   PRICE 80 CENTS (in China)   NUMBER 10

LEFT AND BELOW:
The *China Weekly Review*
reports on the Badlands
policing fiasco and
gang warfare
(China Weekly Review)

THE CHINA
WEEKLY
REVIEW

報論評氏勒密
A Weekly Newspaper Established in 1917

February 22, 1941

Professor "Bill" Sung Takes Over
Helm of St. John's University

Gang Warfare Opens

Occidental Predicament

Mme. Chiang Warns West

Puppet Efforts to Gain Seats on
Shanghai Municipal Council Defeated

VOLUME 95   PRICE 80 CENTS (in China)   NUMBER 12

New Order in Shanghai's
Night Life

Shanghai Evening Post

ABOVE:
Badlands gangster cartoon, 1941
(North-China Daily News)

WESTERN
AREA
POLICE
ACCORD

Now a Bit of Mopping-up ?

ABOVE:
Cartoon by the famous White
Russian artist Sapajou, 1941
(North-China Daily News)

Road—the shooters hop the barricades and disappear into the Badlands as the SMP are left gawking. The pro–Free China *Shun Pao* newspaper is bombed for the third time in six months—a Fah Wah village gang pulls up in hijacked rickshaws and lobs four hand grenades into the lobby. Number 76 pays them a measly fifty Chinese bucks for it. More *lieu-maung* hold up the Brenan Road Post Office and relieve a White Russian woman of a diamond ring. When a British customer intervenes, they shoot him in the back with an Imperial Army–issue pistol. The ambulance takes more than an hour to arrive, though the Country Hospital on Great Western Road and St Luke's on the corner of Yu Yuen are both only minutes away. The man dies in the ambulance, and the Japanese police make no arrests.

The newspapers don't have enough hacks to cover the crime wave. A pro-puppet Chinese lawyer is gunned down on a Frenchtown street by assassins from a passing black Citroën. A Little Tokyo businessman is shot in the head at point-blank range on Nanking Road. The owner of the Sung Chi Egg Company is shot repeatedly while sitting at his desk on Kweichow Road—even eggs are a racket now as the price triples, quadruples. A number 76 officer kidnaps and then kills a Yu Yuen Road businessman; a Chinese SMP constable goes rogue and shoots a fellow officer before being disarmed. A young Chinese man, loaded down with gambling debts from the Badlands, drugs and murders his aunt, steals her money and jewellery, and gets caught trying to fence the trinkets to pay his bad debts; six *lieu-maung* raid a house on Sinza Road, shoot the owners and steal jewellery; a gun battle breaks out in broad daylight on a Frenchtown street as yet another gang attempts to rob the home of the manager of the Great World Amusement Palace; three pedestrians are robbed at gunpoint on Shantung Road in the heart of the Settlement in one day.

Even in the midst of this, the SMP are still on the hunt for Shanghai's public enemy number one. Jack Riley is thought to be residing in the Badlands under Japanese protection, crashing at the Six Nations. Sam Titlebaum gets over there with Little Nicky close behind, but Jack has moved on by the time they arrive. John Crighton strongarms Joe, but Farren says he has no idea where Jack is—that partnership is finished.

The snake slithers on—politics, thievery, war, and gangsterism intermixed and unstoppable. Bodies that fall in disputed territory, gunned down on a Saturday, are still lying there on Monday. And still the SMP raids on the foreign-run Badlands casinos haven't come. The Municipal Council is demanding action on the escalating crime rate; the foreign consuls in the city want something done about the murders; the Settlement's Ratepayers' Association is threatening a tax strike if the crime wave on their doorstep isn't tackled. Commissioner Bourne can't let the situation stand much longer.

SHOPPING NEWS
—'BREVITIES'—
MONDAY, JANUARY 27, 1941

Shopping News has gotta call it like it is. Our ruling Municipal Council is failing to deal adequately with Shanghai's trade. Given the current shortages of everything, one would imagine our Settlement's trade to be booming, but no—just the opposite. The Council has failed to negotiate import and export terms with the Japanese and consequently the Settlement's access to raw materials is nearly non-existent. Cotton mills have reduced their output 30 per cent; the tea trade and the silk filatures are at a standstill; American oil companies are faced with a Japanese monopoly. And yet the Council allows the Gas Tycoons to raise prices and the phone company to charge more. Just whose side are the Council on?

Shopping News got a 'for our eyes only' peek at a new SMP memorandum that notes that 90 per cent of armed crimes in the Settlement in which pistols were seized or bullets recovered were committed with 'hot' weapons stolen from Chinese or Sikh Constables while they were on duty in the Badlands. Can this be purely accidental? We think not, as all patrols are now four-men strong by order of Commissioner Bourne for protection. Could it be, as has been whispered to us, that the traffic in SMP armaments is now brisk with foreign constables profiteering greatly, middle men amassing fortunes, desperadoes arming themselves easily, and constables claiming to have 'lost' their weapons before being issued with new weapons at the ratepayers' expense? Where do all these 'lost' firearms go? Surely a full and searching enquiry is required immediately.

Action is needed <u>NOW</u>—1940's deadly tally? Nine SMP officers killed in the line of duty including a foreign probationary sergeant, a Sikh, and seven Chinese, of whom two were superintendents. Last year's medals tally was the highest ever—two Class I and 51 Class II medals awarded.

Regular readers will no doubt be delighted to hear that, with Carroll Alcott's departure from Station XHMA, you can still tune over to XGRS and hear, 'The Call of the Orient'—nightly at 8 p.m.— with your host *Shopping News* Editor D. Chisholm. Just in case you're not on the airwaves we've arranged a 30% discount on all Zenith radios, including the newly arrived 1940 model, through our friends and partners at the Radio Service Company, 142 Museum Street. But hurry, the show's about to start and supplies are limited—call 12997 NOW, tell them you're a *Shopping News* subscriber and reserve your discounted Zenith Model 5-S-313.

Just dying to tell someone? Editorial: Rm 540, 233 Nanking Rd. Tel: Shanghai—10695

35

Six weeks after the SMP raid the Pai Loh, they finally start to try and get serious with the Badlands at last. On February 3, the edict goes out:

> WASP FORCE ORDERS ALL GAMBLING
> ESTABLISHMENTS AND OPIUM DENS
> TO CEASE ACTIVITY AND CLOSE
> FORTHWITH BY OFFICIAL ORDER.

But it's one thing to order something, another to make it happen. Most of the Chinese joints close, but those joints that pay the big taxes, and those patronised by number 76 chiefs, stay open. Chinese cops look the other way for squeeze or if a Mauser is waved in their faces. Bulletproof-vested SMP cops figure it's not their beat anyway and back away from confrontation.

The big earners keep their neon switched on: the Eventail, the Welcome Café, the Argentina, and Farren's. Word gets out from a belligerent and determined Joe: Farren's is staying open, come hell or high water. Inside, the lucky few, those still in Shanghai with cash to spend, sip champagne and snatch the caviar being passed round the tables on silver salvers. They're still willing to fight through the crowds and the music of the Badlands pavements to get there, past a Jewish refugee violin player, an old Russian in tattered tsarist costume from the last war, singing mournful songs of a homeland long gone, a blind Chinese scraping a sad melody from a homemade *huqin* fiddle. All of Shanghai's street music is sorrowful, all songs of the lost, the refugee, the dead, and the forgotten. But inside Farren's it's the music of America, black America, played by Manilamen and Macanese Eurasians for those left to listen.

How did Jack come to this? The money has run out; the slots aren't paying. With the Marines shipped out of town, the take at the few Mickey's got back in action is way, way down. The Velvet Sweet Shop dope cash is long gone. Jack's staring into the abyss. He needs more stake to get out of Shanghai . . . and Farren's is where he'll get it. Joe has done nothing to help him; Jack considers that partnership null and void. Farren is running the wheels and banking the take. His sources tell him the Kempeitai are letting Joe keep the lights on and the doors open in return for heightened daily taxes, while Jack Riley can't even walk in the door. He hears the tables are still raking it in, that Joe's got Al Rosenbaum running the roulette wheels and acting like he doesn't need and didn't ever need Jack. Joe needs to pay.

Slowly, a plan forms. At three a.m., wide-awake on his crash cot, he knows it's a shit one, but it's all he's got. He can set up a joint with Evelyn Oleaga fronting it—Badlands-protected, corner of Great Western and Edinburgh Roads. Evil Evelyn is in tight with the Japanese Naval High Command through her Axis connections, an Italian commander who's stupid sweet on her.

She has the kind of connections that can ring-fence the operation, pay off the Kempeitai, get number 76 to back off and scare away the WASPs. But he'll need twenty-five thousand American dollars to make it happen. There's only one place Jack knows of with that kind of cash inside: Farren's. Joe owes him that and more besides.

36

On February 15 Farren's is packed to the rafters—there are six hundred punters, mostly Americans and Brits who've decided not to evacuate. It's the only foreign-run casino in the Badlands to have a full house despite the Japanese wire, despite the curfew, despite the war, stagflation, gunmen at large, kidnappers rampant, the junkies and dealers on the street outside. Gentleman Joe remains the dapper host of the Shanghai night.

There's no plan but to get to Joe's safe, relieve him of the night's take, escape the city, wait till things calm down—and then Evil Evelyn's new casino. Mickey stays loyal, Schmidt too. To make up the numbers Jack pulls in gun-for-hire ronin from Hongkew and AWOL Fourth Marine mercenaries. Jack would like more reliable men, but Mickey says nobody wants to be part of it; Joe is too connected, his security is loyal, Rosenbaum knows everyone, and Carlos Garcia will cast you out and feed you to the wolves for this.

Jack is jagged on his usual strong coffee and Benzedrine. There's an itch under his skin that won't go away, his current predicament sitting heavy. If tonight goes well, he's got a way out, but one that will cost more than just cash. He'll be forever outside the syndicate afterwards. He figures, so what? He's been on his own since that shitty orphanage, Tulsa, McAlester, and the early days of Shanghai. It's nothing new.

Jack and his hastily assembled crew cross the Avenue Haig and cut through the rookeries and laneways onto the Great Western Road. Farren's neon is bright as they storm the door with canister bombs, split into two groups—blue flames spit up into the air from their Red 9s like wisps of opium smoke; Jack, Mickey, Schmidt, followed by men carrying baseball bats, black leather coshes, and pickaxe handles. It goes bad right from the start.

Schmidt knows Lunzer's reputation and makes a decision to up the odds. No delay at the door to warn those inside. The two men are eye-to-eye: Schmidt's pupils are dilated like a rabid dog's; Lunzer squints to stare him down—trying to communicate that this is not the way. Wally Lunzer reaches for his shoulder holster, and Schmidt raises his Red 9, aims, and pulls the trigger. Schmidt's calculation: men like Lunzer don't give second chances—hit fast, hit hard; always outnumbered, never outgunned. A correct assessment, but one that burns all possible bridges for Jack. Lunzer goes down with a bullet through the left eye, dead in an instant on the pavement of the Great Western Road. The noise of the shot registers faintly over the jazz and hubbub inside Farren's. The raid is on, the point of no return passed. Jack screams at Schmidt. There'll be no asking Joe nicely now.

Jack, Mickey, and Schmidt head upstairs, to the gambling floors, to the office where the safe is. BOOM—ceiling plaster falls, screams upstairs in the club's casino rooms. BOOM—the mirror behind the bandstand shatters, raining jagged glass blades on the heads of the Manilamen band, blood seeping through their white silk suits. BOOM—woodwork splinters off the bar. The raiders move through, smashing bottles, upending tables, kicking over music stands. Punters flee, crushed at the door aiming for the Great Western Road, tripping over Lunzer's body, kicking shards of skull and brain across the cobbles of the Badlands outside. Farren's staff gets clubbed with rifle butts, ronin knuckledusters land on boychik skulls, and best-quality Pyongyang leather coshes on exposed knees, elbows, necks. Jack and Schmidt hit the gaming floors, watch the punters and croupiers huddle under the roulette tables. Only Alice Daisy Simmons, Farren's regular and rich-girl daughter of one of the city's top Brit bullion sharks, stands there looking surprised to see him. She smiles slightly, and Jack involuntarily smiles back. Both Jack and Schmidt raise their Red 9s and fire towards the ceiling. More plaster falls. Then Jack looks back to Alice and sees her staring straight at him, but unseeing. Alice takes a richocheting bullet to the back; it severs her spine, and she drops dead by the roulette table she's been playing at. Jack walks towards her lifeless body—it wasn't meant to go like this—but Schmidt grabs him by the arm and motions upwards. To the top floor; to Joe's office.

And the office is where it finally plays out. The office where Joe and Jack once tallied the night's total and laughed out loud at their good fortune—taxes plus five; taxes plus ten; night after night while the going was good. The office where the dapper Ziegfeld of Shanghai and the Slots King buried the hatchet, forgot past enmities, and came together to become Solitary Island millionaires. Now Jack wants what's his.

Joe is standing by his desk, and there's no exit from the office but out into the club and the melee. Schmidt steps forward and cracks Joe's skull with the stock of his Mauser. He crumples on the floor, and Albert Rosenbaum, who's been dragged in too, raises his arms high in surrender, recognising Jack. Schmidt points his Mauser straight at the man's forehead.

Jack kneels and spins the wheel of the safe—he knows the combination, he'd been the one to set it—1-5-3-8-0; the telephone number for the Gordon Road Police Station, home of the SMP Anti-Gambling Squad. His little joke. The door swings open—*bupkis*; a couple of thousand Chinese bucks and some jewellery.

He stares hard at Rosenbaum. Hands still high, Rosenbaum tells Jack he's picked a bad night—Joe cleaned out the safe a half hour earlier to pay the local Kempeitai who are taking pretty much everything as tax now, thanks to you, Jack. The rest is on the tables. No time to stop and scoop it up; the call will have already gone out to the Riot Squad. Schmidt gun-butts the side of Rosenbaum's head and watches the man fall to the floor next to his boss. They turn and leave.

What Jack wanted, what he desperately needed, is gone. Jack, Mickey, Schmidt, and the new Friends head back downstairs and exit the club, over Lunzer's corpse. They step out onto the Great Western Road, now a crazy freakshow of hopped-up, terrified punters and Badlands trash in a state of total confusion. They separate, merge into the crowd, get lost among the mendicants, hustlers, whores, and Japs. In the lawless Badlands there's not even a siren—even the Riot Squad now to have negotiate their way through the Japanese barricades, and there's nothing the bluejackets like more than watching the squad fume while they check their paperwork. They slip into the zigzag lanes and alleyways of the Badlands; some head into Fah Wah village, up towards Yu Yuen Road and the Settlement beyond, others go across the Avenue Haig and past the French Garde Municipal barricades into Frenchtown. They melt into the rues and avenues, away from the Badlands, leaving behind their chaos.

The November 1940 truce between the foreign gangs that ruled Shanghai is over; it hadn't even lasted six months. The unprecedented syndicate of Shanghai's casino bosses and nightlife kings is laid waste in one night, courtesy of Jack T. Riley.

Scaremongers say the Japanese Imperial Army's biological warfare Unit 731 has released a million fleas infected with bubonic plague in the nearby port of Ningpo, tested in Manchukuo, perfected in Chekiang. Shanghai is next—the International Settlement will be targeted. The citizens of the Solitary Island avoid public transport and eye each other warily on the trams and the trolley-buses. Taxis do record business and hike their fares accordingly. Children are kept from school, food carts are deserted, gas masks sell out, windows are sealed and doors locked. A plague is coming. Thousands, hundreds of thousands, maybe, are dead in Ningpo. The rumour in Shanghai says the dead lie in the streets, that corpses are heaved into the canals and creeks, that ships are avoiding the port. Every fly, flea, nit—insect of any kind—is feared. The Japanese, of course, are immune. Everyone knows they take special pills flown in from Tokyo; they inject their soldiers with serums that protect them.

Every plane arching over the Shanghai skies is suspected. The stone houses of Shanghai's laneways and alleys reek of burnt Shanshi vinegar; the Chinese believe the fumes are an antidote. Unscrupulous black-marketeers sell jars of fake vinegar, promising that it will keep the fleas at bay, sending them to another house, another family, another body to infect. Soon the shops and markets of Shanghai sell out of vinegar, real or fake. There's a riot in Hongkew when supplies are rumoured to have arrived. The rumour mill continues to churn—America has ordered all of its nationals to evacuate Ningpo, and other foreigners are escaping too; even the missionaries are fleeing. The countryside is destroyed, and food shortages will accelerate. A Japanese plague will engulf Shanghai; the Japanese will march into the Settlement, crunching the bones of the dead beneath their boots. Resistance is futile.

This, people believed . . .

37

The Kempeitai and the thugs from number 76 are swaggering taller than ever after the Farren's raid—the syndicate looks to be in tatters. They up the daily taxes again, and the previously agreed ten grand daily limit is history now. Joe is furious and stubborn. He refuses to pay any more to the Kempeitai and the puppets—fuck the ronin; fuck the Kempeitai, they're just yakuza in khaki. The Badlands is now too bad to make money in. People stay away from Farren's, away from the Badlands; the take is seriously down.

The first repercussions of Joe's decision to refuse to pay taxes to the Japanese make themselves felt fast: the Kempeitai hassle his Chinese staff not to work for the 'number one Jew man', jostle the punters pulling up outside, cut his electricity, and try to send in troublemaking *lieu-maung* to start fights in the joint. Others pay the escalating taxes, which means the puppets only hate Joe more for holding out. John Crighton sits Joe down and says that the SMP might be able to help, if only they knew where Jack was. Joe stays schtum. Truth is he doesn't know and doesn't care where Jack is, and he doesn't believe John Crighton, senior and respected as he is in the SMP, can do anything about the Japs or number 76 now anyway.

As times get tough, the dope gets cut and then cut again, invariably with strychnine, leaving junkies and hopheads dying by the score. Cabbage Moh and the Cantonese Shumchun triads come north to carpetbag in Fah Wah village, boost their dope prices anyway despite the deteriorating quality and maintain their profit margins to kick back and fund Wang Ching-wei's crony regime. Illicit hooch becomes a lethal blend of eighty per cent ethanol, an old Prohibition trick, and drunks stagger and collapse on the Avenue Haig. Mike and his Music Masters dust off the old 'Jake Walk Blues' and lampoon the poor lushes outside, but nobody's laughing much now. A backfiring car has the remaining punters and the bar staff ducking involuntarily; a slamming kitchen door gets everyone tense. Number 76 thugs walk in and brazenly demand payment; WASP patrols cross the road and let it be known they're not going to get involved. The boychiks are plenty tough and face down the number 76 goons and their demands, but it can't happen indefinitely. The Badlands is awash with guns—.32s, .45s, Mauser Red 9s . . . they seep in, changing hands for just a few dollars, with ammo for cents; where they all come from is a mystery. A gun now costs the same as a catty of rice. Food inflation; firearms deflation—that's the Badlands' law of supply and demand.

In the wake of Jack's raid, the unofficial leader of Shanghai's foreign hack pack, J. B. Powell, declares '*GANG WARFARE OPENS*' on the front page of his anti–number 76 *China Weekly Review*; before, it was just the usual Chinese gangs fighting for turf, but white men blasting each other away on the Great Western Road is something altogether different for Shanghailander society to cope with. Chicago has come to the Whangpoo. What happened at Farren's shows up the SMP's paltry attempts to control the gambling joints, their lack of effective raids and closures. Commissioner Bourne must be shamefaced—two foreign racketeers just went head-to-head and left a dead body on the Great Western Road in sight of numerous Settlement swells. When any Badlands holdup man can rent a gun for two bucks fifty, where do you even start looking for the culprits? The WASPs, never much to start with, have degenerated into a force of bogus cops who turn the other cheek for a few shillings and put cotton wool in their ears when the shooting starts. They'll gladly kick a beggar into the shadows or run a freelancing doper off the strip, but they're not detectives. The papers reveal that phone calls from Farren's to the SMP station, a stone's throw away on Great Western Road, had gone unheeded; the SMP had only turned up after the fact because an armoured car, passing nearby, was stopped in the street by fleeing customers. There's an outcry in the *North-China Daily News* letters page, excoriating editorials in the *China Weekly Review*.

Bourne reacts by ordering John Crighton's Crime Squad into the Badlands in force—it's finally, at long last, time to send in the heavies. It's gone beyond Chinese and foreign ne'er-do-wells. Alice Daisy Simmons, just turned twenty-eight, lifeless on a gurney, determines his decision. Old man Simmons is creating merry hell, demanding action and reminding all and sundry that his bullion profits have served the Settlement nicely over the years. He calls Bourne personally to demand that his daughter's killers be brought to book.

The SMP print boys have been all over Farren's and lifted a million dabs—punters, employees, gunmen, boychiks. It's almost useless, as there's no way to print those who fled the scene, whether customers or raiders. But one set keeps coming up again and again . . . smudged, unreadable, corroded, and deformed. Crighton thinks back to the FBI and their nifty detective work. He gets the scenario almost right: Jack and Joe fall out; Jack tries to take out Joe and claim the business for himself—from Slots King to Badlands King? Crighton's got Joe and his boys in his interrogation room on constant rotation, and it's always the same question: where's Jack? They stay defiantly silent. He brings U.S. marshal Sam Titlebaum on board, who's been part of the search since Jack skipped bail. Titlebaum and Crighton take the prints they figure must be Riley's to Little Nicky, who cables them to his fed contacts in D.C. Can they work their magic again?

The grand buildings of the Country Hospital on the Great Western Road represent the Badlands' only still-functioning medical facility—cautious nurses and doctors refused to work at the others; even the missionaries have moved out and seemingly given up on the district. Sam Titlebaum and John Crighton come to see the dead. In the morgue, reeking of formaldehyde, the pair from the Farren's raid lie side by side: Alice Daisy Simmons and Walter Lunzer, both on slabs, naked and pale, their identical regulation SMP rubber body bags dumped in a corner. They hadn't known each other in life; their trajectories to Shanghai and their relative positions on the Settlement's social totem pole were distant, but they are now close in death. John Crighton is shocked to see Alice's body isn't covered; he finds a sheet and throws it over her to at least provide some dignity. Both have nicotine-stained fingers and dyed black hair. Lunzer is missing his top plate, making his face look like it has fallen in, the left side of his head bloody still, the back of his skull completely missing. Alice looks almost as if she's sleeping. The pathologist had extracted a Mauser slug from her spine.

It's not only Commissioner Bourne who's in a permanent rage; the Honourable Judge Helmick's about fit to have a stroke. Forget Farren's; forget a Badlands casino getting turned over. Alice represents the 400, the families who had built the treaty port of Shanghai from a fishing village to a great metropolis of staggering wealth in a single century. She was not one of Helmick's 'vice merchants, sharks, or bucaneers' and her death is like a call to arms. The Settlement is the bastion that must be protected. Helmick is fuming, spitting across the table, veins popping—with immediate effect, every effort of the U.S. marshal's office and the Shanghai Municipal Police is to be directed towards finding, capturing, imprisoning, and extraditing bail jumper and crime kingpin Jack T. Riley.

38

By order of the police commissioner, all leave is cancelled. The plan of attack takes shape at a late-night meeting of the SMP's top brass, the elite of the Settlement's forces of law and order—Commisioner Bourne, of course, with John Crighton beside him. The other men are all Brits, all Shanghai cops of long standing, all proven thief-takers, rackets busters, and known to be incorruptible. They're joined by Martin Nicholson of the U.S. Treasury and Sam Titlebaum, recently appointed U.S. marshal, along to represent the U.S. Department of Justice in Shanghai.

It's Crighton's office, but Bourne is in charge. Crighton is trying to open a window as Titlebaum lights a cigarette, blowing smoke up into the fluorescent lighting, passing around his hip flask. Crighton takes a swig and gags on the sweet-sour mash bourbon, but it keeps the February cold out. It's no joke—SMP HQ is a cooler for real, as the Japs work hard to ensure there are no coal deliveries. The main subject for discussion this evening: the indictment, apprehension, and prosecution of Shanghai's most notorious fugitive from justice, officially still referred to—for the moment—as Jack T. Riley.

Little Nicky lays out the story of the prints at Farren's, and Crighton and Titlebaum get the irony—a thousand prints tell no story, but one indistinct set might reveal a clear and concise narrative. By seeking to obliterate his past, Jack Riley has reinforced his current predicament and screwed his future.

The feds in D.C. have cabled back a no-go, though—the prints are too partial, too smeared, and they can't make a match with Becker/Riley's prints on file. It's a judicial dead end, but the cops know Jack is desperate. By opting not to offer him sanctuary, the Japanese have disowned Riley and ended all negotiations with the syndicate; for breaking their rules, the syndicate has cast him out and will also offer no protection. If he's behind the raid, then that only further proves his desperation. The Kempeitai let the SMP know they will not get in the way of their apprehension of one Edward T. Riley. Jack's pretty much alone now. With the countryside around Shanghai under Japanese occupation and all civilian non-Japanese shipping on the Whangpoo at a standstill, that means he's still in the city . . . somewhere. They will seek him out; the Riot Squad's Red Maria armoured truck is at their disposal, and there's no time like the present to shake up Shanghai's underbelly. In capturing Riley, the SMP can shut down everyone else too.

They target the gambling dens immediately. The Anti-Gambling Squad, with the SMP riot van in tow, crashes the doors at the Silver Palace, José Bothelo's long-running gambling dive. Nine Chinese croupiers are arrested, wheels confiscated and plenty of dope, but no Jack. Bothelo skips town for neutral Macao on a Portuguese-flagged tramp steamer early the next morning. They bust the Portuguese mob–run 37427 club, and this time they throw supply and sale of opium onto the charge sheet along with running illegal wheels. Next morning the Portuguese Consular Court doesn't budge, dispensing only small-time fines all round, which indicates Tony Perpetuo has been greasing palms monthly to good effect for years. Lisbon loyalties stand strong; Powell's *China Weekly Review* claims the Portuguese consul had a financial interest in both the 37427 and the Silver Palace. Still, Fat Tony's joint is shuttered.

The next night they change tack and raid the Burlington Hotel, where Bill Hawkins runs illegal roulette wheels in the fancy suites. The squad picks up fourteen Chinese croupiers, but no Jack. They bust an illegal poker game that Jack occasionally sat in on at the Stock Exchange Building on Kiukiang Road. Five card players go down for two months each—but no Jack. Later that week it's a busy night again for the Red Maria: they bust a Chinese-only casino and dope den on a lane off Hwakee Avenue; a tip-off said Jack was holed up there. No Jack, but they arrest an old woman, who turns out to be Cabbage Moh's mother. It's just gangster score-settling. Cabbage Moh gets his ma bailed and moves her into the fortress of Fah Wah village, vowing he'll chop any copper ever comes for her again.

Titlebaum is swearing to the papers he'll take down Jack Riley and restore the good name of Uncle Sam in Shanghai. While the SMP is crashing gambling joints, Titlebaum sweats what's left of the Riley crew. He picks up Schmidt, Riley's Mauser-toting Teutonic henchman, but the tough German says *nichts*. Sam bangs Mickey O'Brien in the U.S. court lockup and goes at him day and night for thirty-six hours, trying to get him to link Jack to the Farren's raid. Mickey takes the blows, the not insubstantial Shanghai telephone book on the head, the squeezed scrotum, and laughs in Titlebaum's face. Mickey O'Brien, righteous bucko mate, chief Friend of Riley, give Jack up?—squeeze the other one, marshal, it's got bells on it. Why do you care anyway? Somebody did you a favour—Jack can't call in your marker now, and Joe's almost out of business. The telephone book comes down hard again.

Day three of the hunt—Titlebaum goes outside his remit and kicks down doors at the Broadway Mansions to pull in the remnants of Elly Widler's crew. They wave their Swiss passports and tell Sam he'll get nothing this side of hell freezing over. Call the consul, he knows us all well. He raids the Burlington again, smashing the wheels, and interrogates Bill Hawkins. The old man tells him he's never told a Shanghai copper anything in forty years and isn't about to start. Hawkins decides it's time to retire and head home—after four decades running casinos on the China Coast, it's back to Manchester. Fellow old-timer Stuart Price says he doesn't remember anything these days and is just an old man and a good citizen. Titlebaum busts the Venus Café, but Sam Levy tells him he's not seen Jack since Al Israel's funeral.

The last few marines left in Shanghai awaiting rotation out say Riley is on the lam and you'll never catch old Jack. Titlebaum causes a diplomatic row by crossing the border and strongarming into a bunch of Frenchtown boîtes and cathouses. He rousts every Blood Alley dive bar and gets nothing but lush-head AWOL marines who think Jack's a kingpin and a stand-up fella. He rousts the Manila and busts Babe at the bar, but she's permanently tight-lipped except for a few choice curses. He turns over the short-time flops at the back of the Great World and finds a bunch of Chekiang whores, some startled Chinese men, one embarrassed German with a swastika armband, his trousers round his ankles, and two Great World prostitutes all dolled up and *déshabillé*. Titlebaum thinks of busting Carlos Garcia at the Canidrome, but then thinks better of it; some people are just too powerful.

Day four: Sam moves westward. Into Fah Wah village, with Crighton's boys and the Riot Squad as backup and all armed to the teeth in case the triads fight back en masse. Cabbage Moh never opens his mouth, never even looks Titlebaum in the eye, spits Canto at him and Sam gets his drift—Cabbage would rather stab his own stinking brood to death than squeal. Rousting his ma didn't go down well with the Shumchun boss. The triads are another ball game anyway, and Sam's not got time to try to learn their crazy rules. He raids the Yu Yuen Road garrets, to number 76's anger—he's causing a scene, he's trampling over Solitary Island protocol. The SMP squirms, but Judge Helmick tells him to carry on busting balls—this is about American prestige. Desperate now, Sam storms the ring-fenced Dennis Apartments on the Bubbling Well

Road—Apartment 35A has been a high-end poker game, dope parlour, and bordello for connected Shanghailander taipans for years. Finally, a step too far. Helmick tells him to stop ruffling the feathers of the remaining 400. Concentrate on the Badlands.

In that case: Farren's. Sam left it till last, knowing it could be embarrassing because of his unpaid gambling debts from before. The boychiks spit in the dance floor's sawdust when they hear Riley's name but say nothing. Joe asks Sam if he'd like to settle his outstanding markers while he's here. Albert Rosenbaum scribbles down the amount for him on a Farren's napkin—multiple zeros and underlined. Sam exits sharpish.

Sam knows Riley hasn't left town. He's here, he's close, Sam can smell the Slots King; hear him laughing. But where's Jack?

39

It's ten days since the Farren's raid. Blood Alley's too hot. Jack signs over the Manhattan to Mickey, who keeps him in cash. The cash is stuffed in Jack's leather baseball bag with that rabbit ball, his mitt, and those old Oklahoma State Pen magic dice for company. Sam Titlebaum just misses him at the 37427—Jack blows in and hangs with the Lisbon *rufiões* for a few days. Their coffee is good but they're breaking in broads all day and boozing all night. He transfers over to the Burlington, but Bill Hawkins, who's been dealing cards and spinning wheels in Shanghai since the turn of the century, is nervous. He'd been repeatedly busted, the gig was up, and he is getting out of town. Anyway, Crighton's boys are watching the hotel day and night. Jack crashes in the Burlington's attic for a couple of days and doesn't like it much—bats, birdshit, and dry bread for supper, and then having to sneak out in a laundry wagon past the SMP prowl car on the street outside. So. . . . a Murphy bed at Broadway Mansions with the Russian card sharps; an upstairs flat over the Isis Cinema in Hongkew, courtesy of Sam Levy; a cot on the floor of the manager's office at the old Fantasio Dance Hall . . . he keeps on moving, handing out ever larger parcels of cash to keep himself safe. Fah Wah's secure and Titlebaum can't get in there easily, but Cabbage and his triads can't be trusted not to sell him out. Jack's years of working virtually solo mean he's on his own.

He catches naps in the back rows of the Paris Cinema on the Avenue Joffre, a second-run house with German movies and a mostly Russian crowd who avoid eye contact. Jack understands not a word, but it's warm and dry and dark, and he can stay out of sight. Schmidt slips in and pushes the cash-stuffed baseball bag across to Jack. He spends nights back with Babe at Leong's place, the Moon Palace: Babe in a dope haze and Jack bored. John Crighton and the SMP raid it on a tip-off but Jack's gone—just. Leong got advance warning, and they miss Jack by minutes; everyone in Shanghai is selling everyone else out in these final days. Still, Titlebaum is moving fast and getting closer. Mickey says Evelyn Oleaga will stash him.

But there's a catch—with Evil Evelyn there's always a catch. Just ask that poor schmuck Paco back in Manila, or any of her subsequent lovers who've been left high, dry, and broke. Evelyn's finally got her long-planned male brothel up and running. She brings in the lonely Shanghailander ladies and lets her stable of pretty-boy Latino gigolos take care of them . . . and then it's light blackmailing with the negatives of their illicit funtime. Riley thinks it's crazy, but he needs a hidey-hole bad. Evelyn wants a cool twenty grand to keep him till the heat dies down. Jack knows he hasn't got much choice, but he doesn't know how fucking long that will be. She'll bleed him dry, and Jack knows he can trust Evil Evelyn about as far as he can throw her, but he's got Titlebaum, Crighton, the Kempeitai, and some seriously pissed-off boychiks all on his tail.

Evelyn is still on board with her long-term plan too: the Axis-friendly casino on Edinburgh Road, the edge of the Badlands, with wheels from Jack's former Macao contacts. All she needs is an additional twenty-five grand to get up and running, and Jack can manage the house, just like at Farren's. Evelyn can square it with the Kempeitai to take Jack back into the fold. He'd be beyond Crighton and Titlebaum in the Badlands with Kempeitai protection and number 76 security to warn off the Settlement authorities. He'll run the risk of boychik revenge, but it's better than a crash cot in an attic. But that's twenty-five grand on top of the twenty grand to stash him—Evelyn's not cheap. Where to get the cash now?

Jack finds himself in a room at the male bordello on the Avenue Joffre, its location and raison d'être so far unknown to the SMP and Garde Municipal. Thanks to the doc, he's got a regular supply of bennies. Evelyn brings him corned beef hash from the Venus, hamburgers done Shanghai-style with a fried egg on top, and a few dollar bills collected from a few final admiring Friends to show solidarity for the old times. Jack sends word via Mickey to his lawyers to pay her the twenty-G stash money in telephone, gas, and tram company shares they've been holding for him. To kill time he chucks those well-worn Okie dice against the skirting board all day, a blanket on the floor to muffle the noise, and wins every time. He tosses the baseball and catches it in his mitt—again and again and again. Comings and goings all day, Evelyn in her trademark Shanghai madam's garishly coloured kimonos, always with that shrill laugh, the whiff of chypre, against a backdrop of married-dame chatter, Tagalog gossip, and Spanish backtalk from her Argentine pretty boys, morning till night. The bedsteads need oiling.

The hunt continues in earnest. The radio says every cop has been issued a photograph of Riley, and traitors Moy and Chisholm demand Jack's capture on XRGS. Moy says he's an example of the rottenness of American society; Chisholm says the new order will weed out all the Jack Rileys from China. Titlebaum says they're getting close. Crighton is liaising with the WASPs; their previous inaction will not be tolerated. The Badlands will not be safe territory for Jack Riley.

Jack still hasn't worked out a way to make money. Until he can, he's on borrowed time. Mickey O'Brien sends notes but can't visit—Crighton's got plainclothes boys on Blood Alley scoping the Manhattan, a squad car outside each DD's branch—Mickey's movements are now extremely limited. Mickey sells the MG to a bachelor griffin with a need for speed. Jack tears up at the news; it's the first time he's had wet eyes since the nightly beatings in that godawful Tulsa orphanage. Jack loved that Brit roadster more than any Natasha, more than even Nazedha. Mickey sells his dog Blood Alley Babe to Garcia, who hasn't forgotten that Jack nobbled his beloved Black Dolly. He tells Mickey Jack can forget any more favours from him. DD's is on the auction block, but war-nervous investors won't bite even at a bargain price. The gendarmes in Frenchtown are installing their own slots and busting the few Mickey managed to get up and running again. It's the end of an era. Jack Riley brought slot machines to the China Coast, and for a decade everyone in Shanghai with change in their pockets—Chinese and foreigner; leatherneck and sailor; society lady looking for a taste of the sporting life and prostitute feeling lucky; even off-duty cops and missionaries praying one of their congregation didn't catch them—has pulled those levers and made Jack 'the Slots King' Riley a wealthier man. The slots bankrolled his step upmarket with DD's; they paid for his stake in Farren's. The slots gave Jack sportscars, his own baseball team, lightning fast greyhounds, tailored suits, handmade shoes, comfortable apartments. The slots were an industry—every bar, boîte, nightclub, café, dance hall, and club took a cut. Hole-in-the-wall bars paid their rent on slots commissions; the Marines Club published its own newspaper funded by their slots proceeds. History now.

Mickey cleans out the Ningpo trust account, with the last of the slots' proceeds delivered to Jack by Schmidt on foot—even the dependable old Packard Jack and Mickey used for the slots run has been sold. As usual, stagflation renders the sum paltry. Evelyn is charging an arm and a leg to keep Jack stashed. She says the twenty grand is all used up and she needs more. Jack has little choice. Mickey gets what he can to her with the bundles larger and larger as the money becomes more and more worthless.

Jack finally cashes in his final twenty-five thousand worth of stock in the Shanghai Power Company for Evil Evelyn's Badland's casino fund—fear not, friend Jack, she says with a smile, I'll cut you in on the house once we've got the wheels spinning on the Edinburgh Road. We'll go back to Manila yet, you and I. Twenty-five thousand doesn't go far now, and the Portuguese want plenty to bring in the wheels from their Macanese suppliers. Number 76 demands a cut, as do the Kempeitai and the Chinese landlords. The Kempeitai want protection money, while Evelyn's security crew of Hitler-loving thugs looks seriously untrustworthy at best. But it's Jack's last roll of the dice.

Now Evelyn is saying maybe they'll relocate to Frenchtown, hire Corsican muscle. The Sûreté are less rapacious than the Japs, and she's in tight with the pro-Vichy clique. This is when Jack knows his twenty-five G is gone, set for Evil Evelyn's retirement fund post-Jack, post-Shanghai. The casino is all bullshit. Jack sensed it was a pipe dream; any other time he wouldn't have gone near Evelyn's plan with a barge pole. But this wasn't any other time, this was the most desperate time, and he realizes he grabbed at anything that seemed a way out. Now he knows Evelyn is not the way out; she's just another money-draining dead end.

And then suddenly it's time to move. Some Brit broad didn't take well to the blackmail scam and grassed on Evelyn to the Frenchtown *flics*. The gig's up before it's even really begun. By squeezing the most respectable in town—or their wives—Evelyn has stirred up a hornet's nest even her powerful contacts can't settle.

The Filipinos and the Argentinian boys have been turfed out, the joint's closing—oh, and by the way, Jack, we spent your stash money and the other cash, and the casino stake you fronted was spent on roulette wheels, now stuck in transit in Macao, expecting Jack to buy that bullshit story. He is past caring now. Move on; another throw of the dice.

Jack's been low before; he can rise again. Mickey grabs what cash he can and stuffs Jack's trusty old baseball bag full of notes. He passes the bag to Babe under the counter at the Manhattan; she saunters out, past Crighton's watchmen, just another China Coast dame smoking a Mei Li Bah on the working girl's evening stroll. She gets the bag down to Jack at Evelyn's with a change of clothes, and tells him she's rigged up a stash pad for him over the creek in Hongkew.

Time to go back to the start . . .

SHOPPING NEWS
—'BREVITIES'—
MONDAY, FEBRUARY 25, 1941

Honestly, could the Shanghai Municipal Police look any more toothless? We think not. Two weeks after the shootout at Farren's on the Great Western Road and the SMP has failed to make one single, solitary, lonesome arrest. Two dead and hundreds terrified while the SMP seems to fear nothing but treading on the toes of No. 76 by venturing uninvited into the Badlands. At this time of heightened and prolonged Emergency for the Settlement shouldn't we be able to rely on our own cops to at least keep us safe? Seems not, and Commissioner Bourne's got nothing to say for himself while Gentleman Joe's still opening the doors nightly.

Coal prices across the Settlement have reached record highs and the Municipal Council is doing nothing to prevent rampant profiteering in times of shortage caused by the emergency situation. Could it be that too many of our esteemed Councilors are mighty matey and real chummy with the major distributors? Our sources report that their fires are burning bright while the rest of us consider bank loans to buy even a brick or two of anthracite from Hongay's. No wonder, despite having to duck the bullets and leave your pearls at the roulette table, so many *Shopping News* devotees still choose to spend their evenings in the Badlands where the fires roar lovely at the Eventail, the Argentina, and even at Farren's, despite a hole or two in the wall!!

You may have spied our esteemed Municipal Council Chairman cruising the Settlement in a green bulletproof V-8 Caddie of 1928 vintage. He says the machine is Al Capone's old limo from back in the day, and that a dashing taipan had it shipped over from Chi-Town special. Everyone's favourite US marshal, Sam Titlebaum, says it looks a lot like the vehicle old 'Scarface' cruised Chicago in when Titlebaum was but a mob-busting beat cop in his younger days. Titlebaum says it'll take a Thompson round or a 'Red 9' slug at close range with only chipped paintwork. Let's hope it doesn't get tested . . .

Suffering through this long, long winter of our discontent? The Siccawei Observatory is predicting a damp and wet winter ahead. Best then to prepare for the coming rain with a new raincoat from Whiteaway, Laidlaw & Co. As they promise—'We can't stop the rain, but OUR RAINCOATS WILL KEEP YOU DRY'. They promise the largest assortment in the Far East with ladies macs starting at \$8.95. Now's the time, get a 20% discount with this week's copy of your beloved *Shopping News*.

Let everyone know the juicy details. Editorial: Rm 540, 233 Nanking Rd. Tel: Shanghai—10695

40

The Garden Bridge is a no-go—bluejacket sentries and barricades, papers demanded. It's the same all up the creek westwards, with every bridge a Japanese barricade. It's possible to cross farther up, into Paoshan via sampan if you can dodge the Japanese river patrol boats with their sweeping searchlights. The corner of Gordon and Markham roads, the far northwest of the Settlement, is the frontline—manned by the American company of the Shanghai Volunteer Corps. And luckily for Jack, these guys still love him.

It's early March when the Volunteers take over the wire that marks the divide between foreign Shanghai and occupied territory. The Markham Road trolley-bus terminus is fully locked down with the American company behind sandbags, a 37mm gun on wagon wheels that can stop a Japanese tank if necessary (and it will be necessary, sooner or later). More Volunteers are up in front pointing rifles at the sentries, who point right back. The bluejackets are edgy—itchy trigger fingers twitching, these philopon-dosed conscripts have been methamphetamined ever since raping Nanking back in the cruel winter of '37.

The Volunteers sort Jack out with some chow and coffee. Jack shares his stash of Doc Borovika's bennies all round to welcome hands. They're sipping bourbon from hip flasks and ragging Moy and Chisholm on XGRS, who are roasting FDR for signing the Lend-Lease Act—sending dollars to London? Why prolong the English people's agony in a futile resistance? Churchill is 'syphilitic' and Roosevelt is 'mentally deranged and idiotic', spouts Moy; Roosevelt's a 'war mongerer', a 'double crosser'; US Steel and Standard Oil's profits are all that will be defended; 'a German victory's inevitable'; 'Why are Americans preparing to fight to defend the British Empire in Shanghai? Put down your guns, get on your evacuation ships, and go home to your sweethearts.' It's easier to flip to another station, forget it all, catch the Big Band sounds—Jimmy Dorsey, Benny Goodman, Glenn Miller . . . American standards tinkle out over the Japanese lines, over the cluster of beggar boats and sampans on the Soochow Creek.

The Volunteers can get people through the wire and across the creek into Hongkew—Free China agents, black-marketeers, refugees with money to pay their way. By midnight the fizzing streetlamps are on reduced power, the Gordon Road Police Post on a skeleton crew with just the Riot Squad waiting for a 'tip and run' call—the tip comes in and the Riot Squad are suited, booted, armed, and out the door in under five minutes. The old Fourth Marines regimental hospital is in blackout, and what used to be the Shanghai Mint is now shuttered—they couldn't mint the coins fast enough to keep up with the falling exchange rate. Towards the border the streetlights disappear completely, shot out by snipers—who's going to be fool enough to go up a ladder and repair them with trigger-happy snipers just yards away?

Enough men are still honoured to help out old pal Jack, Lucky Jack, Tulsa shitkicker Jack, stand-up guy, fellow American, veteran—*Semper fi!* Just down the line, just beyond the wire, just past where the Jap sentries are, they have a friendly sampan waiting, no questions asked. Jackpot Riley dips into his trusty baseball bag for some cash for the boys. Get a drink on old Jack and speak of me kindly, fellas. There are a few coppers for the old woman on her sampan, her 'honey barge' piled high with Settlement shit for transportation upriver as fertiliser—the stink's so bad the river patrols never search it. They travel across the Soochow Creek, until just beyond the searchlights, when Jack is off and over the wall of the Cantonese Cemetery, avoided by patrols that fear opium ghosts and *kuei huo* fireballs.

Chapei is a total wasteland. Body parts are scattered about the cemetery where bombs have landed, uprooting the corpses from their flimsy papier-mâché coffins. Beyond the cemetery walls just about anyone who can has gone, fled. Riley tramps east, across the ruins to Hongkew and the Northern External Roads, to Jukong Alley, back to the Trenches and then . . . where? Boats out are non-existent, the Whangpoo now almost totally silted up.

Here he is back in Hongkew, where it all started, knocking heads at the Venus for Sam and Girgee, tossing dice out back of the Isis picture house on the North Szechuen Road, where the Joe and Jack show began. It's war-ravaged territory now, but it might be a bolthole, buy Jack time to think.

41

It's the end of March. Jack's been holed up in a small flat at the Young Allen Court apartment buildings on Hongkew's Chapoo Road for two mind-numbingly boring weeks with nothing but time to reflect and ruminate on his life's turning points. Life comes like snapshots from a Kodak box Brownie. That shithole orphanage in Oklahoma, with drunk custodians who half starved the little bastards so they could skim the charitable donations for their all-night hooch and craps sessions. Hitting out and heading for Denver to polish brass in a brothel at just seven years old, calling the punters 'sir' and the working girls 'sister'. A decade later, standing on the deck of the U.S.S. *Quiros* on Yangtze patrol duty, maybe his only settled time of order and belonging. His honourable discharge in '21, barhopping the ports of the west coast, each night ending with a hangover, a flophouse, and the big Q: What now, buddy? On the midnight shift driving taxis on Tulsa's mean streets. The wrong crowd offering him easy money to work as a wheels man. Bad, bad decision, Jacky boy. The inside of a cell, furnished by the Oklahoma State Penitentiary, a Sodom of seriously disturbed men and convicted sexual predators. Stepping out that morning with the baseball team, outside the gates, walking away, waiting for the bullet, waiting for the dogs. Jumping that freight to San Francisco and becoming a new man, becoming Edward T. 'Jack' Riley. He knows now there has only been one place that felt like home, that offered sanctuary and asked no questions: Shanghai.

All so long ago. And now . . .

Young Allen Court is run by some Russian woman who rented rooms to Babe back in her Hongkew days, before she moved up and over to Frenchtown. The place is near deserted, with just a few down-at-the-heels Japanese working girls and some itinerant Chinese short-timers. Mickey sends a final ten grand in Chinese de-valued dollars with Schmidt, whose German passport gets him through the Jap wires and into Hongkew without a bag search from the Kempeitai. They're all good Axis friends now—Schmidt's raised arm and *heil Hitler* gets a *tenno-heika banzai*—'Long live the Emperor!'—in return. He gets the cash to Jack and heads back, but his luck runs out when he finds John Crighton, Sam Titlebaum, and Little Nicky waiting for him with open arms on the Bund side of the bridge.

Jack has grown a moustache, just like the papers said Louis Lepke did while hiding out in Brooklyn, just like Dillinger did before Hoover's feds caught up with him and gunned him down. He's ditched the trademark pinstriped suit for khaki trousers and a brown lumber jacket Babe picked up at the Pennywise store. No more Slots King, no more gambling kingpin, no more Farren's pit boss—just a regular working stiff bedding down in Hongkew, with missing shirt buttons and broken shoelaces knotted together. He's registered with the landlady under the first name that came to mind—Lawrence Frank, the name Babe dreamed up for his bogus lease on his old Frenchtown pad, all those years ago with Nazedha. It's another alias, one more nom de plume in a long, long list. He's been on the run since the start of December, three and half months, and he's down to just ten thousand Chinese bucks in his pocket. Jack's only plan now is to stow away on a tramp steamer to Manila, or maybe a Portuguese blockade-runner to Macao. It's a pipe dream: Shanghai's surrounded, the docks locked down; the Whangpoo is silting up as the Chinese dredgers have been scuttled. There's no way out.

Broken furniture and a vermin-ridden bed. Broth and bread twice a day, plus the occasional sticks of yakitori from the Chapoo Road street stalls. They're brought by a Japanese girl working out of the building who does him favours for pay. She doesn't speak any English; he talks to himself at night. A fly-speckled light bulb provides an hour or two of erratic electricity, and then a stinking, leaking old kerosene lamp does for light. The walls bulge with damp, covered with graffiti in Japanese kanji, and sniper holes let in drafts. Outside, bats swoop against the moonlit grey clouds— bats were good joss, said the Chinese. Once-Lucky Jack is in dire need of some good joss.

42

Jack's seen it all in his mind's eye before it happens. Someone has dropped a dime, claimed the reward. Who? Babe, unlikely; Mickey, never; Evelyn, quite possibly; a Friend turned Judas, most probably; Joe? Certainly, if he'd known where Jack was. The last Friend he'd seen was Schmidt, and he'd bet a year's slots takings that the German had talked—it's each man for himself now. He knows the procedure: Crighton will have sweated Schmidt till he broke down. Then Crighton would call Titlebaum before dialling Shanghai-15380, a 'tip and run' call to raise the Red Maria. A bell would ring in the Gordon Road Police Station, and the Riot Squad would assemble, receive their instructions, be issued their arms, pull on their bulletproof vests, pile into the back of the Red Maria and head across the Settlement to the Garden Bridge and across into Hongkew. Crighton would alert the Japanese police they were heading north of the Creek, laissez passers prearranged to prevent any misunderstanding, and then . . .

They'll cordon off the street, surround the complex, cover the entrances on Chapoo and the side streets, and put snipers on the buildings opposite with .303s and P14 Enfields with scopes. There'll be a five-man entry team, an armoured raiding party to kick in the door, with tin helmets and metal shields. They'll be backed up by the snipers, a fourteen-man rifle squad and more vans with a couple of dozen SMP Chinese constables out of the Dixwell Road Station armed with batons. The entry team will let the snipers pick you off as you contemplate a window jump or appear on the roof. But if they get close to you on the stairs, they'll shoot you in the guts as a standard takedown technique. If it gets dark they'll bring up floodlights, tighten the cordon, and bring the snipers in closer. The riflemen will then mask up and lob the tear gas and the stink bombs in, and start shooting through the smoke at anything and everything.

He hears the rumble of the Red Maria. Crouched down and looking out the window onto Chapoo Road he sees the Riot Squad come out the back, armoured vests on, rifles held close across their bodies, looks of grim determination on their faces under their protective tin helmets. Snipers enter the buildings opposite. In a minute he sees them appear on the roof across the road. He hears the quick march of police boots, a squad of oilskin-caped Chinese constables with batons closing off each end of the street. And then he sees the temporary barrier pulled back and a black SMP Nash pull up by the Red Maria—Crighton, Little Nicky, and Titlebaum inside. Crighton motions to the Riot Squad officer in charge; Little Nicky and Titlebaum move round to the trunk of the Nash, open it, and pull out shotguns they start loading. They don't waste any time.

Tear gas comes rolling in, and Jack heads out of his room, through the hole in the wall with a screen over it into what had been apartment number 25. The girl is in the room but she's frozen rigid, too scared to speak, nothing except a quiet sob. Titlebaum is down behind the Red Maria with a megaphone, telling Jack to quit. He can hear Crighton and Little Nicky barking orders and coordinating the entry squad with their shields. Shit, they've even brought along some Japanese Kempeitai. He knows it will be hand grenades next, if they decide to up the ante, and random shooting.

Jack ducks under the metal frame of the bed—he's not hiding, just wants a chance if they come in guns blazing. The Japanese girl cowers in a corner covering her head, whimpering. Jack feels bad—this isn't her trouble, but she's in the middle of it now. There are things to consider; those snipers sure like to test their skills, and Bourne ordered the armourers to modify every SMP-issued gun so no officer can ever put the safety on and get caught coming up slow.

Titlebaum comes up the stairs and kicks in the door of number 24, shouting for Jack to give it up. John Crighton follows him, beige mac billowing out behind him like a cape. He's got Little Nicky with him too, carrying a pump-action that looks to be half his height. It's getting crowded out there. He can hear them shouting to one another—he can hear they've got his baseball bag, they've found his last stash. Jack lies under the bed and waits. The U.S. marshal comes through the hole in the wall and into the room with his Winchester pump-action lowered; Crighton is right behind with Little Nicky in tow. The girl might have motioned to the bed, or maybe it's just that there's no place else he could be. Titlebaum points the rifle underneath the bed frame, motioning for Jack to come on out from there.

Dead ain't me, thinks Jack; I'll take my chances. Shanghai is the ultimate city of second chances. There's always the opportunity to live another day, to win another round . . . but not today. Jack scrabbles out from under the bed, the brown trousers and lumber jacket over his pyjamas, tan brogues with no socks on, flashing the marshal his best stained-teeth Tulsa grin, a nod to John Crighton behind him. It wasn't meant to end this way, but then it isn't over just yet.

Titlebaum gut-slams Jack with his Winchester and drops him to his knees. He swings back for a head shot, but Crighton holds him back. This is not how we do it. The SMP man slaps the cuffs on Jack, pats him down, takes the few yen he's got in his pocket.

Titlebaum and Crighton walk Jack Riley out of Young Allen Court, one on each side, holding an arm apiece. Titlebaum is never one to miss the press; he's made sure the snappers are lined up for the walk. Crighton, mac done up tight now, has his hat on, pays the hacks no mind. Sam hands his own hat to Jack, allowing him to cover his face from the flashbulbs while making sure they get the brave marshal's profile full on. At the curb they stand back as two big khaki-turbaned Sikh constables manhandle Jack Riley into the Red Maria, where he knows a righteous kicking will ensue for putting the Riot Squad to all this bother. The doors of the Red Maria slam shut.

43

It's a Shanghai procession: SMP cop cars, bells clanging, with Crighton's jet-black Nash leading the way. They are taking Shanghai's public enemy number one to his court date, March 29, 1941. Riley is in handcuffs and ankle straps back in the Red Maria, motorcycle outriders with Thompson-wielding cops on the pillions as escort. His blood is still on the floor from the Sikh-administered kicking the day before. He's wearing those brown workingman's trousers and lumber jacket, but the moustache is gone—they made him use blunt clippers, and his top lip's got a nasty nick. The Riot Squad's on duty outside the court, Chinese constables with truncheons to push back the crowds. Riley is escorted in by the six-foot Sikhs, the Thompson sniper on the Red Maria's roof scanning the crowd for any breakout attempts from Riley's Friends.

Jack's back in the dock at the U.S. court facing seventeen counts of gambling, but they can't pin the Farren's shootout on him. Surprise, surprise, Schmidt coughed, after feeling the weight of the Shanghai phone book on his head, to Jack's whereabouts—but he isn't talking about the Farren's raid, given his starring role, and neither will anybody else. Incrimination. By now everyone knows that this time around the feds can't match the partial acid-seared dabs from Farren's to Jack's Navy records. The court can levy a sentence for the gambling charges, but it'll be the time due to the Oklahoma State Pen that'll rack up Jack Riley's prison years.

The judge hands down eighteen months, one for each count and an additional thirty days for luck—chickenfeed. Jack's lawyer says okay—he'll do the time without appeal in Ward Road over in Y'Poo. But Judge Helmick says no. He's to do the time stateside. It's Helmick's revenge for the grandstanding, the runaround on Jack's nationality, that stunt with the fifty grand. He'll do the time at McNeil Island, and the judge insists that there's those twenty-three years from McAlester still to do. You can bet the guards from the Oklahoma State Pen will catch the ferry across the Puget Sound and be waiting outside McNeil's gates after eighteen months to reclaim their man. Federal judge the Honourable Milton J. Helmick hands down the sentence with a smile on his face. 'It is unfortunate that you could not apply your talents and intelligence to more legitimate pursuits, Mr Becker.'

Jack pays him no mind. His eyes wander up to the gallery, where what remains of the crew sits. Babe, Mickey, a Friend or two . . . and Joe, dapper as ever with his horn-rimmed glasses on. They make eye contact while Helmick drones on about good and bad, right and wrong. Jack grins up at Joe, but Joe just stares back, cuts him dead and heads for the door.

44

The S.S. *President Cleveland* of American President Lines weighs anchor downriver from the Bund, sailing for home. Aboard are American evacuees from the Solitary Island. Jack is glad to be out of Ward Road Gaol—it's been twenty years since he's seen the inside of a prison cell.

Ward Road, the Shanghai Bastille, the world's largest purpose-built prison, a thousand convicts crammed inside with tough White Russian and Sikh guards. Riley's cell is spitting distance from the execution chamber, where the drop from the noose efficiently went straight down into the jail's morgue. Inmates are stripped of tie, collar, shoelaces, suspenders, belt, and razor blades, and put in a ten-by-six-foot cell with one wooden bench, a two-inch-thick mattress with regulation blanket, a board secured to the wall as a table, a stool nailed to the floor, and a dung hole the Brits called a lavatory, which stinks day and night. The food is shit—you can't tell the coffee from the tea from the cocoa. Cause trouble and it's the isolation room, with 'rubber wallpaper' for the guards to bounce you off. Lockdown at five p.m.; lights out at eight p.m.; rise and shine at six a.m. One library book and one illustrated magazine permitted per week; one half hour's outdoor exercise a day, in enforced silence; one shower a week in tepid water. Brit tradition means you get a pint of beer a day—Jack passed his on to the old lags.

Jack's few days in Ward Road saw him get the shakes till Mickey greased some palms and Doc Borovika gets in some bennies via a pliable guard. Friends sent in packs of Craven A so Jack could trade; Babe sent in fried chicken and corned beef hash; Evelyn sent a note saying she was sorry it hadn't worked out. Jack cursed ever meeting her. He should have walked away and let old Paco kill her all those years back in Manila.

Now on board the ship, here's Jack Riley, lying on his bunk in first class (the only rooms with secure doors and metal beds), freshly delivered to the docks in John Crighton's armoured Nash—the *Cleveland*'s celebrity passenger. Cuffs off, but steel hoops around his ankles, chained to the bed, and he's watched over by an SMP detective sergeant. This time he's registered on board as Fahnie Albert Becker, returning home courtesy of the United States Department of Justice. After stopping to pick up two hundred repatriated American missionaries from Kobe, it's straight to the port of San Francisco. Been a long time, Jack; a long time since that lodging house on the Embarcadero.

This is the twentieth evacuation ship for American citizens in China to leave, with the last dregs now—only the die-hard evangelist missionaries, managers of American factories, old China hands finally wrenching themselves away from the Middle Kingdom after decades. Stalwart missionaries who steadfastly refuse to leave are lined up dockside singing 'God Be with You Till We Meet Again'. It's the *Cleveland*'s last passenger voyage, as she's been commandeered by the U.S. Navy. Trouble is brewing in the Pacific.

The boat docks stateside on April 24, with a welcoming party of state troopers. Jack's ready for the press—hair slicked down, shaved, and in a shirt, tie, and suit. He's ready to do his time. The long arm of the law has finally caught up with him—and he wonders who else might it catch up with too. Back there, dockside in

Shanghai, John Crighton and Jack Riley had taken a minute together—old adversaries with a mutual grudging respect for each other. Crighton told Jack he'd had a good run; those Fourth Marines and Badlands highrollers were going to miss him. Jack told him some would and some wouldn't. One of them in particular, he knew, wouldn't be sorry to see him sail. And then Jack Riley told John Crighton one last Shanghai tale, one for the road, for old times' sake. Crighton was skeptical, but Jack looked him straight in the eye and told him to ask Albert Rosenbaum if he didn't believe him, that Rosenbaum knew it all. And, while you're at it, why not talk to Joe too, and tell him no hard feelings from me. Jack handed John Crighton a little black book and gave him a pat on the shoulder before walking down the gangplank. Sayonara from Jack Riley to Shanghai.

As the summer heat of 1941 engulfs the city, alligators come to Shanghai for the first time in a hundred years. They ease down the river at night and settle in the mudbanks as the Whangpoo has silted up, undredged. It is said that their black, slow-blinking eyes are Japanese-like. People claim that they snatch the rats and abandoned babies left on the shoreline at low tide, the bloated corpses of dogs, cats, and washed-up suicides, before slipping back into the mudbanks and waiting for nightfall. Only bubbles from their snouts and a reflective shine from their reptilian eyes break the surface. Nobody has actually seen one of these *Alligator* sinensis, but stories of them spread throughout the city, among Chinese and Shanghailanders. They are blamed for missing pets, suspected of snatching away the mudlark children who sift the shoreline for treasure; they supposedly upturn nightsoil sampans and beggar boats, and devour the occupants whole.

It is said that if you go down to the waterfront along the Bund in the early hours of the morning, you can hear their rasping bellows as they mate and give birth to fully formed offspring. You can hear their claws scratching along the edge of the Bund's stone embankment, trying to come ashore to roam the city streets. They are said to be a portent of death in Shanghai, that they swarm towards the city, knowing it will be a profitable hunting ground.

This, people believed . . .

45

Joe's business is down, but not quite out. Farren's is humid in the July heat of 1941: the air conditioning has packed it in and shorts the fuse box when they try to crank it up. During storms the roof leaks—the timbers are rotten. Coolies climb up on the roof and nail tarp over the holes. Tonight's a stinking hot Shanghai night, finally broken by a typhoon storm rolling in from across the East China Sea. Ferocious cloudbursts pelt the Badlands, and the sewers back up; the stink of human shit pervades. Typhoon rains bring mosquitoes—arms, legs, ankles, necks are bitten and scratched red raw. Joe and the remaining boychiks huddle at tables between strategically placed buckets to catch the rainwater until they finally open and see who turns up, who's left in Shanghai. It's a long curfew till four a.m. The barricades into the Western Roads District mean nobody can get in or out without laissez passer; rickshaws and pedicabs no longer work after dark—it's just too dangerous.

The Badlands has shifted from exotic and tempting to just plain scary and dangerous. There have been constant SMP raids since March on the edge of the Badlands, coming ever closer, and Joe has no choice. He decides to pack up the roulette wheels and the baccarat shoes, the cards and the dice. Now he's left with just the band and the floor show; the takings are way, way down, though he's legit in the eyes of the SMP, even if the Kempeitai and number 76 still demand their taxes.

The Kempeitai and number 76 created the Badlands; the Kempeitai and number 76 are killing it. The Avenue Haig Hwa-Wei parlours don't pay out; the dope is cut and cut again and then further adulterated with strychnine and baking powder. Only the most impoverished now frequent the back-alley whores off Avenue Haig—they've been untreated by doctors too scared to enter the district for months now. The Badlands is to be avoided: it's just one big nightlife slum. It's too dangerous to go west of the Settlement now—an SMP deputy commissioner gets gunned down on Tifeng Road.

It's not just cops who are targets. Joe's paranoia heightens when a rival casino operator gets shot in the back of the head walking down Canton Road near the supposedly respectable Bund; another gets snatched off the street, and his severed finger is sent to his family with a ransom note. Ciro's nightclub gets bombed with a phosphorous and gasoline incendiary. A taxi dancer from the Paramount disappears and is found in the Soochow Creek, in a blue satin dress with a knife between her shoulder blades. Farren's security is stretched to the maximum.

Joe and the boys are finding it tougher to keep it together, and Joe's starting to look rough. His hacking cough is exacerbated by the homemade Russian émigré *papyruski* cigarettes, rolled ever more loosely. He's ageing, soft around the jowls, getting a paunch. He's not the man he was back in the Majestic in '29, no longer the man who danced through Batavia, Yokohama, Singapore, and back to Shanghai. Not the man who once guided Mary Pickford round the floor or held Nellie close. His teeth are hurting, but you can't find a decent dentist for love nor money in Shanghai now. It's been a summer of eye and ear infections, as the water that flows from the taps is contaminated. He can't sleep, it burns to piss, and Doc Borovika's got nothing to ease the pain.

There was a time he was a man whom everyone knew. He was the boss—with a driver, maids, cooks, tailors, security, bootmakers, printers, butchers. Across town barmen knew his drink—the stengah was on the bar the moment he walked in; waiters knew his order—schnitzel, no rich sauces, or straight-up ham and eggs; barbers knew his style—high on the back. They shaved him with cutthroat razors and applied Bay Rum cologne; his fingernails were manicured in Little Russia.

The hard water makes the boychiks' hair stands straight up, as though they've been subjected to electric shocks. It takes masses of pomade, buckets of brilliantine now, to smooth it down. They've got red eyes, Hong Kong foot, itchy fucking everything, snot the consistency of coal dust, phlegm like tar. Suits and shirts start to fray as the tailors close down for lack of cloth. Shoes go unsoled, the heels worn down. They gather round a shortwave radio to hear news of the war, but there's nothing much but pro-Axis bullshit on the local stations now—the Allied XHMA is off the air for good; the BBC Far Eastern service repeatedly jammed. Moy and Chisholm rant victorious and unchallenged.

The Farren's neon light fizzes and clicks with the erratic electricity supply. Inside, the lights dim, the power cuts and then surges, the fuses blow. You eat now in Farren's on a reduced menu and by candlelight—five- and ten-watt bulbs only, due to the electricity restrictions. Joe's remains the one venue that has solidly refused to pay the spiralling taxes. Now the vultures want their carrion from the Badland's 'number one Jew man'. But now, even if he submitted to their demands, he's not pulling in enough cash to pay; they're feasting on a body with only a thin trickle of lifeblood still flowing through it. It's just a matter of time.

They'd go—they'd all go if they could . . . but where? No passports, no exit visas, nowhere to depart, nowhere to arrive. Vienna is a Nazi town; Austria, under the Anschluss, part of the Reich and no place for Jews. This is it: Shanghai is all there is. Joe's run out of all options but one—to stay put.

John Crighton's been busy since March. There's always a final twist in any Shanghai story; there's always unfinished business. It takes a while to line it all up and work it out. It takes time to put the sting together. Jack's little black book is an incredible repository— a little black leather-covered marvel filled with the names, dates, and details of every marker ever issued by Jack at Farren's. Here's every loan, credit, and advance; every debt, unpaid chit, and absconded defaulter. The single largest bad debt at Farren's? U.S. marshal Sam Titlebaum. The icing on the cake? He'd offered to pay one time with confiscated guns and ammo; guns and ammo that should have gone to the marshal's lockup for decommissioning by the SMP eventually; those same guns and ammo that tied Shanghai criminals to murdered SMP officers and were in the hands of every thug in the Badlands.

46

Crighton, black book in hand, confronts Joe Farren. Joe, happy to stick it to Titlebaum, confirms the debts, then calls Albert Rosenbaum and tells him to talk to Crighton. Okay, Jack went rogue and now he's gone, but Titlebaum's a *fakakta mamzer* who owes. More important, putting him in the shit doesn't open any other cans of worms for Joe or the boys of the syndicate that was; in fact, it'll create the mother of all shitstorms for the U.S. Department of Justice in Shanghai.

Rosenbaum advises Crighton to ask around. Titlebaum owes large all over town—a grand at the American Club poker tables; four grand at the Palace Hotel on meals and rooms alone. He owes plenty of Badlands gambling joints too—the Arizona, the Argentina, and the Ali-Baba, before they got shuttered, Tony Perpetuo's 37427 and Bothelo's Silver Palace. Bar bills were racked large and left unpaid at Vertinsky's Gardenia before it closed; there are more unpaid chits at the Handy Randy, Ma Jackson's Tavern—hell, all over town. Carlos Garcia, off the record, confirms Titlebaum has been losing bad at the pari-mutuel at the Canidrome. Half of the joints have been offered illicit weapons as partial payment of debts— weapons confiscated from criminals and in raids by the U.S. marshal's office and supposedly decommissioned and destroyed.

According to Rosenbaum, the schmuck even loves the Hwa-Wei lotteries and is maxed out at the grind shops down Paramount Alley.

It's not until August that the sting is set up. Rosenbaum tells Titlebaum his Farren's debts are still owed, and Joe wants them paid or he'll talk to Crighton. Titlebaum offers once again to pay in guns and ammunition; Rosenbaum says he'll broker a meet at his Route Remi stash house in Frenchtown to introduce Titlebaum to one of the local captains from number 76. Titlebaum sells the number 76 man guns for forty-four hundred American dollars and the ammunition for another thirty-five hundred, paid in Yankee hundred-dollar bills. Rosenbaum tells him to bank it and settle his debts with Joe with more illicit guns. Rosenbaum calls in a favour, and number 76 send a tame *lieu-maung* along to SMP HQ to register a couple of the guns, an unheard-of thing—a number 76 thug registering weapons! Crighton is waiting. He watches the armourer check the serial numbers against the files and . . . bingo. The guns are registered to the U.S. marshal's office in Shanghai and supposedly decommissioned.

The swaggering marshal and big-mouth-about-town Titlebaum was as crooked as one of Jack Riley's slots. Surprised, he is arrested, printed, and handed over to the U.S. court. The court demands five thousand American dollars as bail, and nobody will stand it for him. Sam finds himself in the SMP Red Maria heading east down to Y'Poo and the Ward Road Gaol for processing. Titlebaum is weighed, measured, examined, printed, searched, and photographed before being assigned Jack Riley's recently vacated cell where the ignominious marshal will await trial. But it gets weirder.

Two months later, on October 11, 1941, Detective Sub-Inspector John Crighton lays out the evidence against former U.S. Marshal

Samuel Titlebaum to the U.S. court. The debts, the missing guns and ammo from the U.S. marshal's safe box, the Rosenbaum-brokered deal to sell the guns to agents of number 76, the amount paid turning up to the exact cent in Titlebaum's National City Bank account. Sam realises he'd been played by Rosenbaum and Joe. They never wanted guns; they just wanted the paper trail to lead all the way to Titlebaum's account. Even the Chinese kid who works at the marshal's office, whom Titlebaum sent to pay the money in for him, stands in the witness box. It's bad news and a major public embarassment. The man who took down Jack Riley is as crooked as his nemesis.

But who the hell is Sam Titlebaum anyway? The prints Crighton takes at Ward Road Gaol are different to those on file for Titlebaum with the U.S. court. Crighton goes to the feds in D.C. again, via Little Nicky, and discovers there is no Samuel Titlebaum—at least there never was in the Chicago police, or ever on the staff of any big Chicago or Seattle newspaper like he claimed. Titlebaum has apparently substituted another man's prints for his own on his Department of Justice application form. Crighton checks the Ward Road medical examination files from when Sam was booked in and learns that Titlebaum is recorded as having a seven-inch scar on his torso, a bullet wound in his hip, and another in his foot, none of which he'd declared when appointed marshal.

It's a packed Saturday in the court, and this time Sam Titlebaum is in the dock. He's up on twelve counts of embezzlement, including taking six .38 Colt revolvers and fifteen hundred rounds of .38 pistol ammunition. Judge Helmick is out of town and President Roosevelt himself appoints the U.S. commissioner, Nelson Lurton, to be a special judge of the court. The DA's special assistant, Charlie Richardson Jr., who'd fast-tracked Titlebaum's application and championed him, makes himself scarce as the press excoriates him daily.

Lurton is unsparing—he declares that the man who calls himself Sam Titlebaum is indeed a U.S. citizen and therefore subject to the court's verdict even though they cannot verify his identity. He sentences Titlebaum to two years' imprisonment on all of the embezzlement counts, plus five years on the false identity counts. He looks the former U.S. marshal square in the eye: 'You have brought shame upon yourself and imposed on the dignity of your country, betrayed men who have recommended you, and heaped humiliation on yourself.' The man in the dock stays silent and makes no effort to defend himself. But the best is saved for last: Titlebaum is mandated to serve his sentences concurrently at Mc-Neil Island Penitentiary, the same jail in Puget Sound now home to a certain Fahnie Albert Becker.

John Crighton takes Sam Titlebaum, who's said nothing, not one single word, during the whole trial, downstairs to the Red Maria and back to Ward Road Gaol. The press scrum on the street outside is rivalled only by that of the Riley trial back in March, when Titlebaum had still been badged and smiling for the cameras. In the van the two men share a cigarette. As they smoke, heading east to Ward Road, John Crighton asks, 'Who the hell are you, Sam?'

The convicted prisoner flicks the smoked-down butt onto the floor of the Red Maria, stubs it out, sits back, looks at the roof of the vehicle and doesn't say a damn thing.

47

By November, Farren's is the only major joint in the Badlands left open: an outpost of the desperate, the needy, and the lonely. The music is as shrill as ever, the jazz as frenetic, but the acts are all gone—the Hartnells leave on an evacuation ship after snagging a tour of the American Midwest, Mike and his Music Masters light out on the last U.S. evac ship to head to San Francisco. The Filipino band is willing to stay, but only for hiked fees. The only others staying are the stateless Natashas, their fiercely powdered and painted faces still as common as blackberries in a good season. The place is also full of equally hopeful young men—stateless White Russian émigrés, Jewish refugees from Nazi Europe—lean in smart beige suits that are now only smart at a distance, only in muted light, only at night. They sleep by day, stick to the shadows after nightfall, cluster around the dance floor, gather on the edge of tables, drowning their miseries in dancing and sex, pretending not to be hungry. All are eager for someone to take them home before the lights go up. There's nobody left in town but the legion of holdup and standover men, petty gangsters, AWOL marines and small-time thieves and hustlers. No money for roulette now, the last spin spun in the Badlands, the final bets placed.

Yet perhaps those inside Farren's were among the lucky. In the winter of 1941, the Shanghai Municipal Council collected twenty-nine thousand dead bodies from the streets of the International Settlement, Chinese and foreign. They died of hypothermia, starvation, tuberculosis, overdoses. Suicide rates shot up—old people not wanting to be a burden simply lay down in frozen alleyways and went to sleep and never woke up; young women, seeing no future, leapt into the Whangpoo; families unable to cope left newborn babies on the steps of churches, but they died before being rescued. They were all buried in unmarked mass paupers' graves outside the city limits and forgotten. But even before the year is out, the end comes for the old Shanghai of treaty port settlements and concessions.

The news from Pearl Harbor is bad. On December 8, 1941, it's '*WAR*' in bold black headlines on the front page of the *North-China Daily News*. The Japanese invade the Settlement hours after their sneak attack on Hawaii. They find it undefended except by the part-time Volunteer Corps, who are disarmed without a shot being fired. After ninety-nine years as an international treaty port, Shanghai has finally fallen—so close and yet so far from the planned centenary. The Japanese Special Naval Landing Force seizes the U.S.S. *Wake*, moored on the Whangpoo, before the captain can scuttle her. The British gunboat H.M.S. *Peterel*, pride of the Royal Navy's China Squadron, is scuttled successfully before the Japs can commandeer her. The Badlands is deserted; what to do now? Open the club, sit, smoke, wait. Joe Farren sits, smokes, waits. Everything will change now—the Solitary Island is no more. The Kempeitai control the town, the SMP are disarmed, and all grudges, bad debts, and scores are to be settled now in Tokyo's favour.

Joe knows they'll come for him. They won't forgive his

defiance—not the Kempeitai nor number 76. He knows exactly where they'll take him: east into the Settlement and out of the Badlands, along the now deserted Bund back across the Soochow Creek, back to Hongkew and the innocuous cream-coloured building on the North Szechuen Road the Kempeitai turned into their own private torture chamber—Bridge House. A former apartment building, subdivided since 1937 into a myriad of filthy holding pens, cells, and interrogation rooms—torture chambers for those who transgress the law of the Japanese Special Higher Police, the Tokkō. People try to ignore the rumours, the screams; ignore the truth of what goes on inside.

And finally, on December 12, they come for him.

48

It's impossible in the half-light from the low-watt bulbs to tell if it's day or night. The windows are boarded up, so Joe doesn't even know if he's on the ground floor or upstairs. Upstairs, he thinks. Second, third floor? He remembers being dragged up, past a portrait of the emperor on horseback—a slight man wearing glasses. Joe lost his spectacles under a Kempeitai goon's boot after they beat him in the back of the truck en route.

They grab him coming out of his nightclub; his boychik security held back at bayonet point by a squad of bluejackets. He lies on the floor of the open-backed truck looking up at the stars, speeding down the Great Western Road. From the Badlands into Frenchtown, along Avenue Foch, watching the plane trees flash past, pruned for the winter and resembling ageing prizefighters' swollen and distended knuckles. Onto the Avenue Eddy; the streets have an almost metallic sheen, the tarmac glistening, shops with iron grilles locked down tight for the night, the weak halos from the streetlights on reduced power, the icy wind chilling the blood on his face, the vomit around his chin from when they'd kicked him hard in the testicles.

The pungent smells of the old town: peanut oil, camphor, brackish water. Shanghainese shouting as peddlers scatter to let the military truck pass. Onto the Bund and he's enveloped in the smell of the river, the plaintive honk of a ship's Klaxon horn, the rumble of the metallic grille as the truck crosses the Garden Bridge, greenish sparks flying. Left onto North Soochow Road, past Broadway Mansions, the building now Japanese Army Liaison Office HQ, all foreigners expelled. Along the creek, past the small red lights of the beggar boats moored by the Szechuen Road Bridge and, if he didn't know it already, right onto North Szechuen Road and towards the large, modern, cream-coloured building called Bridge House. As Joe Farren is bundled from the truck, half blind, bloody, and bound, he sucks in the night air of Shanghai, his last fresh breath of oxygen in the city he's called home since 1929.

They strip him of his belongings—his gold pinky ring, the platinum lighter Nellie gave him the night they opened the Canidrome Ballroom, his silver tie pin, the roulette-ball cufflinks the boychiks got him for his birthday after Farren's opened. His shoes are taken, along with his socks, jacket, tie, overcoat—they leave him in his suit trousers torn at one knee, a cotton shirt and vest. They confiscate his belt. They rifle through his pockets and empty them. They don't bother to fingerprint him.

He's cold. He can sense—his eyes too swollen from the beating to see properly—other men in the cell. He can hear their groans, hear English, garbled Shanghainese, Japanese shouting. From below he can hear women screaming in the basement. Soon after, they come for him, and it begins. They strip him to his underwear and beat him. He's punched, slapped, kicked. They stub their cigarettes out on his bare chest and thighs. He hears the hairs on his legs sizzle. They light more cigarettes and shove them up his nostrils, lit end first. He screams—he doesn't care if they know he's in pain, he knows it won't stop anything.

It gets worse. They rig up some kind of metal plate and wire it to a battery. They place the plate on his thighs, arms, and chest.

They shove it against his balls, and he screams louder than he thought possible. He blacks out. They throw him back in his cell, and he joins the other groaning men. Others are taken periodically. He hears their moans, pleas. Each time he thanks God it isn't him they've taken, but he knows they'll come back.

And so they do. He's beaten again, with more cigarettes sizzled painfully on his body. They concentrate on his genitals this time. It hurts worse than the clap, worse than one of Doc Borovika's quack cures. They fire up the metal plate again, poking it in his kidneys, his spleen, his testicles. He blacks out. They throw stinking water in his face and slap him back to sense. More prods, more lit cigarettes. He thanks God he blacks out yet again.

They never take him to an actual interrogation room. The Tokkō have no questions to ask Joe Farren; he holds no secrets they want to know. He has simply defied them, refused to cooperate with them, pay them what they demanded, and they hate him for it. It's all just revenge.

Then, finally, he is forced to lie along a wooden bench on his back with his head hanging over the end, straining his neck backwards. One fat Japanese sits astride him to stop him moving, another binds his legs at the ankles to stop him kicking. They thrust a gun barrel into his mouth, cracking his teeth. They push it down his throat, causing him to gag. They put some sort of log under his neck, forcing his head backwards even further. Then they pull the gun out and place a wet towel over his face, covering his mouth and his nose. Now he gags from the pain in his throat and the sour taste of gunmetal oil. With no warning, a soldier pours water onto the towel so that it floods up his nostrils and into his mouth, drowning him into the dirty towel. He feels his heart bursting, his head pounding. He swallows as much of the water as he can. They laugh and keep on pouring. He passes out eventually, and they roll him on his side and leave him.

Back in the cell, his stomach bloated and hurting, he is unable to crawl even to the small bucket left as a toilet. The guards insist the prisoners sit cross-legged—every muscle burns like hell. He's unable to clean himself and sits in his own filth, although he can't smell anything, his nose burnt out by the scorching cigarettes. Rice comes sometimes, once with a rotting fish head. He manages to swallow some tepid congee, Chinese rice porridge. He stares at the walls, a Union Jack scratched into the chalk. He isn't sure how long he's been here—a day? Two?

Again they come, again the bench, the towel, the water, beatings with bamboo poles and rifle butts. They mix the water with kerosene that stops him from swallowing it, forcing him to retch. They mix in pepper, which burns like holy fire. They keep on pouring, pouring, pouring . . .

The filthy conditions take one of his cellmates in the night—malaria, scurvy, or dysentery? He can no longer feel his extremities—beaten and freezing, starving and in pain. He goes inside his mind, as far away as he can from the pain, the groans, the rats, the screams. His eyes squeezed tight, he travels until he no longer feels the cramps in his gut, the burns on his genitals, the sores on his legs. He no longer feels the unfamiliar stubble on his chin—Joe Farren, a man who shaved every day of his life since he was fifteen. His fingers hurt where his fingernails have been pulled out—Joe Farren, a man who went once a week without fail, for a decade, to a manicurist in Little Russia. He is so distant he can no longer smell the sweat and the shit. He goes to another place.

He recaptures his past, retraces his journey. He goes to the streets of Leopoldstadt, the cheap stalls of the Raimund Theater, the Prater cafés. He sees that long voyage from Trieste to Singapore, to the Adelphi, and dancing in custom-made tails from Tomes the tailor at sixty bucks a suit in front of the Majestic crowd. The spotlight tracks him and old Whitey Smith conducting. Woo Foo Lane. Now it's the Astoria, the Oost Java, Manila, Yokohama, and always back to Shanghai. The Follies, the Peaches, the Paramount, Frenchtown, the Canidrome, the spinning roulette wheels of Farren's, a thousand showgirls in his bed . . . and Nellie. Nellie's smile, her laugh, her anger, her tantrums, the sounds she made in bed, the times they'd shared afterwards, the faint scent of Mitsouko. His life was entangled with hers from Singapore to Shanghai, entangled on the dance floor and in bed in their old cold-water flat and their better days in modern apartments. Nellie: dancing, gliding. Nellie . . . gone now, who knows where.

When friends of Joe's approach Bridge House, the Japanese name a price. His friends pay it. On December 15, 1941, a large black car emerges through the blacked-out streets and pulls up outside Bridge House. Two European men in heavy overcoats get out and hastily enter the building, leaving a third in the driver's seat with the engine running. Inside they make themselves known, hand over a bag of cash, and wait. After some time a naked body is thrown at their feet with an old blanket alongside. The body is barely recognisable as the man who once ran the biggest nightclub in the Badlands, the largest casino the city has ever seen. Bruised, cut, covered in dried blood and sores, glasses long gone, those immaculate fingernails all pulled out, stomach distended. The men tenderly wrap the body in the blanket and carry it out the door to the waiting car.

It's unclear whether he died in Bridge House or shortly afterwards on the back seat of the car. What is clear is that by the time the car has driven off down North Szechuen Road to cross the bridge back into the Settlement's central district, Joe Farren is dead.

EPILOGUE

The Fallen City

The city is conquered. The Japanese Imperial Army rolls along the Bund, up the Nanking and Bubbling Well Roads to the Great Western Road and out into the occupied Chinese hinterland. The Kempeitai burn the shacks of the Badlands and warm themselves on the blaze. In place of casinos, nightclubs, dope dens, and lottery shacks they construct barracks for the Imperial Japanese Army, which is pouring into the city before heading inland to suppress the last remnants of Free China.

Wang Ching-wei and his thugs in number 76 believe that Nationalist guerillas are hiding in Fah Wah village. The puppet corps raid the rookery; Free China gunmen shoot three of them dead. The puppets are backed up by ceremonial sword–wielding Kempeitai. They take the dope shacks and brothel sheds for themselves and heave Cabbage Moh's murdered corpse into the creek, but not before they sever his head and stick it on a pole as a reminder that nobody gets to play both sides in their Shanghai.

Over the Garden Bridge in Hongkew, Wayside Road and Broadway are incorporated into an expanded Little Tokyo, and whores and backroom-brewed arrack *shamshoo* joints for the victorious bluejackets proliferate. The statues of once-esteemed Europeans on the Bund are torn down for scrap metal; the Quai de France becomes a mooring for Japanese river patrol craft; the Pootung wharves disembark yet more Imperial Army troops to police the conquered city.

The Settlement is now a strategic point in Tokyo's Greater East Asia Co-Prosperity Sphere. Japanese officers cut down the legs on the billiards tables at the once-elite Shanghai Club on the Bund to suit their diminutive height; they corral Jewish refugees in Hong-kew and create a ghetto for the luckless and the stateless. Allied nationals are interned in similar camps—Ash Camp on the Great Western Road holds more than five hundred, Chapei over fifteen hundred; hundreds are at the old Columbia Country Club, yet more on Haiphong Road; Pootung holds two thousand, the same again in Yangtzsepoo; a thousand on Yu Yuen Road, and a further two thousand out by the old aerodrome at Lunghwa. The lucky few scramble ingloriously for places on the last evacuation ships organized by the Red Cross; the less lucky are put on trucks and taken to Bridge House.

Pearl Harbor is the ignition for the volatile gas tank of the Pacific, and total war is declared. There will be fighting from Hokkaido to Darwin in the coming years. The killing fields of Batan and Guam, the body pits of Manila, the jungle slaughter of Malaya, are all still to come. Hong Kong sees street-by-street fighting until finally, on Christmas Day, surrender, defeat, and internment. The lowering of the Union Jack; the raising of the Rising Sun. The wreckage of the once-invincible Royal Navy in Singapore harbour will match that of the Seventh Fleet at Pearl Harbor; an army defeated. Years of battle and slaughter will follow until the firestorms across Tokyo, and then Little Boy and Fat Man. It is only the devastation of Hiroshima and Nagasaki that finally ends Tokyo's dreams. By then the old Shanghai of a century is gone, as quickly as a puff of blue smoke from an opium pipe, that same pernicious substance that drove the very creation of the International Settlement of Shanghai. Nothing will ever be as it was in the City of Devils.

And as the city falls, Jack Riley throws dice on the cellblock at McNeil while Sam Titlebaum shoots his bogus nostalgia shit two tiers down. Joe Farren lies in an unmarked mass grave in Hungjao. The International Settlement is gone; Frenchtown is gone; honky-tonk Hongkew is gone; the Badlands is gone; Old Shanghai is gone, gone, gone . . .

The devils have won the city, the wolves come to feast on the weak, the alligators to snap up the dead, the opium ghosts to roam, the phosphorescent *kuei huo* to dance on the city's fallen ramparts.

AFTERWORD

Joe Farren was buried in Shanghai in an unmarked grave. Farren's nightclub was shuttered, closed, looted, and then eventually pulled down. Not a trace of its existence remains. After the war someone did look for Joe—an advert appeared in *Aufbau*, a New York–based journal for German-speaking Jews around the world. *Aufbau* printed lists of Holocaust survivors and ran countless advertisements for Jewish families looking to reunite or discover the fate of their loved ones in the aftermath of the war. The advertisement ran on October 26, 1945:

> After the painful losses suffered by our family in Europe, we received from Shanghai the incredible message of the partly violent death of our last relative abroad: our unforgettable man, father, brother in law, brother and uncle Ing. Ernst (Bob) Lichtenstern (formerly of Vienna); our dearly beloved brother, brother in law and uncle Joe Farren (Josef Pollak) Shanghai; beloved nephew and the son of our sister, unforgettable Paula Heniz (Harri) Gonda (formerly of Vienna).
>
> Else Lichtenstern, geb. Pollak
> 123 Louden Avenue, Amityville, L.I., N.Y.
>
> Paul Stefan Lichtenstern
> Currently in Palestine
>
> May und Caroline Pollok
> 101 South Grand Avenue, West Springfield, Ill.
> Otto & Rose Pollak
> 317 W. 99th St., N.Y.C.
> . . . and all other relatives.

I looked high and low for the Pollak family and came to believe that most of them, as Viennese Jews, had been swallowed up in the Holocaust. And then one day I received an email from Jacqui Mills in England, a relative, who had always wondered about Uncle Josef/ Joe and what became of him. It turned out one of Joe's brothers had made it out of Nazi-occupied Austria and reached Great Britain, settled in the West Country, become a successful typewriter salesman, and raised a family in the safety and security of England. Joe Farren's family had not known his true fate or the circumstances of his tragic death in Shanghai until I began researching this book.

Jack Riley, at age forty-five, served eighteen months for his conviction in Shanghai. Upon completion he was transferred to McAlester to serve out the remaining twenty-three years of the original sentence he skipped out on. But in August 1942, he petitioned the governor of Oklahoma for clemency so he could enlist to fight in the war. It was a popular tactic, tried by many with long sentences to serve. The governor didn't let Jack Riley join up. Yet on August 17, 1942, Jack Riley was granted a pardon, as part of a wartime amnesty in some states, and walked out of McAlester (after serving just fifty-two days) a free man. Lucky Jack once more. Fahnie Albert/John Becker/Jack Riley walked out of the gates and disappeared. A new name, a new state, a new country, a new racket?

Sam Titlebaum was shipped out of Shanghai in handcuffs on a U.S. Navy vessel returning from duty on the Yangtze to California. At San Francisco he was transferred to a U.S. Prison Services cutter and taken to McNeil Island to serve his two-year sentence. Titlebaum served his full term and was still on the McNeil cellblock when Jack Riley walked free from McAlester. The U.S. court never did fully uncover who he was. The crusading journalist and editor of the *China Weekly Review* J. B. Powell did some digging and found out what the authorities thought they knew. The FBI in Washington, D.C., believed Titlebaum was approximately thirty-two years old, probably from the Great Lakes area, had been convicted previously on various charges, including grand larceny, in New York City, and had served time in the United States Penitentiary, Atlanta, Georgia. But maybe that was someone else?

The gangs scattered as the Badlands came under total Japanese control. It was rumoured that Tony Perpetuo headed down to Macao and eventually back to Portugal. The ever-faithful Mickey O'Brien is thought to have left Shanghai shortly after Jack Riley's conviction. O'Brien was rumoured to be a deserter from the U.S. Navy, and so his name may have been as genuine as Jack Riley's. Schmidt, or Smith as he was sometimes called, was a German national, perhaps called Dieter. He would not have been interned after Pearl Harbor, but he seems to have dropped off the radar after Jack's arrest. Albert Rosenbaum also proved difficult to trace. The SMP had reported Rosenbaum as an international drug trafficker back in the early 1930s when he first arrived in Shanghai, and Martin 'Little Nicky' Nicholson had been keen to arrest him. He did link him to telegraphic transfers of money to and from Mexico City, New York, and Shanghai, but couldn't secure a conviction. After the war, an Albert Rosenbaum did apply for a visa to America in Shanghai at the offices of the United Nations Relief and Rehabilitation Administration (UNRRA), but there were many Albert Rosenbaums amongst the city's postwar Jewish refugee community seeking visas to the United States, and there is no way to definitively prove this was him.

Don Chisholm stayed at liberty during the Japanese occupation of Shanghai, continuing to pump out pro-Tokyo propaganda and to publish the *Shopping News* with Japanese support. He became known as 'Shanghai's Lord Haw Haw'. Yet the Japanese came to despise him and eventually interned him in Shanghai's Haiphong Road Camp. There he was beaten up—first by the Japanese guards and then by his fellow American internees. With the liberation of Shanghai in 1945, Chisholm was arrested and held in Bridge House (now under American control). He languished there for ten months till August 1946. Chisholm remained combative and brought a legal challenge against the U.S. Army for holding him incommunicado for so long with no specific charges being brought. Despite considering him an 'A-1 traitor', the U.S. Department of Justice ordered him released without charge, and he promptly left Shanghai. Chisholm's radio sidekick, Herbert Moy, who appears to have been a true believer in fascism (rather than simply an opportunist, as many thought of Chisholm), committed suicide by jumping out the window of the XGRS radio station studio on the day the Nazi defeat in Europe was announced in Shanghai.

Bill Hawkins planned to leave, but evacuation ships were few and far between, and he never made it out before the Japanese invasion of the International Settlement. He died in Shanghai shortly after Pearl Harbor. He'd been running roulette wheels in the Settlement since the start of the twentieth century. The other veteran of Shanghai's foreign underbelly, the American Stuart Price, in his late sixties by the time of Pearl Harbor, was interned during the war by the Japanese authorities. He'd been in and out of court in Shanghai since 1904.

Carlos Garcia avoided internment during the war (probably by obtaining a neutral Spanish passport). In the late 1940s, having relocated to the United States and set up shop in Reno, Nevada, he got back in the casino business. His partner in the Canidrome, the French banker Louis Bouvier, died in 1945 in Shanghai. His son George was a resistance fighter with the Free French and returned to Shanghai after the liberation of France. George was later arrested by the Chinese Communist Party, accused of being a 'financial criminal', stripped of his assets and deported from China. The Canidrome Garcia and Bouvier had built became an internment camp in 1951, holding three thousand suspected enemies of the Communists and 'counter-revolutionary criminals'. Many were tried and executed in the former stands where the crowds had once cheered the greyhounds.

Jack Riley's first employer in Shanghai, Shalom 'Sam' Levy, remained in business at the Venus Café through to the Japanese occupation of the International Settlement. Sam had started the Venus with his sister-in-law, Girgee Moalem, though they later apparently parted on acrimonious terms. Sam bought Girgee out and ran the Venus on his own. After Pearl Harbor he was forced to close shop. As an Iraqi citizen he was not interned, but his movements were severely limited, and he was forbidden to leave his home except for essential trips. After the liberation of Shanghai, Sam went to Palestine, eventually becoming a citizen of Israel. His health deteriorated, partly due to the privations of wartime China, and he passed away in the 1950s. Girgee had married a man from Aden, a British Crown Colony at the time, thus rendering her a British subject by marriage. The family was imprisoned by the Japanese in the Lunghwa Internment Camp. They later moved to Australia after the war and settled in Sydney.

Thurman 'Demon' Hyde ran the Del Monte after the murder of his brother-in-law Al Israel in 1938 until it was closed down in 1940. He made it back to America and died in Fresno, California, in 1951. The Del Monte was for a time a shuttered relic of the old Badlands. In December 1941 an eleven-year-old J. G. Ballard, later to tell his own story of the occupation and his wartime internment in the best-selling book *Empire of the Sun*, living nearby, dared himself to walk through the gutted building and recalled seeing the floor strewn with busted-up roulette tables and toppled, smashed statues that could have come from the gardens of Versailles. The Japanese dynamited the Del Monte in 1942 to clear the land for new barracks. The Chinese forced labourers on the site smuggled in dynamite and blew up the newly built barracks, killing many Japanese soldiers. Almost all the slave labourers turned guerillas escaped to Free China in the ensuing chaos.

In 1942 Alexander 'Sasha' Vertinsky married Lidiya Vladimirovna Tsirgava. Vertinsky was fifty-three years old; Harbin-born

Lidiya was barely twenty. They had met in 1940 and been secretly seeing each other since then. Their oldest daughter, Marianna, was born on a train later that year leaving the city to eventually reach the Soviet border in Manchuria. Having left the Soviet Union in 1920, Vertinsky returned in 1943 courtesy of a visa personally organised by the senior Soviet leader Vyacheslav Molotov. Vertinsky had been a favourite singer of Stalin, who was reputed to own all his pre-1920 recordings. While many White Russians who returned to the USSR ended up in the gulags or executed, Stalin's fondness for Vertinsky's music and his worldwide fame offered him some security. Still, the times were dangerous: in 1948, during a purge of intellectuals, Vertinsky was blacklisted by the communist ideologue Andrei Zhdanov. However, Stalin is thought to have personally crossed his name off the list. Vertinsky performed more than two thousand concerts in the USSR as well as appearing in many Soviet films, often playing pre-revolutionary aristocrats—his trademark monocle firmly in place. His daughters, Marianna and Anastasiya, both became movie stars in Russia.

Perhaps the last recorded mention of Vertinsky is the sad portrayal of him in Truman Capote's essay *The Muses Are Heard*. Capote encountered the Vertinskys in 1956 in Leningrad, and recalled them as the Nervitskys. Lidiya 'spoke English with the spurious elegance, the strained exactness of Liza Doolittle' and introduced her husband as 'the crooner', a 'gentleman twice her age, somewhere in his sixties, a vain, once handsome man with an inflated stomach and a collapsing chin line. He wore make-up—powder, pencil, a touch of rouge.' Vertinsky/Nervitsky told Capote, *'Je suis Nervitsky. Le Bing Crosby de Russie.'* Capote goes on to tell of how Lidiya attempted to buy winter coats from Capote and his party. Vertinsky died shortly after this encounter, at the Hotel Astoria in Leningrad, in 1957. Lidiya Vertinskaya died in 2013 in Moscow, age ninety-one. The fate of Vertinsky's longtime Shanghai girlfriend, Boobee, is unknown. She was probably called either Boobee or Bubi Fominykh or Fominyh. There are rumours that she did manage to leave Shanghai and move to Hong Kong, but they're not confirmed.

Despite her Russian surname, Evelyn Oleaga was British-born. She appears to have remained at large in Shanghai after Pearl Harbor, probably living in Frenchtown. Despite her supposed close relations with several leading Axis country officials in Shanghai, around August 1944 she was arrested and interned by the Japanese in the Chapei Civilian Assembly Centre. After the war her trail goes cold.

Dr. Borovika is mentioned in a number of memoirs of the period, notably Buck Clayton's autobiography *Buck Clayton's Jazz World*. It is highly likely that he was in fact Doctor Ludovicko Borovicka, an Austrian by birth, but technically an Italian citizen following the collapse of the Austro-Hungarian Empire after World War I. This Borovicka was arrested and detained on an immigration violation in January 1941 in the United States. He was transferred to Fort Missoula, Montana, where the Americans were holding various interned German and Italian nationals during the war. The Immigration and Naturalization Service (INS) records this Dr. Borovicka as age fifty and a well-trained clinician, fluent in German and English and with research interests in venereal diseases, tuberculosis, cancer, and tropical diseases. He was subsequently moved to Fort Lincoln in North Dakota, a similar camp for interned Axis nationals, where he took over the medical service. It was reported that he soon gained the trust of his patients and the confidence of INS administrators. The American government rewarded Borovicka with a detainee officer's pay of $2.50 per week and accolades for good service.

It seems everyone lost touch with Babe Sadlir after Pearl Harbor. She was later immortalised in an article for *Esquire* magazine by Bob Patterson simply called 'Babe'. Patterson (who also wrote under the pen name Freddie Francisco), a journalist in Shanghai with the *China Press* newspaper, reports she was last heard of heading into the Chinese hinterlands and towards Free China. The Nationalist authorities, when approached for information on her whereabouts, responded 'no disposition whatsoever'. Though Patterson tried to trace her after the war, she was never found, and rumours came back to Patterson that she had died somewhere out in the vastness of China. Despite her claim to have come to Shanghai after almost killing another woman in San Francisco in a knife fight, Patterson checked with the SFPD and found that they had no open warrant on her and had never been looking for her in connection with any crime. Perhaps she never needed to be a China Coaster after all.

John Crighton and his wife, Julia, were interned by the Japanese in Shanghai's Yu Yuen Road Camp, which held mainly former SMC and SMP employees. Towards the end of the war, internees at Yu Yuen Road were moved to the Yangtszepoo Camp. This compound was surrounded by twelve-foot-high walls and contained five rat-infested, two-storey buildings, in decaying condition. Due to its proximity to Shanghai's major gasworks, waterworks, Japanese army barracks, and armament stores, the camp was imperilled by Allied bombing in 1945, during the liberation of the city. After the war Crighton was one of a number of SMP detectives seconded to the South East Asian War Crimes Investigations Unit, and served in Sumatra and Burma investigating Japanese war crimes. Crighton moved to Hong Kong in 1947 and died in the late 1950s. Crighton's boss, the SMP commissioner Kenneth Bourne, took long leave from Shanghai in mid-August 1941, departing, with his family, for a vacation in Canada. He did not return to Shanghai, spent the war in British Army Intelligence (mostly in India), and later took up a post with the Royal Canadian Mounted Police. He died in Limehouse, Ontario, in 1968.

Treasury agent Martin 'Little Nicky' Nicholson died suddenly of a heart ailment in his Shanghai office only a few days before Pearl Harbor. His body was still unclaimed at the undertakers' when the Japanese took over the city. J. B. Powell (who was brutally tortured by the Kempeitai in Bridge House himself) wrote that 'perhaps it was fortunate that "Nick" had escaped the Japs, as he probably had tracked down more international dope smugglers, including many Japanese, than any other man in the narcotic-suppression division of the Treasury Department. I had known Nicholson for many years and had spent many evenings in his home, when he recounted his adventures with desperate smugglers of narcotics. Three notorious gangsters recently executed at Sing Sing . . . were exposed as members of an international dope ring by the unadvertised activities of Martin Nicholson, Treasury Agent at Shanghai.' One of those three men executed at Sing Sing was Louis Buchalter, whom Nicholson had linked to opium smuggling out of the Shanghai Badlands.

General Kenji Doihara was prosecuted for war crimes at the International Military Tribunal for the Far East after the war. It was disclosed that, as a general in the Japanese Army and a member of the Supreme War Council, he had voted his approval of the attack on Pearl Harbor. He was found guilty, sentenced to death, and hanged in Tokyo's Sugamo Prison in December 1948. Wang Ching-wei, China's wartime puppet ruler, died in Japan on November 10, 1944 while undergoing medical treatment. By doing so he managed to avoid being put on trial for treason. Many of his senior followers who survived until the end of the war were executed.

The woman who drove Joe Farren's relationship with Nellie almost to the breaking point was Larissa Andersen, who was born in Harbin around 1912. She continued to get work as a dancer in various cabarets around Shanghai and, in 1940, was even hired by Sir Victor Sassoon to headline at his Tower Club in the Cathay Hotel. Her agent claimed she was the highest paid dancer in Shanghai in 1940. After her career in Shanghai's nightclubs, she focused on her true interest writing poetry. Larissa married a French Shanghailander called Maurice Chaize and published a single volume of poems, *Po zemnym lugam* (*On Earth's Meadows*), in Shanghai in 1940. In her poem 'I am Silent Because . . .' she wrote:

> *I dance for various foreigners*
> *In theatres, clubs and cabarets.*
> *My dance is charitably called*
> *Exotic dance.*

During the war and afterwards the couple lived in Saigon and Tahiti before moving to Yssingeaux, Haute Loire, France. Larissa Andersen-Chaize died in France in 2012, and is generally considered one of the finest poets to emerge from the Russian émigré community in China between the wars.

The ultimate fate of Nellie Farren is unknown.

GLOSSARY

Akuma—A fire demon in Japanese folklore; capable of flight.

Alligator sinensis—The Chinese alligator, also known as the Yangtze alligator, that was once concentrated in eastern China and is now a critically endangered species.

Americanski durak—Russian slang for an American idiot.

Annamite—A person from Annam, the more common name for Vietnam before 1945, when it was a French protectorate and a division of the French Indochina empire.

Arrack—A distilled alcoholic spirit typically produced in various Asian countries and made from either the fermented sap of coconut flowers, sugarcane, grain, or fruit, depending upon the country of origin.

Ayah—A nursemaid or nanny usually employed by Europeans or Americans in British India and East and Southeast Asia.

Blind pig—An American term for an illicit establishment selling alcohol.

Boychik—A Yiddish term of endearment for a young boy; in slang terms often used to denote a gang member.

Bucko mate—A term most commonly used in late nineteenth and early twentieth century American for a sailor who worked his crew hard but fair.

Brigade des Stupéfiants—The French police drugs squad.

Bupkis—A Yiddish word meaning 'nothing at all'.

Cadillac—American slang term used in Shanghai to describe a pill containing opium.

Canto—Slang shortening of 'Cantonese' for a person from Canton (Guangzhou) or that city's environs in southern China.

Catty—A traditional Chinese unit of weight measurement for various foodstuffs; one catty equals approximately six hundred grams.

Compradors—From the Portuguese word for 'buyer'; members of the Chinese merchant class who aided Western traders in southern China in the late eighteenth, nineteenth, and early twentieth centuries.

Coolies—A general word for an unskilled native laborer in China and some other Asian countries; it was widely used at the time and has since become a considerably more derogatory word than it was in the early twentieth century.

Cosh—A term most commonly used in Britain to describe a thick, heavy stick or bar used as a weapon.

Crib—Originally an English term for a house occupied by criminals, though later, by the 1930s, had become a term used by African-Americans to describe a home.

Cumshaw—China Coast pidgin English for a tip or gratuity.

Demimonde—Literally the French for 'half-world'; a late nineteenth/early twentieth century term denoting a group of people living a hedonistic lifestyle.

Déshabillé—Originally from the French; the state of being only partly or scantily clothed.

Dime-dropper—American slang for a police informer; someone who gives the police information in return for a reward.

Driftwood—A term regularly used in Shanghai to describe those foreigners who came to the city and were feckless, refused to work, and often became engaged in petty crime.

Emo—Spirits in Japanese folklore.

Entrepôt—A port to which goods are brought for import and export, and for collection and distribution.

Fakakta mamzer—A Yiddish term meaning 'worthless bastard'.

Fan-tan—A Chinese gambling game in which players try to guess the remainder after the banker has divided a number of hidden objects into four groups.

Flic—A French slang word for a policeman; the police being 'les flics'.

Fox demons—From both Chinese and Japanese folklore; can shape-shift to human beings at night and invariably lead people to destruction.

Frauenzimmer—A German term, literally 'woman's room'; used to describe bourgeois women in a humorous and derogatory way.

Gauleiter—German; a political official under the Nazis.

Gee-gees—English slang for horse racing.

Gelt—An older German term, more commonly used in colloquial Yiddish, to mean money.

Gitanes—The French word for a Romani (gypsy).

Godowns—From the Malay word 'godong' meaning storehouses or warehouses and used throughout Asia in the late nineteenth and early twentieth centuries.

Gonef—A Yiddish word for a dishonest or untrustworthy person; from the Hebrew word for 'thief'.

Grind shops—American slang for illegal gambling dens usually specializing in slot machines and low-limit games of chance.

Gudao—Chinese meaning 'solitary' or 'lonely' island; the term applied to the foreign concessions of Shanghai during the period from the initial Japanese attack on the Chinese areas of Shanghai on August 14, 1937 (Bloody Saturday), until December 9, 1941, when the Japanese Army finally occupied the International Settlement following Pearl Harbor.

Hawk-spit—The act of loudly clearing mucus from one's throat.

Hitodama—From Japanese folklore and meaning 'human soul'; balls of fire that float in the night and are said to be the souls of the dead that have separated from their bodies.

Hong Kong foot—A fungal infection of the skin that causes scaling, flaking, and itching of affected areas; known elsewhere as athlete's foot.

Hongs—The term originated in southern China to describe the early trading houses at Canton (Guangzhou); the term was also applied to large foreign trading concerns in Hong Kong, Shanghai, and throughout the treaty ports of China.

Hutongs—The ancient narrow streets of courtyard houses or alleyways associated with Beijing.

Izvinite—Russian for 'excuse me'.

Joss—From the Portuguese word for God, 'Deus'; can relate to a Chinese temple (joss house) or incense (joss sticks); nineteenth century China Coast pidgin English word for 'luck'.

Hanjian—The Chinese word for a traitor; but specifically a traitor to the Han Chinese race; the term was used to attack those Chinese that collaborated with the Japanese during World War II.

Hwa-Wei lottery—The Hwa-Wei (or 'flowery') lottery was one of several numbers rackets that operated in Shanghai at the time of these events.

Jai alai—The Basque game, where a ball is bounced off a wall at considerable speed through the use of a curved hand-held device called a cesta; the game was always referred to as *hai-alai* in Shanghai.

Kaffee und kuchen—German for 'coffee and cake'; a ritual usually undertaken between lunch and dinner and accompanied by conversation and gossip.

Kalderash—A subset of the Romani (gypsy) people mostly originating from Romania, Ukraine, and Russia.

Kanji—The adopted logographic Chinese characters that are used in the modern Japanese writing system, along with hiragana and katakana.

Kasha—A buckwheat dish extremely popular in Russia.

Kempeitai—The military police arm of the Imperial Japanese Army from 1881 to 1945.

Kepi—A French word simply meaning 'cap' and invariably denoting a form of peaked headwear worn by the police and military.

Khuy—Russian slang for penis

Kuei huo—From Chinese folklore; 'kuei' or 'kwei' meaning a ghost and 'ho' means fire; a fire spirit arising from the blood of the dead; takes the form of *ignis fatui* (will-o'-the-wisp), a hovering phosphorescent light.

Laissez passer—A form of travel document issued by a national government or the League of Nations allowing for passage.

Lathi—From the Bengali word for 'stick'; a *lathi* is made of bamboo and is between six and eight feet long; lathis were used by Sikh constables in the Shanghai Municipal Police for crowd control purposes.

Latifundia—The large landed estates in Latin America, typically worked by peasants or slaves.

Lieu-maung—A Shanghainese dialect term invariably translated at the time as 'loafer'; denoting general unemployed young ne'er-do-wells likely to engage in various forms of criminality; common enough to be included in the Shanghai Municipal Council's publication *One Thousand Phrases in the Shanghai Dialect for the use of the Municipal Police* (1926).

Longtou zha—A Chinese phrase meaning 'faucet dregs' and being the tarlike residue found at the bottom of opium pipes after opium has been smoked; these dregs are then boiled with water and sold to addicts and the poor.

Manouche—A French term for Romani (gypsy) people.

Meiyu—A Chinese word denoting the East Asian rainy season or, in China, the Plum Rains that come to China in late spring.

Meshuggeneh—A Yiddish word to describe someone who is crazy.

Mopu/moge—A Chinese term used in Shanghai in the early twentieth century to describe those young Chinese people (usually of some financial means) who had embraced modern ways, meaning invariably American, European, and Japanese fashions, music, and tastes; a *mopu* was a 'modern boy' and a *moge* a 'modern girl'.

Nansen passports—Internationally recognized refugee travel documents issued by the League of Nations to stateless refugees; known as 'Nansen passports' after their promoter, the Norwegian statesman and polar explorer Fridtjof Nansen.

Naptha-lit—Naphtha flare lamps predated todays paraffin (Tilly) lamps; they were widely used by showmen, market-stall holders, and circuses until World War I to create dramatic lighting effects.

Nichts—German word for 'nothing'.

No wantchee—Nineteenth-century China Coast pidgin English for 'do not want'.

Nobble (a horse)—English slang phrase meaning to influence a horse race by underhand or unfair methods, usually doping or in some way slowing a horse.

Old lags—British-Australian English slang; hardened or habitual prisoners and former convicts.

Okami—The Japanese name for the creature commonly called the Japanese wolf (*Canis lupus hodophilax*), which became extinct in 1905 and is a major figure in Japanese folklore.

On the lam—A slang term originating in America meaning to hide; attempting to escape from the police or an enemy.

Panier—The historic waterfront of Marseille composed of myriad narrow alleyways and long a hide out for the city's criminal fraternity.

Papyruski—A papyruski is composed of a hollow cardboard tube extended by a thin cigarette paper tube containing tobacco; the cardboard tube plays the role of a disposable cigarette holder; it was seen as a very cheap and inferior smoke in Shanghai at the time.

Pari-mutuel—From the French term for 'mutual betting'; a betting system in which all bets of a particular type are placed together in a pool and the payoff odds are calculated by sharing the pool among all the winning bets.

Partido—From Galician, meaning the division of a game of *hai-alai* (jai-alai)

Philopon—The original brand name for mass-produced methamphetamine (or shabu) in Japan, where it was invented, consumed in large amounts by the military and exported to other East Asian countries.

Picul—A unit of measurement for rice dating back to the early days of the eighteenth century China trade; one picul is defined as a shoulder-load, or as much as a man can carry on a shoulder-pole; a picul is always equivalent to 100 catties (see *catty* above).

Pi-seh—A Shanghainese dialect term for a beggar, usually noting a particularly physically aggressive beggar who may turn swiftly to crime; common enough to be included in the Shanghai Municipal Council's publication *One Thousand Phrases in the Shanghai Dialect for the use of the Municipal Police* (1926).

Pongee—A soft, thin woven cloth suitable for lightweight and summer suits mostly manufactured in the mills around Shanghai and eastern China for local consumption and, primarily, export to the United States.

Quiniela—From Spanish; a bet in which the gambler picks the first and second place finishers but need not designate their order of finish in order to win.

Rabbit ball—Also called a jackrabbit ball; a rather lively baseball; considered a form of cheating.

Rin-kwa or *kin-kwa*—From Japanese folklore; ghostly lights that hover; often a gold color and associated with places were many have died.

Ronin—Originally a Japanese samurai warrior without a master, but in the 1930s in Shanghai the term was used by vigilante groups of Japanese in the city who officially operated as auxiliaries to the Japanese army but in reality behaved arbitrarily with no restraint.

Rufiões—The Portuguese word for 'ruffians'; young gang members.

Samogon—Russian moonshine; high-proof illicitly distilled spirit made from grain.

Sampan—Flat-bottomed wooden Chinese style of boat; often used as conveyances across rivers and creeks in Shanghai at the time as well as for transportation and as homes by the poor on 'beggar boats'.

Schlemiel—A Yiddish word for an awkward or unlucky person.

Schtum—A German word meaning 'silent'; though commonly used in Yiddish to denote maintaining silence in the face of the authorities.

Schvantze—Yiddish word for penis.

Shabu—A slang term for the drug methamphetamine, normally at this time associated with Japanese-manufactured narcotics.

Shamshoo—Chinese moonshine; high-proof illicitly distilled spirit made from rice.

Shanghailander—A foreigner (either by birth or nationality) residing and working in the International Settlement and French Concession of Shanghai.

Shanghainese—A Chinese resident of the city of Shanghai; also the Chinese dialect spoken in Shanghai.

Shebeen—A term originating in Ireland but used throughout the Anglo-Saxon English speaking world to denote an illegal drinking den.

Shlyukha—Russian slang term for a prostitute.

Shroff—A cashier; the word is derived from the Hindustani word *saraf* (bullion merchant); was widely used throughout British India, East and Southeast Asia in the nineteenth and the first half of the twentieth century.

Slumgullion—Of nineteenth-century American derivation; a cheap and insubstantial stew of indeterminate ingredients (though usually with some meat content), usually eaten by the poor.

Smuts—A spot or soil caused by soot or coal dust.

Sojourner—A person who resides temporarily in a place.

Speak—Speakeasy; an American term for an illicit establishment selling alcohol, though in prior use, the term came to prominence during Prohibition.

Squeeze—A China Coast pidgin English term for an augmentation of servants' or workers' wages through purchasing something at one price and receiving repayment at a higher price; alternatively, receiving a commission from a shopkeeper or service provider in return for placing their firm or employers business with them.

Standover men—Australian slang; criminals who steal or extort money by intimidation from other criminals knowing they cannot go to the police.

Taipan—A Cantonese term meaning literally the 'big boss'.

Tchotchke—Yiddish term meaning a bauble or small miscellaneous item but also used to refer to gigolos.

Tonk—A fast-paced matching card game that can be played at intervals and by varying numbers of players, making it perfect for actors between scenes and musicians between sets.

Tonkinese—Denoting people from the Tonkin region of North Vietnam, at that time a part of the French Indo-Chinese Empire; many Tonkinese served in the French Concession's Garde Municipal police force and in France's Colonial Regiments.

Tooth glasses—The common term at the time to describe a glass for holding toothbrushes.

Tukhes—The Yiddish word for 'backside'.

Triads—Organized crime syndicates originating in China.

Trusty—A prisoner, usually having served a lengthy sentence, who is given special privileges or responsibilities in return for good behavior.

Ublyudok—Russian word for 'bastard'.

Vig—Or the vigorish (from the Russian word for 'winnings'); the amount charged by a bookmaker for accepting the bet or the interest on a loan granted by a loan shark.

Voor vrouw—A Dutch word meaning 'wife', but with the implication of a somewhat tough demeanor.

Vunbottlvine—A phrase that became a Shanghai joke in the early twentieth century to mimic how the many White Russian émigrés working in bars and nightclubs asked the question, 'one bottle of wine?'

Weianfu—The Chinese term for 'comfort women', those women and girls forced into sexual slavery by the Imperial Japanese Army in its occupied territories during World War II.

Weiansuo—Chinese for 'comfort houses'; the locations for Japanese army brothels filled with coerced Chinese women and girls in Shanghai.

Yakitori—A Japanese type of skewered chicken grilled over a charcoal fire.

Yakuza—Organized crime syndicates originating in Japan.

You-tiao—Chinese fried dough sticks cooked in oil by street vendors, a traditional breakfast.

Zakuski—Russian term for hot and cold hors d'oeuvres invariably intended to follow shots of vodka; the word literally means 'something to bite after'.

Zitterer—German term that came into use during World War I to describe those soldiers suffering the particularly severe post-traumatic stress disorder that causes the body to shake uncontrollably; usually referred to as 'shell shock' in English at the time.

APPENDIX—
OLD SHANGHAI INDEX

Chinese Cities/Provinces

OLD	CURRENT
Amoy	Xiamen
Canton	Guangzhou
Chekiang	Zhejiang
Chungking	Chongqing
Dairen	Dalian
Foochow	Fuzhou
Hangchow	Hangzhou
Hankow	Hankou
Kiangsu	Jiangsu
Mokanshan	Moganshan
Nanking	Nanjing
Ningpo	Ningbo
Peking	Beijing
Shanshi	Shanxi
Shumchun	Shenzhen
Tientsin	Tianjin
Weihaiwei	Weihai

Shanghai Districts

OLD	CURRENT
Chapei	Zhabei
Hongkew	Hongkou

OLD	CURRENT
Hungjao	Hongqiao
Kiangwan	Jiangwan
Paoshan	Baoshan
Siccawei	Xujiahui
Yangtszepoo	Yangpu

Shanghai Streets

OLD	CURRENT
Avenue Road	Beijing Road West
Baikal Road	Huimin Road
Blood Alley	Rue Chu Pao San
Brenan Road	Changning Road
Broadway	Daming Road
Broadway East	Daming Road East
Bubbling Well Road	Nanjing Road West
Canton Road	Guangdong Road
Rue Cardinal Mercier	Maoming Road South
Chapoo Road	Zhapu Road
Rue Chu Pao San	Xikou Road
Rue du Consulat	Jinling Road East
Route Courbet	Fumin Road
Dixwell Road	Liyang Road
Route Doumer	Donghu Road
Route Dupleix	Anfu Road
Edinburgh Road	Jiangsu Road
Avenue Edward VII	Yanan Road East
Fah Wah Village	Fahuazhen Road
Ferry Road	Xikang Road
Avenue Foch	Yanan Road East

OLD	CURRENT
Tifeng Road	Wulumuqi Road North
Route Voyron	Yandang Road
Ward Road	Changyang Road
Wayside Road	Huoshan Road
Woo Foo Lane	Wufu Alley
Yangtszepoo Road	Yangshupu Road
Yu Yuen Road	Yuyuan Road
Yuan Ming Yuan Road	Yuanmingyuan Road
Ziang Teh Road	Shanyin Road

Other

OLD	CURRENT
Batavia	Jakarta (Indonesia)
Hongkew Park	Lu Xun Park
Jessfield Park	Zhongshan Park
Sawgin Creek	Shajing Creek
Siccawei Creek	Xujiahui Creek
Soochow Creek	Suzhou Creek
Whangpoo River	Huangpu River

ACKNOWLEDGMENTS

Many people contributed anecdotes and stories from old Shanghai that have been incorporated into *City of Devils*. They include Robert Bickers, for his wealth of knowledge on the Shanghai Municipal Police; Douglas Clark, for his understanding of Shanghai's labyrinthine justice system; Andrew Field, for his deep investigations of the city's dance-hall cultures; Fred Greguras, for his research on the Fourth Marines in Shanghai; Katya Knyazeva for her exhaustive knowledge of the city's White Russian community; Greg Leck for his voluminous knowledge on the internment of allied civilians in China during the war; and Sue Anne Tay, for her work uncovering the city's 'comfort houses' (and her photography). Thanks also to longtime Shanghailanders Graham Earnshaw, Duncan Hewitt, Peter Hibbard, Tess Johnston, Ned Kelly, Lynn Pan, Bill Savadove, and Mike Tsang.

Thank you to George Krooglik, whose father served in the Shanghai Municipal Police in 1941 and served in the SMP Special Reserve Unit (Riot Squad) while his mother was an usherette at the Majestic Theatre. Jacqui Mills, the great niece of Joe Farren, is part of the Pollak clan that ended up in England, and always wondered what happened to the 'black sheep of the family'. I'm so glad she got in touch; it made rediscovering Joe so much more pertinent.

Dan Moalem, the son of Girgee Moalem, née Ghazal and once Sam Levy's partner in the Venus Café, generously shared information and photographs from Australia. So too did Vera Loewer from California, the daughter of Clara and Vasia Ivanoff, a Paramount Peach and a clarinet player in the Paramount's White Russian house band respectively. They were witnesses to the whole thing. Steve Gensler—a distant relative of poor Daisy Simmons, who was in the wrong place at the wrong time—also added some details. Vadim Zaliva allowed me to see the memoir of George Radbil (a resident of Shanghai between 1930 and 1946 and an employee of the Jessfield Club, 1484 Yu Yuen Road in the Badlands, as its cashier and manager between 1938 and 1940), which included his recollections of Alexander Vertinsky and Boobee Fominykh. Daphne Skillen, the daughter of Kyriaco Dimitriades, proprietor of the Astoria Confectionery and Tea-Rooms on Hongkew's Broadway, kindly shared her treasure trove of old Shanghai mementoes with me over tea and cake in Highbury, North London. And Jim Cunningham, a relative of Elly Widler, long fascinated by his most interesting ancestor, generously shared details of Widler's amazing China experiences and the photographs that prove it. Sadly, space prevented a full telling of Elly's amazing life and times—anyone looking for a worthy subject for a rollicking good biography need look no further.

I must also acknowledge the previous work done on the Shanghai Badlands by the great Sinologist Frederic Wakeman (1937–2006), whose books *Policing Shanghai, 1927–1937* (1995) and *The Shanghai Badlands, Wartime Terrorism and Urban Crime 1937–1941* (1996) first led me to be intrigued by this aspect of Shanghai's history. I'd also like to acknowledge the staff of the British Library, Hong Kong University Library, and the Shanghai Library Bibliotheca Zi-Ka-Wei, as well as the London Library, where the bulk of this manuscript was researched and written.

My thanks to Jo Lusby for being so patient in waiting for this book. Also Patrizia Van Daalen, Lena Petzke, and Anya Goncharova at Penguin in Beijing for production help and Nerrilee Weir at Penguin Australia for handling rights. I am grateful to both Stephen Morrison at Picador in New York and Jon Riley at Riverrun in London for their support and suggestions and for becoming my publishers. Especial thanks to Arwen Summers in Melbourne and Emily Murdock Baker in New York for editing the manuscript and both being a lot of fun to work with . . . again. Much thanks to Anne Witchard for reading and commenting on the manuscript throughout its incarnation. I'd like to note the support of my agent, Clare Alexander, as well as Lesley Thorne at Aitken-Alexander Associates in London, and also Sue Swift, Diederick Santer, and Ollie Madden at Kudos Film and Television.